**"Achieving the Good Life After 50 should be the first book
on every baby boomer's reading list!"**
–Howard Putnam, Former CEO Southwest Airlines; author, *The Winds of Turbulence*

Read What People Have to Say About *Achieving the Good Life After 50*,
The Five O'Clock Club, and Renée Lee Rosenberg

With so many books and choices, one can be very confused by which one to read
and whom to believe. *Achieving the Good Life After 50* takes all the confusion out of
this important process in your life. Many books deal solely with financial issues.
Achieving the Good Life After 50 includes finance, but goes far beyond and provides
insights to help with the retirement transition, what to expect, how to plan for
it, how to deal with it, and most importantly how to "look forward to it" and
"enjoy it."

> —Howard Putnam, Former CEO Southwest Airlines;
> author, *The Winds of Turbulence*

Achieving the Good Life After 50 is a book we have all been looking for! Renee has
counseled hundreds of retirees, and is superbly qualified to guide and advise the
over-50's crowd about how to grow and blossom in later life. **A pleasure to read,
with practical tools and creative suggestions that offer hope and optimism for
the after years.**

> —Natalie H. Rogers, author, *The New Talk Power—The Mind Body Way*

At The Five O'Clock Club, [members] find discipline, direction and much-needed
support.

> —*Modern Maturity*

Achieving the Good Life After 50 is a guide and <u>**an inspiration for all of us as we**</u> <u>**face the confusion of re-inventing ourselves**</u> in our wisdom years. Using both her personal and professional savvy, Renee gracefully steers us step-by-step so that a journey inherently fraught with perils, pitfalls and possibilities becomes a time of powerful potential and calm choices. No matter how ready you are to consider your future, this book will power your reflection, your strategies and your positive outcomes. Highly recommended for those who are ready to take a holistic view of their work and life, and the legacy they want to leave behind.

—Gail Liebhaber, author, *Purposeful Listening: Spiritual Coaching Techniques for Career Development Practitioners*

Renee's coaching and The Five O'Clock Club approach has put my résumé on track and instilled me with <u>**optimism, focus**</u> and <u>**direction**</u>.

—M. K., financial services supervisor

Achieving the Good Life After 50 presents <u>**a new**</u> and <u>**unique approach**</u> to the changes and transitions individuals face when dealing with retirement. Every retiree needs to read this book!

—Lynn Berger, author of *The Savvy Part-Time Professional*

I dragged myself to my first Five O'Clock Club meeting, totally demoralized. Ten weeks later, I chose from among job offers and started a new life. <u>**Bless You!**</u>

—Senior editor, not-for-profit

Having retired four years ago from my career as a manager in city government, I found *Achieving the Good Life After 50* useful in helping me to realize that I'm on the right path in my second career (after retirement) as an artist. It has helped to keep balanced and gave me the courage and advice to possibly go on to a second retirement and third career if and when that opportunity and desire might occur. It was also <u>**fascinating**</u> and <u>**helpful to read**</u> about other individuals' retirement challenges and how, with wise counseling, they were able to make informed decisions, resolve their issues, and forge ahead.

—Anne Stanner, former Director, Management Planning and Financial Analysis

If you are planning to retire, be sure you first read *Achieving the Good Life After 50*. It will not only inspire, it will also motivate you to plan a positive future.

—Diane W., retired office manager

I have doubled my salary during the past five years by using The Five O'Clock Club techniques. Now I earn what I deserve. I think everyone needs The Five O'Clock Club.

—M. S., attorney, entertainment industry

The personal vignettes in *Achieving the Good Life After 50* complement the text. These **real-life illustrations put a human face on the problems we all face approaching retirement.**

—Dr. Allan J. R., retired physician

Renee helped me to focus my resume and gave me advice for getting interviews. She encouraged me to articulate what I'm passionate about. **Her think-outside-the-box approach has helped me find the 'hidden job market**.' Thus, I knew how to find the contacts that *matter*, either for informational interviews or for jobs.

—Lawrence N., M.D.

Renee looks at the whole person—including skills, values, interests, and even emotional profile—to provide individualized, real-world guidance. She has never steered me wrong!

—Stuart W., attorney and professional services marketing

The Five O'Clock Club has been a fantastic experience. I couldn't have done it without you. Keep up the good work.

—Former restaurant owner who found his dream job with an organization that advises small businesses

What Human Resources Executives Say About
Five O'Clock Club Outplacement!

"**This thing works**. I saw a structured, yet nurturing, environment where individuals positioned themselves for success. I saw 'accountability' in a non-intimidating environment. I was struck by the support and willingness to encourage those who had just started the process by the group members who had been there for a while."

— Employee Relations Officer, financial services organization

"**Wow! I was immediately struck by the electric atmosphere** and people's commitment to following the program. Members reported on where they were and what they had accomplished the previous week. The overall environment fosters sharing and mutual learning."

— Head of Human Resources, major law firm

"The Five O'Clock Club program is **far more effective** than conventional outplacement. Excellent materials, effective coaching and nanosecond responsiveness combine to get people focused on their central tasks. Selecting the Five O'Clock Outplacement Program was one of my best decisions this year."

— Sr. Vice President, Human Resources, manufacturing company

"**You have made me look like a real genius** in recommending The Five O'Clock Club [to our divisions around the country]!"

— S.V.P., HR, major publishing firm

"Selecting Five O'Clock outplacement was **one of my best decisions this year**."

— S.V.P., HR, major not-for-profit

ACHIEVING THE GOOD LIFE AFTER 50

TOOLS AND RESOURCES TO MAKE IT HAPPEN

✓ A New Approach to Retirement
✓ Discovering Yourself and Where You Want to Go
✓ Maintaining Your Motivation and Morale

RENÉE LEE ROSENBERG

With a Foreword by Kate Wendleton

Five O'Clock Club Books
www.FiveOClockClub.com

The
Five
O'Clock
Club®

Achieving The Good Life After 50: Tools and Resources For Making It Happen by Renée Lee Rosenberg

Copyright ©2007 The Five O'Clock Club,® Inc.
Some of the contents of this work appeared previously in somewhat different form in other Five O'Clock Club® works. The Five O'Clock Club®, Seven Stories Exercise and Forty-Year Vision are registered trademarks of The Five O'Clock Club®, Inc.
Printed in Canada

1 2 3 4 5   09 08 07
Five O'Clock Books is a part of The Five O'Clock Club, Inc.
For more information contact Five O'Clock Books,
300 East 40th Street, New York, NY 10016
Or find us on the World Wide Web at
www.FiveOClockClub.com

For information, please contact:
The Five O'Clock Club®
300 East 40th Street
New York, New York 10016 www.FiveOClockClub.com

Library of Congress Cataloging-in-Publication Data
Rosenberg, Renee Lee.
  Achieving the good life after 50 : tools and resources for making it
happen / by Renee Lee Rosenberg ; with a foreword by Kate Wendleton.
     p. cm.
  Includes index.
  ISBN 978-0-944054-14-7
  1. Retirees--Life skills guides. 2. Retirement--Planning. I. Title.
  HQ1062.R67 2007

  646.7'9--dc22

                                          2007001984

NOTICE TO THE READER
Publisher does not warrant or guarantee any of the products described herein or perform any independent analysis in connection with any of the product information contained herein. Publisher does not assume, and expressly disclaims, any obligation to obtain and include information other than that provided to it by the manufacturer.

The reader is expressly warned to consider and adopt all safety precautions that might be indicated by the activities herein and to avoid all potential hazards. By following the instructions contained herein, the reader willingly assumes all risks in connection with such instructions.

The Publisher makes no representation or warranties of any kind, including but not limited to, the warranties of fitness for particular purpose or merchantability, nor are any such representations implied with respect to the material set forth herein, and the publisher takes no responsibility with respect to such material. The publisher shall not be liable for any special, consequential, or exemplary damages resulting, in whole or part, from the readers' use of, or reliance upon, this material. The authors and The Five O'Clock Club affirm that the Web site URLs referenced herein were accurate at the time of printing. However, due to the fluid nature of the Internet, we cannot guarantee their accuracy for the life of the edition.

President, The Five O'Clock Club: Kate Wendleton
Chief Operating Officer: Richard C. Bayer, Ph.D.
SVP, Director of the Guild of Career Coaches: David Madison, Ph.D. Cover Design: Andrew Newman Design
Interior Design and Production: Bookwrights

We are face to face with our destiny
and we must meet it with a high and resolute courage.
For us is the life of action, of strenuous performance of duty;
let us live in the harness, striving mightily;
let us rather run the risk of wearing out than rusting out.

—Theodore Roosevelt, U.S. President (1858–1919)

Table of Contents

Foreword xi
Acknowledgments xvii
Preface xix
Introduction xxi

Part One:
Understanding the Process: Coming to Terms with the Financial, Psychological, and Emotional Issues Connected with Transitioning into Retirement

1. The Changing Face of Retirement: A Perspective 3
2. Dispelling the Myths of Aging 9
3. Your Finances: Coming to Terms with What You Need 21
4. Transitioning into Retirement 31
5. Learning to Manage Change 47
6. Developing Positive Thinking 57
7. Five Strategies for Positive Thinking 65

Part Two:
Moving Forward: Discovering Who You Are, What You Want and How to Find It

8. Together at Last: Where Do We Go from Here? 81
by Marjorie Hendrickson, M.S. in collaboration with her husband, Allen Hendrickson

9. Discovering Your Needs and Finding Your Purpose 91
10. Assessment and Taking Action 101
11. No Matter What Your Age:
The Value of Having a Long-Term Vision 113
by Kate Wendleton
12. Want to Retire to Something?
Will it Be Working for Pay or Volunteering? 125
13. Easing the Transition into Your Retirement Career 153
by Harvey Kaplan, Ph.D.
14. Age Discrimination—or Is It? 163
15. Exploring Volunteer Vacations and Leisure Travel 175
16. Education, Life-Long Learning and Other Pursuits 185
17. Keeping the Balance: Taking Care of Yourself 193
18. Reflecting on Retirement 207

What Is the Five O'Clock Club?
America's Premier Career Coaching Network

How to Join the Club 213
Questions You May Have About the Weekly Job-Search Strategy Group 219
The Way We Are 229
Lexicon Used at the Five O'Clock Club 231

Appendixes

I. Inspirations and Quotes from Retirees 239
II. Quotes from Experts 243
III. The Seven Stories Exercise® 245
IV. Your Fifteen-Year Vision® and Your Forty-Year Vision® 259
V. Suggested Additional Reading 267

Index 269
About the Author 000
About the Five O'Clock Club and the "Fruytagie" canvas 000

Foreword

The best is yet to come. That's true for those who plan for their retirement years and then execute that plan. Your future may involve full-time or part-time work, volunteer work, family involvement or hobbies. Renée Lee Rosenberg is the best person to help you consider your options. She has been a Five O'Clock Club coach since 1996, and has over twenty years of experience helping people develop satisfying lives after their primary work life. Other Five O'Clock Club coaches also specialize in retirement careers, and *Achieving the Good Life After 50* represents The Five O'Clock Club approach to this process.

Following The Five O'Clock Club process, you can have the best. But to have the best, you need to plan. Often, unplanned years are full of self-oriented pursuits: shopping, traveling, and keeping physically fit. People think, "I'll travel or play golf." But 30 years of self-indulgence is a long time. Where is the sense of momentum and purpose?

Self-oriented pursuits are not considered the healthiest for the long haul. If you have been working hard for years and deserve a break, take a break. Cut back. But stay involved with life, especially in pursuits that *help others*. Herbert Rappaport, Ph.D., an expert on aging, says that one of the common themes he sees among depressed adults in his psychiatry practice is the deep sense of regret for not "stretching oneself" at different life stages. It is not too late to become deeply immersed in something that matters. Rappaport found that those who engage in meaningful activities are happier than those who engage only in self-indulgent activities.

Yet the evidence at hand suggests that ultimately life does not appear satisfying or socially valuable when approached as an opportunity to be free of responsibility.
—Herbert Rappaport, Ph.D.

Many older people are depressed and bored. Life seems to drag. That's because the retirement dream was too vague and not well thought out, *i.e.*, "travel." They're not productive and contributing. More and more people are in great physical health and not as well off emotionally because they're *drifting*. They lack goals.

We are not in a position in which we have nothing to work with. We already have capacities, talents, direction, missions, callings.

—Abraham Maslow

You have the time to learn and be productive for many, many years. You could have your greatest life accomplishments after the age of 50 or even older. Why give up now? You have plenty of time to make great progress toward whatever you plan. Most people can now expect to live into their 80s and 90s. You have thirty years. What are you going to do with that time?

Twenty years from now you will be more disappointed by the things you didn't do than by the ones you did. So throw off the bowlines. Sail away from the safe harbor. Catch the trade winds in your sails. Explore. Dream. Discover.

—Mark Twain

Landing Good Volunteer Work Takes Effort

Take Bill, for example. His situation seemed ideal. He retired at age 55 after having made millions on Wall Street. Some senior executives decide they want to serve on for-profit or not-for-profit boards, but through the Five O'Clock Club's self-assessment process, Bill decided he wanted to do what he considered volunteer work: He wanted to "impart his knowledge" to younger people by teaching at a private high school. "This will be easy," he told me, "high school principals will jump at the chance to have someone like me." He even developed a syllabus for the course he wanted to teach, a course covering his approach to life.

Bill was going about this all wrong. He knew Wall Street, but he knew nothing about high schools from an administrator's point-of-view. No principal would want him to come prancing in like the king of the hill teaching a course that did not fit in with their curriculum. Bill himself did not fit in: He didn't look or sound the part of a high school teacher. Even though he had earned his Ph.D. when he was much younger, he came across as the stereotypical Wall Street big shot. I begged him not to contact any schools until he settled down a bit, learned about high schools and studied The Five O'Clock Club process.

So Bill relaxed for a few weeks, let his hair grow into something softer than his "greed is good" Gordon Gekko look, dressed more like other high school teachers, and became a little more humble. Then he met with a number of principals, and found out what their needs were, rather than telling them what he wanted to do. By the end of his initial search, he was glad to have found two part-time assignments teaching history in private schools. He learned that getting valuable "volunteer" assignments takes a lot of effort. But that effort was worth it. He is now living his dream, and he has twenty-plus years to pursue it.

Self-assessment The Five O'Clock Club way will help *you* uncover what you want to do and what is possible for you, and then we'll show you how to make it happen.

Don't Give Up Too Easily

In some respects, those who are older are very similar to recent college grads. College grads often feel like they have already paid their dues and that others should quickly recognize their talents. Older folks may feel they've paid their dues, have a terrific record of accomplishments, and should not have to put in as much effort as a younger person. But this attitude is unrealistic and can keep an older worker out of an ideal volunteer or work situation—and it's tempting to blame the lack of headway on discrimination. So be prepared to pay your dues to get to the next level in retirement—and always be guided by your plan.

To have a fulfilling next thirty years, you will *need* to plan and you will need to execute that plan. This book will show you how to do that.

Part-Time Jobs Take Effort Too

Let's look at the part-time issue. Plenty of students find part-time work, and their work requirements are often more unpredictable than yours. For example, their schedule may change each semester, so they have to find employers who are willing to put up with that. Small companies may be more inclined to hire older part-timers because they can't afford someone of your caliber full time. So don't ignore small companies.

Large companies may not want to put up with hiring part-timers, and only allow people who have been there for a while to work part time. For example, many years ago, I wanted part-time work because I was busy in the early stages of running The Five O'Clock Club. I applied at a large firm and they refused to hire me unless I was willing to work full time. Since my field is very small, I was stuck. I reluctantly accepted the full-time job, worked hard to build relationships inside the company, and one year later—when I felt I had more power—asked for part-time work, and was able to get it then. This was not prejudice because of my age (I was in my early 40s), but had to do with the realities of large corporations. I was in no room to negotiate, and neither are you if you are chasing large employers.

Finding good part-time work will take some effort.

Full-Time Jobs Are Open to Older Workers

Finding a job when you're 55 or older is only *slightly* more difficult than when you were young. According to the most recent survey on older workers from the Bureau of Labor Statistics (BLS), those aged 55 to 64 who *actively search* for a job, typically take only 4 weeks longer to find a job than the population as a whole. This is a trick figure because they include only those who are searching. Many people over 55 stop searching because they fear discrimination, or think every rejection they get is a proof of discrimination. But those who *keep searching* don't have that long to wait to become employed again *if they are searching correctly.*

So, those 55 and up who want a job are more likely to have one—*if they're looking.* But they're NOT! Of those 55 and older who are not in the labor force (that is they are not employed and they are not looking), 73.6 percent said they did not search during the previous year, yet *82.4 percent said they are "available now" for work!*

It's not discrimination if someone 55 and over is *not* looking for a job, yet says he or she would take a job if it were offered. Thus, for many older people, it's the hopelessness of not seeing a positive response and *giving up too quickly.* The major obstacle for the 55-and-up group is discouragement. Assume you will have to put in the same effort—or just a little more—than those who are under 55, and you will have a better chance.

Taking a Lower-Level Position Takes Effort

Some older people want to take a step back in their careers, not wanting the stress and responsibility of their past jobs. But employers may be afraid that you will leave when you find something better if they think you are not really eager to take a job that is lower level than the kind you have held in the past. It's your job to reassure them: "At this age and stage, I want something where I simply do the job rather than manage other people who are doing the job. I have found that that is what I love best. The benefit for you is that you get someone with this terrific experience, who understands what you go through as a manager, but who wants to support you and does not want your job." Now that sounds believable.

Do You Want That Good Life?

If you *do* want the good life for the next thirty or so years, and understand that achieving that good life will take both planning and execution, then you are reading the best possible book on that subject. Get started now on your next thirty years. The best is yet to come!

It is not the critic who counts: not the man who points out how the strong man stumbles or where the doer of deeds could have done better. The credit belongs to the man who is actually in the arena, whose face is marred by dust and sweat and blood, who strives valiantly, who errs and comes up short again and again, because there is no effort without error or shortcoming, but who knows the great enthusiasms, the great devotions, who spends himself for a worthy cause; who, at the best, knows, in the end, the triumph of high achievement, and who, at the worst, if he fails, at least he fails while daring greatly, so that his place shall never be with those cold and timid souls who knew neither victory nor defeat.

—Theodore Roosevelt

Kate Wendleton
President, The Five O'Clock Club
A national career coaching and outplacement organization
www.FiveOClockClub.com

The original Five O'Clock Club was formed in Philadelphia in 1883. It was made up of the leaders of the day, who shared their experiences "in a spirit of fellowship and good humor."

Acknowledgments

To all those who helped me move through my personal retirement journey and who encouraged me to write this book to help others move through their journey.

To my friend and colleague, Daralee Schulman who was always available to critique my ideas and encourage me through the challenges of completing this book. Her insight, constant kindness, always-present laughter and positive attitude were a source of energy and inspiration.

To my brother, Allan Rosenberg and my nephew, Aaron Rosenberg, for their expertise, technical assistance and good humor.

To Julie Kern-Smith and Julie Maxwell for their insight and editing.

To Kate Wendleton who provided the opportunity to write this book. To Claire Cohen, former director of the Peer Intervention Program and the late Carol Feit Lane, founder and president of the Career Development Specialists Network, both of whom mentored me to become as good as I could be in performing the work that I love.

To special friends Gail Wisan, Anne Stanner, Lorraine Marx Singer and my colleagues at the Career Development Specialist Network who assisted me throughout the process of researching and writing.

To the clients whom I have coached and counseled over the years and to all the individuals whose stories appear on these pages.

And most importantly, to my husband, Michael, for his patience and support in helping his computer phobic wife write an entire book on the computer.

Preface

I have been a career counselor and career coach for over twenty years. I worked at a teachers' union for ten of those years. One of my primary tasks was helping teachers transition into retirement. I have also assisted hundreds of clients, from various industries and differing professional levels, move into fulfilling retirement careers.

While working with the teachers, I witnessed an interesting phenomenon that seemed to go against the common wisdom offered by many of the books written about retirement. Even though the teachers had pensions and secure financial futures, many of them were confused and anxious about their next steps. It became apparent to me that, for many, *the major retirement issue* was not really money; emotional and psychological issues needed to be addressed. Although teachers and other clients were looking forward to the freedom of not working, most were actually fearful about the future.

When I retired, I also found myself in a state of disorientation. I had the same concerns as the retirees I was coaching. I wondered how this could be. I had helped *others* understand what needed to be done. Why couldn't I move out of my state of confusion and get on with my new life as a retired person?

What a shock to experience first-hand the truth that *intellectually understanding an issue* is not the same as having a personal solution. I too needed to accept the changes brought on by retirement and work through the steps of the transition process in my own way, just as I had taught my clients to do. I needed to be patient, to take the time to explore who I was and what I needed. I realized that my feelings were not unique; I could anticipate them.

I wrote this book to provide a road map for this journey. By combining my personal *experience* and professional *knowledge* I felt I could offer focus and direction for others. This is a book of insights—of what to expect, and of the stops and detours you'll encounter along the way to a successful retirement.

The book is divided into two parts. Part One is about understanding and coming to terms with financial, psychological, and emotional issues that surface in retirement transition. It deals with the emotional roller coaster of retirement and developing the inner resources needed to cope with the personal transformation that needs to take place.

Part Two is about assessment—*discovering who you are* (believe me, it's *never* too late for that!), identifying what you need and want, setting goals and developing plans to create a successful blueprint for your future. What drives you? What are the threads that run thru your life? What would you like to do next? This section contains Five O'Clock Club assessment inventories as well as exercises I have developed and adapted specifically for retirees. It also provides internet resources, and ideas and information to assist in your exploration. You will find lists of resources for job search, volunteering, vacation volunteering, travel, education and life-long learning programs.

The book is rich with the true stories of real people sharing their insights, experiences, and their journeys. In most cases, however, I have changed the names.

Lastly, I would like to acknowledge and thank the two Five O'Clock Club coaches who contributed chapters: Harvey Kaplan, "The Transition into Your Retirement Career," and Marjorie Hendrickson, "Together Again: Where Do We Go From Here?" Thanks also to Kate Wendleton for her chapter, "No Matter What Your Age: The Value of Having a Long-Term Vision."

I urge you to read this book cover to cover and use it to launch your next thirty years: the journey *begins* now at fifty! Enjoy the journey!

Renée Lee Rosenberg, MA
Five O'Clock Clube Career Coach

It's not the years in your life that count. It's the life in your years.
—Abraham Lincoln, U.S. President (1809–1865)

Introduction

Welcome to Retirement!

This time, like all times, is a very good one,
if we but know what to do with it.
— Ralph Waldo Emerson, American author, poet, philosopher (1803–1882)

Every exit is an entry somewhere else.
— Tom Stoppard, Czechoslovakian born British playwright (1939–)

You are probably reading this book because you're one of the seventy million plus baby boomers, born between 1946 and 1964, already retired or heading rapidly toward retirement. Reports show life expectancy figures are growing to new highs. By 2050, the number of centenarians is projected to reach 834,000 (U.S. Census Bureau). This means the chances are good that you'll live many years past your retirement age.

Given the fact that you will be around for many more years, I encourage you to develop a proactive, positive attitude and tell yourself, "I am in charge of my future and I will work to make these the best years of my life." "Work?" you say. "But I just retired" or "I'm looking forward to retiring, soon!" Yes, retirement is work. The twist is *you* are the organization, as well as the employer and the employee. You are now in charge of determining your mission, work load and daily projects: all designed to meet your future goals. The essential question of your "organization" is to ask yourself, "What do I need to do to create a fulfilling, meaningful, enjoyable life after I retire?"

In this book you will find the tools and resources needed to successfully answer that question.

This book isn't about finances. (However since it is such an important retirement issue, a discussion about money and retirement is covered in Chapter Three.) This book is about exploring who you are, what is important to you and providing you with resources and strategies to help you work through your personal retirement concerns. To guide you through this process I have included stories of people 50 plus, some struggling with the issues of aging and retirement others accepting and enjoying their new state of being.

Retirement isn't easy, as I've learned from my own experience as well as from the many people I have counseled—but you don't have to be afraid to face it either.

The big question is whether you are going to be able to say a hearty yes to your adventure.

—Joseph Campbell, American writer (1904–1987)

Retirement Is Different Today Than It's Ever Been Before

Retirement is no longer seen as only a time of leisure and relaxation, sitting daily by the pool in some warm climate, playing with the grandchildren, getting good at golf or shuffleboard, spending your days at movies or museums, or meeting friends for coffee or tea. Although these activities may still be part of your life, today's retirees want more.

Retirement is being redefined by a cohort of millions of boomer retirees who are better educated, healthier and more vigorous and energetic than any previous generation. Boomers, winding down their careers, are beginning to view retirement as a time of:

- continuing to work (some because they have to, others because they want to),
- exploring new activities,
- taking on new challenges,
- becoming life-long learners,
- developing hobbies,
- renewing dormant dreams,

- becoming more in touch with their spiritual side, and
- discovering their purpose and passion.

Your reaction to retirement will depend on *your* circumstances. If you have made plans, you will be busy and feel content. Without plans you may become let down and depressed immediately or euphoric at first, only to feel let down later. Even *with* plans, adjustment to retirement can take from several months to several years. (My retirement transition took me almost two years before I could adjust to a new role and new identity.)

To Prepare for a Happy Retirement Answer the Following Questions:

- What are your expectations for retirement?
- Are you prepared to cope with the changes that lie ahead?
- Have you begun to plan for your retirement lifestyle?
- Do you know how you want to live your life during your next 10, 20, 30 plus, years?

If you are having trouble answering any of these questions, or haven't thought about them, read on. This book was written for you.

My *Professional* Experience with Retirement

In my 20 plus years' experience as a career coach/counselor I have worked with many clients who were either moving into retirement or beginning to think about it. They ranged in age from 45 to 84, and had worked from 10 to 45 years at the same job. Most voiced similar concerns. I have used some of their stories in this book to illustrate the ups and downs they experienced while moving into and through the retirement process.

In 2003, I presented a study on my work at The International Career Development Conference in Sacramento, California. My talk described my client's predominant emotional and psychological issues around retirement. Each client presented a variety of conflicting feelings about his or her retirement: loss vs. freedom, fear vs. excitement, confusion vs. focus. They had dreamed of the day they would retire. Yet, when faced with the reality, fear set in, leading to inertia and an inability to make decisions and move their lives forward. They wanted meaning and fulfillment in their lives but were not sure what form that would take. (Renee L. Rosenberg, Retirement Talk, "Transitioning into Retirement", International Career Development Conference, Sacramento, CA. 2003.)

My *Personal* Retirement Experience

You can't no more teach what you don't know, than come back from where you ain't been.

—Mark Twain, American writer (1835–1910)

I became personally familiar with the topic of retirement change and transition confusion when I retired from my fulltime employment position at a major organization. My retirement path had many bumps and turns, not unlike those of the clients I'd counseled. When I told people I had retired, many responded with variations on:

- "Wow, how lucky you are; you can sleep late and go to the movies during the day and do what ever you like."
- "I can't wait to catch up to you. When I retire I'll stay home all day and take it easy."
- "I wish I could retire now. I would never have to worry again about meeting deadlines and having other people telling me what to do."

People thought I had it made. Actually that couldn't have been further from the truth! As I mentioned, it took almost two years for me to move through my retirement transition process, and it wasn't easy. I needed to read about, understand and accept the different stages of transition that I was living through. See Chapter Four, for a description of how William Bridges' three-stage transition process can be used to describe the retirement transition. (W. Bridges, *The Way of Transition*, Perseus Publishing, Cambridge, MA, 2001.)

When People Think About Retirement They See It as:

- A time to literally and figuratively clean up the mess in the house:
  "I'll sort through the pile of articles I've been collecting and finally get to read them."
- A time to begin or complete projects started but never finished:
  "I'll finally finish repairing the bookcase I started working on years ago."

- A time to create, to experiment, to be more flexible, and do things differently: "I'll sign up for that woodworking class I always wanted to take."
- A time of greater fulfillment, acknowledgement, and self-acceptance:
- "I'll speak with my long lost relatives about our family history."

- A time to relax:
  "I'll get up each day when ever I want, have my coffee, read the paper and then decide what I want to do."
- A time to explore new possibilities:
  "I'll travel to places I have never been but always dreamed of visiting"

Retirement *can* be all of the above, but generally, it's not so simple. A client said to me recently, "This is harder than working. I still haven't made a dent in the old magazine pile." Another client stated, "I'm really surprised at my reaction. I wake up and immediately feel disconnected, aimless and unfocused."

Many people think that when they retire they will quickly fill the empty time and replace work with something new. Unfortunately, most retirees will instead experience their transition into retirement as a difficult and painful time. Many who at first enjoyed a new sense of freedom will often discover after several months (or sometimes it may be after a few years) they feel empty, isolated and depressed.

Learning to Deal with Retirement

Even if you didn't like your job and were ready to give it up, your identity has been tied to your work. You may have feelings of no longer knowing who you are and what you want to do, or feel that your life has lost its purpose. To deal with these feelings create a meaningful plan of short-term and long-term goals and a schedule of daily activities. A plan for the future will inspire you to build and maintain feelings of personal fulfillment. (To create a plan, see Chapter Ten and Chapter Eleven.)

It is up to you to redefine, reinvent and redirect the second half of your life. In many African cultures, and in the Native American Indian culture, the "elder" is someone who achieves the highest status of respect because he or she lived a purposeful life. So create purpose in your life and as you age become proud of being an "elder".

What to Expect from This Book

Part One of this book deals with understanding and coming to terms with the financial, psychological and emotional issues connected with transitioning into retirement.

Part Two deals with helping you to move forward, discovering who you are, what you need and want and how to get it. Those chapters list resources for job search, volunteering, vacation volunteering, travel, education and life-long learning programs. (The web sites listed have been researched and updated up to the printing of this book. However since information changes so rapidly, you may find some of the websites have changed.)

It is my hope in reading this book you will learn the appropriate tools and strategies to remove obstacles that may litter your path toward an active, meaningful and purposeful life.

Retirement is a time of changing familiar roles and doing things you have always done differently. I invite you to read this book from cover to cover and then delve into Appendix I and Appendix II in the back. There, you will find affirming and uplifting quotes and suggestions from retirees, mid-life career changers and well known inspirational writers. I listed them as a reference to use whenever you find yourself stuck in a negative mindset and unable to motivate yourself to move forward and enjoy your life.

You may find it helpful to keep a notebook at your side to record your observations and thoughts as you read through this book, reviewing and adding information as you learn more about yourself and your journey into your best years ahead.

On retirement, we become permanent exiles from the world in which we have spent most of our waking hours and move completely into the smaller quarters of our private life, which we must consequently reorganize for continual occupancy.
—Jules Willing, *The Reality of Retirement: The Inner Experiences of Becoming a Retired Person,* Lively Minds Books, Chapel Hill, NC, 1989.

Part One

. . . .

Understanding the Process:

Coming to Terms with the Financial, Psychological, and Emotional Issues Connected with Transitioning into Retirement

1
...

The Changing Face of Retirement: *A Perspective*

What Does Retirement Mean to You?

When you hear the word "retirement," where do your thoughts go? Typically you will think of the economics of the event. When financial planners suggest you start planning for retirement as early in your career as possible, they are talking about savings and investments. They are not looking at retirement from a developmental, psychological or emotional perspective. When contemplating retirement, take into account your whole person and not just your financial issues.

Looking at the Word "Retirement"

William James, the 20th century philosopher, wrote that the words we use influence our thinking, which in turn influences our actions. Negative words create negative thoughts and produce negative actions. According to Webster's Dictionary, "retirement" means to retreat, to withdraw—two words with negative connotations. Certainly this is not a very uplifting thought for entering the next phase of your life. No wonder many people feel frightened and insecure when approaching retirement. Who would want to withdraw and retreat when starting a new period of life that may last for another 30 or more years?

Much has been written about replacing the word "retirement" with words such as: rewiring, non-retiring, un-retiring, the retirement zone, moving on, the next stage, the third age, renewal, advancing, moving forward, redirecting. These are attempts to break the negative mindset created by the word itself. But why spend time and energy worrying about "the word?" Instead accept and understand retirement for what it really represents:

- The end of a stage of work usually defined as long-term employment.
- An ongoing process of exploration and change into a new life of "new beginnings" for the next 30 plus years.
- An opportunity to plan and set goals for the rest and best years of your life.

A Historical Perspective

The Social Security Act of 1935 made retirement a household word, part of the American dream of the "good life" to be spent in one's "golden years." The Act established 65 as the age at which an individual could collect a monetary reward for work he or she no longer performed. For eligible individuals, retirement represented, for the first time in the nation's history and for over half a century after its passage, a time of leisure with no structure or responsibility. The ideal image became that of enjoying a relaxing leisure-filled life in a warm climate with a community of peers.

The Social Security Act is still extremely important to working Americans today. For many it is the main and sometimes only source of income, while for others, it provides a much needed supplemental income. But few actually know what the Act says. A close look at the written language of the 1935 Act might surprise you.

Title1 of the Social Security Act created "money payments to aged individuals" while Title 11 provided "more adequate (monetary) provision for aged persons, blind persons, dependent and crippled children." It lumped the "aged" 65-year-old with blind and crippled adults and dependent children, creating a not-so-subtle implication that being 65 was considered a handicapping disability.

Betty Friedan, in her book the *Fountain of Age,* points out that the Social Security Act was not based on humanitarianism, but rather on a need to force the older worker out of the workforce to make room for the younger worker. (B. Friedan, *The Fountain of Age,* Simon and Schuster, New York, NY, 1993.)

The Social Security Act of 1935 provided individuals with a monthly rate up to $85. This was considered adequate in 1935. How times have changed! In 2004 the estimated average monthly benefit was $915 and for many people this amount isn't considered adequate. These figures can be found at: www.ssa.gov/budget/2004bud

Until the 17th century, it was rare for anyone to reach old age. In the 17th and 18th centuries, attitudes were more positive toward the 60+ generation, then they are today, possibly because so few lived that long. According to social historian David Hackett Fischer, only two percent of the population lived past 65. Those who did, Fischer states, "were revered and respected, and even given the best seats in church." (D.H. Fischer, *Growing Old in America,* Oxford University Press, New York, NY, 1977.)

With increases in urbanization and industrialization, attitudes about the aged changed for the worse. In 1882, the British novelist Anthony Trollope, well-aware of the hardships of growing old in the nineteenth century, wrote an allegorical novel entitled, *The Fixed Period*, in which he sarcastically recommended that those who had passed their prime of 67 should be euthanized. No retirement planning for them!

In the nineteenth century, older workers were no longer highly regarded or useful. Factory owners only wanted young and virile workers. Mandatory retirement laws came into effect, forcing older workers to leave their jobs. Derogatory labels such as "codger, fuddy-duddy, feeble-minded" and "geezer" were freely used. Age discrimination devalued older workers and strongly barred them from working. No retirement planning for them either!

Age discrimination was noted again in a 1976 poll by Louis Harris, which showed that from 45% to 65% of all polled retirees *had not wished to retire.*

Modern times have certainly not been kind to older workers, who are forced out of their jobs and quickly lose both status and identity. Ursula A. Falk and Gerhard Falk, in their book on ageism write about the fate of the elderly who are healthy and want to find work but are refused because of their age: "Since occupation and work are the principal criteria of social prestige in America, the old, by being excluded from work are therefore devalued." (U. Falk, G. Faulk, *Ageism, the Aged and Aging in America: On Being Old in an Alienated Society,* C.C. Thomas Publishing, Springfield, Il, 1997.)

Female elephants past their fertility don't leave their herds, animal behaviorists have discovered, but remain on as "elders" who educate the young in elephant ways. Orcas, known as Killer Whales (in error, since they are dolphins, not whales), form pods that are often led by Orca seniors, some in their 90s.

We could and should learn from the animals!

Things Have Changed

It is a relatively new concept to be productive when you retire from work, or even think about working. When social security came into being, people didn't plan to continue working beyond their actual retirement days. Why should they? The life expectancy in 1935 was 45.

However, life expectancy in the United States today continues to rise. People are living into their 80's, 90's and beyond. What's more, the cohort of baby boomers, born between 1946 and 1964, are fast becoming the majority and are rapidly changing the face of retirement. U.S. census bureau statistics report that on January 1, 2006, nearly 76 million boomers began turning 60. *Fortune* magazine writes that on January 1, 2011, "The biggest retirement wave in U.S. history will officially begin."

The baby boomer generation came of age with different cultural influences than its parents' generation. The boomers grew up listening to the music of Bob Dylan, Joan Baez, Jim Morrison and the Doors, Jimi Hendrix, Janis Joplin, The Incredible String Band, The Mamas and The Papas, Donovan and Cat Stevens. Their familiar names and pictures were of Rev. Martin Luther King, John Kennedy, Bobby Kennedy, Malcolm X, Bobby Steele and the Black Panthers, the kidnapping of Patty Hearst, Angela Davis, Woodstock, Vietnam and the first man walking on the moon. The image is of hippies, freethinkers and flower children all rolled into one.

This first wave of boomers turning 60, and those boomers who follow close behind, are described in the media as more energetic, more skilled and more spirited than prior generations. The members of this cohort are no longer defined by, nor do they follow, a predictable linear life-stage model: college, work, retirement. According to the media, the new buzz-word has become "life stages" not "aging." Boomers don't see themselves "aging" as their parents did nor does their age define where they are in their life cycle; men are becoming fathers at 50, women are turning to careers after raising a family or even combining career at the same time as raising a family. Large numbers are returning to school for second degrees. Many are changing careers; doctors are becoming educational advisors, teachers are becoming nurses, nurses are becoming lawyers, bankers are becoming small business owners, sanitation workers are becoming social workers, and the list goes on.

What Does All This Mean?

According to Census Bureau predictions, the boomer generation has at least thirty or more good years ahead. A large percentage of the sixty-plus generation is choosing to either work or be involved in a meaningful activity well into their 70's, 80's and 90's, and in some cases even beyond. This means that you and your cohorts, for the first time in history, will each be responsible for taking charge of your individual journey to discover who you are and to then create what you want to do with the rest of your life.

Boomers Are Active

The Roper Starch Worldwide survey conducted for AARP in 2000 concluded the following about boomers planning to remain in the workplace:

- 30% wanted part-time work, not out of necessity but for enjoyment,
- 25% wanted part-time work for both enjoyment and supplemental income,
- 23% felt they had to work because they needed the additional income,
- 9% were not considering retirement at all, but wanted to continue at their present jobs.

Al Lewis, who played Grandpa in the 1960's TV series, *The Munsters*, ran for governor of New York when he was in his 80's and ran for a seat in the New York State Senate two years later. Betty Friedan, the founder and first president of NOW, wrote books and taught at Cornell University well into her 80's. Senator Claude Pepper was active in the U.S. Senate until his death in office at age 88. He was an advocate of eliminating ageism, and a good example of what he preached. When South Carolina Senator Strom Thurmond retired at 100, in 2003, he was not only the longest serving senator in American history (48 years) but also the oldest person to ever serve in congress. Lillian Carter, President Carter's mother, joined the Peace Corp at 84 and spent two years in India working as a nurse. Jack La Lanne, the bodybuilding and fitness guru, came to Times Square in New York City on his ninety-second birthday to promote his new food juicer and sign copies of his new cookbooks—*Celebrating 90-Plus Years of Healthy Living* and *Cooking with Jack: Eat Right and You Can't Go Wrong.*

Sidney Harmon, 88, founder and CEO of Harmon International Industries, Inc. and a pioneer in the high fidelity industry, is quoted in the October, 2006 issue of *AARP Bulletin*, as telling the Washington Post, that he didn't need a replacement but rather a successor because he was "planning to retire in 25 years."

The world has changed, and so have we. Whether it means continuing to work, developing new interests, going back to school, traveling or spending it in leisure pursuits, your goal should be to create a retirement life of redirection that is productive, healthy, happy and fulfilling as possible. To create this life, it is best to start early to plan for retirement.

What if you haven't started planning? Don't dismay. You can begin today. No matter what your "life stage," start now to gather your information, do your research, read this book and begin planning your next steps.

Remember "retirement" is not only a word. It is a process. Be patient with yourself; take the time you need to plan and experiment. This is your opportunity to move forward and explore and meet the challenges that lies ahead, to make the next 30-plus years of your life the best yet. This book was written to be your guide.

You have brains in your head. You have feet in your shoes.
You can steer yourself any direction you choose.
You're on your own. And you know what you know.
And YOU are the guy (or gal) who'll decide where to go.

—Dr. Seuss, American Children's Writer,
Illustrator, *Oh, the Places You'll Go!* (1904–1991)

We either make ourselves miserable or we can make our selves strong. The amount of work is the same.

—Carlos Castaneda, Brazilian/American
anthropologist, writer (1931–1998)

2

...

Dispelling the
Myths of Aging

*To be 70 years young is sometimes far more cheerful and hopeful that to be 40
years.*
　　　　　—Oliver Wendell Holmes, Chief Justice US Supreme Court (1809–1894)

*When I was young I was called a rugged individualist. When I was in my fifties I
was considered eccentric. Here I am doing and saying the same things I did then
and I'm labeled senile.*
　　　　　　　　—George Burns, American comedian (1896–1996)

When you were 20, what were your thoughts about people over 50? Out of shape,
inflexible, asexual, inactive.

What did you think about people over 60? Has-beens, elderly, slow thinking, not
physically fit, difficult to communicate with, stuck in their ways.

Over 70? Ancient.

If you are 50 plus it may be true that you are no longer young, but are you old?

You can't help getting older, but you don't have to get old.
　　　　　　　　　　　　　　　—George Burns (1896–1996)

We turn not older with years, but newer every day.
>   —Emily Dickenson, American poet (1830–1886)

We Are Influenced by Cultural Attitudes and Perceptions Toward Aging

Many of the characteristics we ascribe to older people are actually stereotypes or myths perpetuated by government, business and the mass media. According to Alex Comfort, society labels older persons as "wanting to withdraw, wanting fewer commitments, wanting less activity and wanting reduced social interactions." (A. Comfort, *A Good Age*, Fireside Books/ Simon and Schuster, New York, NY, 1978.) Comfort calls these negative roles assigned to older people "sociogenic aging." He believes that these false beliefs are responsible for creating the biased attitudes toward older persons. The adage, "you are only as old as you feel" reminds us that if you believe you are "old" you will act "old', conversely believe in feeling "young" and you will act young."

To me, old age is always 15 years older than I am.
>   —Bernard Baruch, American statesmen, presidential advisor (1870–1965)

When it comes to staying young, a mind-lift beats a face-lift any day.
>   —Marty Bucella, contemporary American cartoonist

Several Different Attitudes Toward Aging

Clara was a vibrant, active woman until she retired at 58. Three months into her retirement she lamented, "I'm afraid I'm growing old and beginning to look my age. I am feeling old and tired. I don't want to be 58. I want to look young and be young, but I'm not. I would do anything to turn back the clock."

Clara can't accept her age. She wants to be seen as young. She is caught up in her regrets and is having a difficult time enjoying her present life or planning for the future. Her fear of aging has convinced her that she is "old" and that the future will be difficult.

By the way of contrast, let's look at Paul, Alice and Robert.

Paul, 62, declared, "I see life as involved and revolving. I feel quite comfortable with who I am and am looking forward to who I will become in my retirement."

Alice, 59, retired two years ago and is planning her next trip to Thailand, where she will be teaching English in a missionary school. She told me, "The experience of working in a different culture in a distant land keeps me energized and excited. I never know what to expect next. It's very different from my old work environment."

Yet another client, Robert, 80, downsized six months ago from his job of 14 years, shared, "I don't think there will be a job out there for me now. I guess I'm retired, but that's okay. I have a rather romantic approach toward life. I can't quantify it, but I always have things to do. I like to stay active. I like to learn new things and keep exercising my mind."

Paul, Alice and Robert accept their age and view themselves as senior adults. They are productive, energetic and optimistic about the future.

Accept Your Age and Move on

There is no old age. There is, as there always was, just you.
—Carol Matthau, American author (1925–2003)

In an interview with *The New York Times* in 1993, Betty Friedan, author of *The Feminine Mystique,* (W.W. Norton and Co., New York, NY, 1963) was quoted as saying she worried that, "people who were in denial about old age, who feel threatened as they see it looming . . . will miss an enormous potential." She continued, they will "miss the surprises, the possibilities and the evolution" that they "are just beginning to know."

Having a positive attitude toward aging and retirement requires a sense of humor and the ability not to be influenced by the mass media messages of trying to convince you that beauty and youth go hand-in-hand. Recently I saw an ad that read, "Who doesn't want to look half their age? Face it; a fresh younger appearance is a hot commodity."

Now, what is the point of looking 32 when you are 64? Or 26 when you are 52? How sad it is to keep struggling for an image that is no longer you, rather than appreciating and accepting who you are *now*. Yet the media is constantly pushing the concept of eternal youth. We must remind ourselves that no matter what our age, we all possess a unique beauty.

It is my hope that as the baby boomers age, we will see more and more advertisements showing mature-looking models as a "hot commodity."

Youth, large, lusty, loving—youth full of grace, force, fascination,
Do you know that Old Age may come after you with equal grace, force, and
fascination?

—From the poem, *Youth, Day, Old Age and Night*
by Walt Whitman, American poet (1819–1892)

Are You Influenced by Your Unconscious Attitudes Toward Aging?

Your beliefs about aging can greatly affect your sense of well-being and your adjustment toward a successful retirement. Read the questions below and answer them honestly:

- Do I regret I'm no longer 20? 30? 40?
- Do I really feel old or am I being influenced by advertising and mass media?
- Am I excited by the future or do I lament opportunities missed when I was younger?
- Do I have a negative attitude about getting older, and is it influencing my ability to take on new challenges and learn new things?
- Do I look forward to the future with optimism and excitement or fear and anxiety?

Any aha's? What did you learn about your beliefs? Are you surprised by your answers?

Eight Common Myths of Aging in Our Culture

Read the following statements and circle your answer, true or false, for each one. Then review the answers below to see how you scored.

1. Chronological age determines how old you feel.
   True   False

2. Most older adults have rigid beliefs and have difficulty adapting to change.
   True   False

3. Older adults can't learn new information.
   True   False

4. Ageism is the main limiting factor for those who have retired and still would like to work.
   True   False

5. Physical strength declines in old age.
   True   False

6. When you become older, your creative and intellectual abilities decline.
   True   False

7. Mental ability declines with age.
   True   False

8. Retirement is the last stage of life; it's all downhill from now on.
   True   False

Now let's look at the answers.

1. Chronological age determines how old you feel.
   <u>False</u>

   Chronological age is the number of years you have lived since your birth. Functional age—how well you psychologically and socially function in your environment—is more important in determining how old you feel. I have met individuals in their 80's and 90's who are independent, creative, vibrant and able to meet life's challenges head-on.

   Recently I worked with two 63-year-old clients, both of whom retired last year. Janet was constantly referring to her age and describing herself as too old to meet new friends or join new groups. She was fond of saying, "I'm over the hill (I always wonder which hill that is) and heading downhill fast. I'm too old to start anything new."

   Susan, on the other hand, had a different attitude toward her life. She paid very little attention to her age, and viewed her retirement as a time to grow and learn. "Retirement has given me the opportunity to take classes at the local community college. I'm taking memoir-writing, ceramics and horti-culture classes. I'm so busy I'm never home. I love being active and learning."

2. Most older adults have rigid beliefs and have difficulty adapting to change.
   <u>False</u>
   Older adults are no more rigid than younger adults. Individuals who were rigid and had difficulty adapting to change as young adults will probably exhibit the same characteristics when they are older.

   > *He who is of calm and happy nature will hardly feel the pressure of age, but to him who is of an opposite disposition youth and age are equally a burden.*
   >
   > —Plato, Roman philosopher (427 BC–347 BC)

3. Older adults can't learn new information.
   <u>False</u>
   Who said, "You can't teach an old dog new tricks?" What an awful phrase and completely untrue! (My dog Lucy, at thirteen, is still learning new tricks.) Older adults are as capable of learning new information as anyone. When Dianne was 63, she was hired to work part-time for a college work-study program. She didn't type and was hoping the computer on her desk would be given to someone else. Today, at 75, she's still on the job and uses the computer daily. "I must admit," she exclaimed, "it was a challenge but now I don't know how I ever got along without it."

   > *The excitement of learning separates youth from old age. As long as you're learning you're not old.*
   >
   > —Dr. Rosalyn S. Yalow, contemporary American
   > physician, Nobel Prize for medicine, 1977

   Neuroscientist, Dr. Marian C. Diamond, who conducted studies of people over 88 years of age, states: "We must disallow negative attitudes that say the elderly can't learn . . . the main factor is stimulation, and the brain can be active at any age." (*Aging Today*, May/June 1998)

4. Ageism is the main limiting factor for those who have retired and still would like to work.

<u>False</u>

Ageism can certainly play a role in limiting opportunities, discouraging retirees from pursuing meaningful employment. It's difficult to stay positive about job-hunting when you hear comments like, "Who will hire you at 60?" and, "You can't be interested in starting something new at your age."

But these are not the strongest limiting factors. The main issue remains the internal, self-defeating, self-fulfilling prophesy of *believing* you are too old.

As one client told me, "I would like to continue working or do something productive, but who will hire me? I'm old." Another client claims, "I only know the old systems, I'm from the old school. Employers want young blood not me." (See Chapter Fourteen, for tips and strategies for dealing positively with negative beliefs about age discrimination.)

5. Physical strength declines in old age.

<u>True, but . . .</u>

Physical strength does tend to decline with age. However, studies have shown that exercise can counteract and even limit physical decline. It's your choice to be a couch potato or continue to remain active and physically fit no matter what your age or physical limitations. Yoga and exercise classes are available for all levels and all ages. A person who is 65 and has a steady exercise routine may be (and probably is) in better shape and physically stronger than a forty-five-year-old who rarely exercises. Even following a regular walking routine can be beneficial.

Charlie, a 92-year-old, who retired in 1974, is a good example of someone who has stayed fit. He walked two miles and swam one hour every day until he was 87. He told me he has slowed down, walks to the supermarket and back—approximately 1 mile each day and swims "only" 3 times a week.

> . . . *take a guy that's 60 years old and hasn't exercised . . . exercise him for 6 to 8 weeks—you can double his strength and double his endurance . . .*
> —Jack La Lanne, fitness guru still going strong at 92, interviewed at 91 by the editor of the online publication, *Share Guide, 2003.*

6. When you become older, your creative and intellectual abilities decline.
   <u>False</u>

   Throughout history it has been proven that intellectual and creative ability are not determined by age. Goethe finished *Faust* at 82; Cervantes wrote *Don Quixote* in his 60's, I. F. Stone authored *The Trial of Socrates* in his eighties. Ben Franklin at 70 sailed to France as a representative of America, to obtain aid for the war against England. At 85 he remained actively involved in the Constitutional Convention. Grandma Moses painted up to her death at age 104. Matisse, in his 80's and physically handicapped, designed stained glass windows for a church in Vence, in southern France.

   > *I never feel age . . . If you have creative work, you don't have age or time.*
   > —Louise Nevelson, artist (1900–1980)

7. Mental ability declines with age.
   <u>False</u>

   Richard Restak, clinical professor of neurology, connected with George Washington University Medical School, states "the brain of an older person is not inferior to the brain of a younger person—it is just organized differently." (R. Restak, *The Secret Life of the Brain,* Dana Press, New York, NY and Joseph Henry Press, Washington, DC, 2001.)

   Many people believe that the brain shrinks and that we lose brain cells as we age, affecting our mental capacity. Research has shown however that even though we do lose brain cells, the average brain can compensate for the loss by staying active. In the article, "The Brain . . . Use It or Lose It", Dr. Diamond states that the "receptive branches of nerve cells, called dendrites, located in the neocortical region of the brain, will increase with use and decrease with disuse." (*Mindshift Connection,* Vol. 1, No.1, Zephyr Press, edited by Dee Dickinson, 1996.) (See Chapter Seventeen for additional discussion on how to keep the brain active.)

   Alex Comfort, in *The Good Age,* bluntly reminds us, "Old people become crazy for three reasons: Because they were crazy when they were young, because they have an illness or because we drive them crazy—and the last reason is more common."

8. Retirement is the last stage of life; it's all downhill from then on.

   <u>**False, False, False**</u>
   Retirement can open up new possibilities and opportunities for you to discover your passions and fulfill your dreams—if you remain open to the challenge.

> *Of all self-fulfilling prophecies in our culture, the assumption that aging means decline and poor health is probably the deadliest.*
> —Marilyn Ferguson, American contemporary writer

How Did You Do?

If you answered "true" to even one question above consider making an attitudinal shift. If you think positively about aging, your future will be happier and you may also increase your longevity. A study conducted by researcher Becca Levy at Yale University's Department of Epidemiology and Public Health and published in the August, 2002 issue of *The Journal of Personality and Social Psychology* reported that, "Older people with more positive thoughts about aging, measured up to 23 years earlier, lived 7.5 years longer than those with less positive self-perceptions of aging." The study found that higher longevity remained even after factors such as age, health, gender, socio-economic status, and loneliness were taken into account. Dr. Levy concluded that, "Negative views operate without a person's awareness because they are internalized since childhood."

The perceptions you develop at a young age are the perceptions you carry with you throughout your life. Some of you may have to work harder than others to disallow your ingrained negative beliefs about aging in order to see it as just another stage in life to explore.

> *We become what we think about most of the time.*
> —William James, American philosopher (1842–1910)

People Incorporate Life Values Based on Earlier Beliefs and Experiences

Several 90+ retirees I interviewed spoke of the influence of living through the Depression. They described living in poverty, with little and sometimes no food on the table, with no heat and cracks in the windows. This created what they described as "depression thinking" or a "scarcity mentality." They spoke of still saving paper bags, string balls and rubber band balls. As one 92-year-old retiree put it, "During the Depression I worked everywhere and anywhere. When I retired I felt like an old farmer. I've got a horse, a cow, a pig and a plow and I'll get along somehow. I wasn't worried about how I would survive. I survived the Depression, I'll survive retirement."

Wisdom doesn't automatically come with old age. Nothing does . . . It's true, some wines improve with age. But only if the grapes were good in the first place.
—Abigail Van Buren, American columnist (1918–1978)

Don't Despair. It's Never Too Late to Change Your Attitude

How can you develop positive attitudes toward aging? Here are some suggestions:

- Read books about people who have achieved success in later life.
- Find role models in your neighborhood who are living full, rich, productive lives in their 50's, 60's, 70's, 80's and even 90's. Talk to them, listen to their stories and follow their advice.

My inspiration was Edna, who retired 40 years ago. She became an accomplished and acknowledged painter at 85. Approaching 95, she was mentally sharp, active, and in charge of planning future events in her life. She took public transportation, traveling by bus one hour each way twice a week to attend art and literature classes across town. Look at websites such as www.healthandage.com and www.civicventures.org for information on optimistic articles, resources, exercises and inspiring stories about aging.

- Read magazines such as *Geezer Jock*, geared to the over-40 athlete or *More*, with a focus on the positive aspects of and opportunities for those over 60.
- Seek out volunteer opportunities in the community, including local schools, cultural institutions, arts groups, libraries.
- Join a book club or a writing group at your local university, 'Y', or community center.
- Take an art class in something you always wanted to learn: painting, wood-working, ceramics, papermaking, photography, metal sculpture or knitting.
- Stay active. Sign up for yoga classes or other exercise classes, swim, ride a bicycle, learn how to use aerobic equipment, and walk whenever you can.

As Deborah Killam, a sociologist at the University of Maine Cooperative extension program, reminds us in the online *Caregiver Factsheet Bulletin # 4209*, "Aging is not a process of decline; it is a process of becoming, of continuing to meet life's challenges and of growing into a powerful and complete human being."

No matter how old you are, there's always something good to look forward to.
—Lynn Johnson, Canadian cartoonist (1947–)

3
...

Your Finances:
Coming to Terms with What You Need

Let our advance worry become advance thinking and planning.
— Winston Churchill, British Prime Minister (1874–1965)

Note: In this chapter I have excerpted interesting suggestions and information from the U. S. Department of Labor publication: *Savings Fitness: A Guide to Your Money and Your Financial Future.* (U.S. Department of Labor, Employee Benefits Security Administration In partnership with Certified Financial Planner Board of Standards Inc.)

This publication is available online at: www.pueblo.gsa.gov/cic_text/money/save-fit/save-fit01.htm or call 1-866-444-3272 to order free of charge.

When you think of retirement do you worry about how to build a secure financial future for yourself and your family? Have you developed a long-term investment strategy based on your personal needs, goals, and tolerance for risk? Have you calculated how much money you will need for a comfortable retirement? Have you determined whether you will *have* enough money or if you will need to supplement your finances by continuing to work?

"Will I have enough money to live the life I want?" is the most commonly asked question about retirement. Financial planners can help you with the numbers, by providing you with forecasts, asset allocation and investment planning.

Money and having enough of it has become a constant obsession in our culture. But how much is enough? What you will need for your retirement depends on several factors: your age at retirement, your economic circumstances and, most importantly, your subjective evaluation of what you really feel about your money needs.

When planning consider the following facts:

1. The cost of retirement is becoming more and more expensive.

2. The average American is living a longer, more active life and will probably live 20 to 40 years in retirement. This means early retirement can be financially daunting since your savings will need to be stretched further.

3. Paying for retirement has become more and more the individual's responsibility. Fewer companies provide pension plans, and those that do contribute less. The employee, not the employer, now generally pays the 401 K defined contribution plan.

4. Studies have found that nearly half of all Americans are unfamiliar with investment basics, and that many workers still believe that Social Security will provide for their retirement needs.

5. Experts recommend putting a mimimum 10% of your annual gross income into retirement savings however if you're 50 and haven't started saving, they suggest putting 20% of your income into retirement savings.

6. To be financially comfortable financial planners believe that you will need at least 70% of your pre-retirement income—a combination of social security, pension, personal savings, and investments. For many, it may also have to include additional income from work, either part-time or full-time.

While these facts represent the current wisdom regarding retirement income, your individual needs and priorities that will dictate your financial plans.

I, Mark Twain being of sound mind, have spent everything.
—Mark Twain, American author (1835–1910)

Barbara, Rosemary and John, like so many of my clients, worried about how much money they would need for their retirement. Their stories offer a clear example of how differently people view their money needs when they retire.

Three Different Views on Finances and Retirement

Barbara

Barbara, at 63, planned on traveling for several months and then purchasing a small condo in a California retirement community. During a pension consultation from her employer she learned that her pension would be close to her working salary. At first, she was delighted to get this news, but after ruminating awhile, she began to feel insecure and worried, "Would this be enough?" She became nervous and started fretting that she needed more money for her retirement plan. She put off her retirement and decided to stay on the job for several more years so that she could continue to increase her pension. She was suffering from what Nancy Schlossberg labels "income withdrawal syndrome," the fear that you will never have enough money when you retire. (N. Schlossberg, *Retire Smart, Retire Happy*, American Psychological Association, New York, NY, 2003.)

Rosemary

Rosemary on the other hand, learned at 62 that her pension would be about a third of her working salary. She had plans to relocate to be close to her daughter and newborn grandchild. She was told if she continued working three additional years her final pension amount would be higher. She was concerned about her small pension, but was determined to go ahead with her plan. She moved to California, found several part-time college teaching positions to supplement her income and down-scaled her life by eliminating unnecessary expenses. She now alternates her time between working two days a week and watching her grandchild grow.

John

John, 63, a sales executive, was downsized after a long career. Although his income was dramatically reduced, he and his wife felt they could make do and enjoy their life together if they took several steps toward simplifying their routines. They began by selling their house and moving into a smaller apartment. In place of eating out in expensive restaurants, they began a gourmet-cooking club with several friends. Each month one group member hosted a gourmet theme dinner in his or her home.

They enrolled in the "My Turn" program at a community college, which, after a small registration fee, offers tuition-free classes to seniors over 60. (Read more about this and other educational programs in Chapter Sixteen.) They became knowledgeable about senior reduced rates and free travel opportunities, such as home exchange programs and Servas. (More about Servas and home exchange programs in Chapter Fifteen.) John and his wife became volunteers at a major cultural institution enabling them to attend concerts and performances for free or reduced rates.

"Our motto now is 'less is good'. We've changed our attitude about what's important in life, and acquiring more is certainly not part of it," John states. He and his wife have less available money and need to conserve for the future, but instead of worrying about their limited finances, they found creative solutions to living full, content lives.

The media scare us into thinking that we may outlive your money, but you can't rely on someone else's financial formula. Your personal needs and view of the world differs from other persons. Financial advisors report that the best way to think about your financial needs is to determine what choices you will be making when you retire and to build a budget around those choices. Of course, this may be hard to accurately predict since so many events of the future are not predictable. Some choices will be in your control but other unknown factors including unanticipated expenses, your life span, your health and the return on your investments, won't be. Lack of certainty is not, however, a reason to avoid planning. Just do the best you can.

Things to Consider to Help You Manage Your Expectations

1. Rising medical and medicine costs and rising health insurance premiums. (To compare health plans go to www.eHealthInsurance.com.)
2. Needed necessities: utilities, rent, health insurance, and food.
3. Wanted necessities: cell phone, car, computer, digital camera, new appliances, new technology gadgets.
4. Discretionary expenses: vacations, hobbies, restaurants, subscriptions and entertainment.
5. Rising inflation.
6. Relocation costs.
7. Capital items that you may need to finance: a new roof, a new car, replacing an old appliance, the cost of emergency or major home repairs.

8. Providing on-going care for an ill or elderly family member or an emergency medical condition to yourself or someone in your family.

9. Changing marital status: getting married, getting divorced, loss of a spouse or significant other.

10. Paying off debts.

11. Retirement or sudden downsizing of spouse or significant other.

Want to Spend Less?

- Think about eliminating all (or most) of your credit cards. Pay for items in cash.
- Downsize your home or large, many room apartment to a smaller apartment
- Downsize your life style. Look around—what can you can do without?
- Shop at second-hand or used-goods stores.
- Attempt to repair broken or damaged items before replacing them.
- Sell your car, and use alternative methods of transportation.
- Learn about and ask for discounts being offered to people over sixty: travel, hotels, movie theaters, colleges, retail establishments.

Tips to Help Plan Your Finances

There are many books and web sites to assist you in handling your financial resources. Most say you should start planning and saving early. But even if you didn't, don't despair. Just get started NOW! The following tips were taken directly from The *Savings Fitness Guide* cited at the beginning of this chapter.

- It's never too late to start. It's only too late if you don't start at all.
- Sock it away. Pump everything you can into your tax-sheltered retirement plans and personal savings. Try to put away at least 20 percent of your income.
- Reduce expenses. Funnel the savings into your nest egg.
- Take a second job or work extra hours.

- Aim for higher returns. Don't invest in anything you are uncomfortable with, but see if you can't squeeze out better returns with a more aggressive portfolio.
- Retire later. You may not need to work full time beyond your planned retirement age. Part time may be enough.
- Delay taking Social Security. Benefits will be higher when you start collecting later rather than earlier.
- Make use of your home. Rent out a room or move to a less expensive home and save the profits.
- Sell assets that are not producing much income or growth, such as undeveloped land or a vacation home, and invest in income-producing assets.

A good financial-fitness plan starts with looking at your current financial resources and calculating your net worth: your total assets minus your total liabilities. Which are greater: your assets or your liabilities? Track your financial stability by reviewing your net worth annually. To help determine your liabilities, monitor how you currently spend by keeping a money diary. Then try to envision and record what your expenses may be after retirement. Will your liabilities increase or decrease? Are your assets enough to cover your liabilities? Your aim is to create a positive net worth that will grow each year.

The Savings Fitness Guide also suggests identifying other financial resources that aren't included in your net worth, but that can help you through tough times. These include the "death benefits of your life insurance policies, Social Security survivor's benefits, health care coverage, disability, insurance, liability insurance and auto and home insurance. *The Guide* explains, that "Although you may have to pay for some of these resources, they offer financial protection in case of illness, accidents, or other catastrophes."

Financial planning is an on-going process. As your life and goals change, so will your financial needs. Financial stability requires research and careful decision-making. Your decisions will be based in part, on your values, goals and plans for your future. Not sure what those are? The assessments in Chapters Ten, Eleven, Twelve, Thirteen, Appendix III and Appendix IV will assist you to explore and gather the information you need to make decisions, set goals and plan your retirement finances.

Free Resources Available

The resources below can give you some food for thought about your finances. For more in-depth information, you can refer to the many books and resources that deal exclusively with financial planning. Included below are several free government and non-government resources available to assist you in monitoring and planning your finances.

Retirement Planning and General Retirement

US Department of Labor Employee Benefits Security Administration, in partnership with The Actuarial Foundation, and North American Securities Administrators Association.
www.dol.gov/ebsa
200 Constitution Ave, NW Washington, DC 20210
Publications: *Savings Fitness: A Guide to Your Money Financial Future*
Taking the Mystery Out of Retirement Planning
Top 10 Ways to Save for Retirement
Women and Retirement Savings
What You Should Know About Your Retirement Plan
Request single copies of above publications by calling 1-866-444-EBSA (3272)

The Social Security Administration
www.ssa.gov
Online resources to help calculate your retirement benefits, and to learn about survivor benefits and Medicare.
Publications: *Understanding the Benefits*
What Every Woman Should Know

The AARP
www.aarp.org
1-888-OUR-AARP (1-888-687-2277)
Publication: *Focus: Your Guide to Financial Planning for Retirement*

The Pension Benefit Guaranty Corporation
www.pbgc.gov
1-800-400-7242

Get help in locating money still in your traditional defined benefit (DB) account.

Publications: *Your Guaranteed Pension*

Finding a Lost Pension

National Endowment for Financial Education

www.nefe.org

Publication: *Guidebook to Help Late Savers Prepare for Retirement*

Savings and Investing

Consumer Federation of America

www.consumerfed.org

202-387-6121

Publication: *Six Steps to Six-Figure Savings*

The Securities and Exchange Commission

www.sec.gov

Publications: *Invest Wisely: Introduction to Mutual Funds*

Questions You Should Ask About Your Investments

The Financial Literacy and Education Commission, US Department of the Treasury

www.mymoney.gov

Publication: *My Money Tool Kit*

The Internal Revenue Service

www.irs.gov/pub/irs-pdf/p590.pdf

Publication: *Individual Retirement Arrangements*

Getting Help

Certified Financial Planner Board of Standards

1-888-237-6275

Publication: *Ten Questions to Ask When Choosing a Financial Planner*

The North American Securities Association

www.nasaa.org/investor education/

Alerts readers to the latest money scams and disciplinary rulings against individual financial advisors.

Publication: *Protecting Your Finances: How to Avoid Investment Frauds and Scams*

The Certified Financial Planner Board of Standards

www.cfp.net/learn

1-888-237-6275

Locate a certified financial planner near you.

Publication: *Financial Planner Resource Kit*

The Actuarial Foundation

www.actuarialfoundation.org

Publications: *Seven Life-Defining Financial Decisions*

Making Your Money Last for a Lifetime: Why You Need to Know About Annuities

The Society of Actuaries

www.soa.org

(See "Research and Publications") Links to information articles in the group's publication, *The Actuary Magazine.*

4
•••

Transitioning into Retirement

One doesn't discover new lands without consenting to lose sight of the shore for a very long time.

—Andre Gide, French writer, recipient of the
Nobel Prize for Literature, 1947 (1869–1951)

Transitioning into retirement is a gradual process that affects everyone differently. Your ability to adjust successfully is both personal and individual depending on many factors: your family life, the role you played at work, the degree of satisfaction you received from work, the timing of retirement (was it forced or voluntary?), your level of pre-retirement planning, your ability to identify purpose and meaning in your life, your health issues and your feelings about financial security.

According to Dr. David P. Helfand there are four basic changes that can be found in any transition:

- change in role
- change in relationship
- change in routine
- change in assumptions about yourself or the world

(D. Helfand, *Career Change*, VGM Careers Horizon, Chicago, IL, 1999.)

Other transitions may include one or two of these changes, but the retirement transition encompasses all four at the same time. Dealing with these four changes simultaneously can be unnerving, confusing, depressing and physically debilitating.

This chapter will offer you tools and suggestions on how you can observe, understand and manage your retirement transition.

The Difference Between Transition and Change

You may think change and transition are the same; they aren't. Change is an event that can happen without your input or consent while transition is the process that helps you to understand and accept the change. In our fast-moving, nano-second, multi-tasking culture, we always tend to be in a hurry to get somewhere or accomplish something. Transition is a process and therefore requires time and patience. However it may be difficult to slow yourself down. Take a few deep breaths and repeat, "This is an important time in my life. I'm worth every minute spent making sure I get it right." If that doesn't slow you down, then think of this: If you rush through the transition process too quickly without understanding *the process*, you may experience negative consequences to both your health and emotional well-being.

Slow down, introspect on your feelings and enjoy the process even if it may seem painful at first.

Basic Differences Between Change and Transition to Keep in Mind

CHANGE

- Change is an external shift in an event or situation
- Change is what you observe.

- Change is focused on an outcome or result.
- Change is very noticeable.

- Change can elicit negative responses, such as anger, depression, illness and low self-esteem.

TRANSITION

- Transition is an internal process influenced by external events.
- Transition is what you feel and experience.
- Transition may not necessarily be outcome or results focused.
- Transition can be subtle and has less definition.
- Transition helps you understand the emotional responses caused by change.

A Closer Look at Transition

Transition is the natural process of disorientation and reorientation that marks the turning points in the path of growth . . . transitions are key times in the natural process of self-renewal.

—William Bridges, contemporary American author, psychologist

Psychologist William Bridges describes transition as a three-phase process; *endings, the neutral zone,* and *new beginnings.* (W. Bridges, *Transitions: Making Sense of Life's Changes,* Perseus Publishing, Cambridge, MA, 1980.) In the first phase, *endings,* you may experience feelings of confusion, loss, emptiness, fear of the future, conflict and ambivalence. Even if you didn't like your job, didn't feel successful in your current work, and were feeling burned out and ready to leave, your job created a role which gave you an identity. Letting go of this identity may not be easy for you.

One of the symptoms of an approaching nervous breakdown is the belief that one's work is terribly important.

—Bertrand Russell, British philosopher, essayist,
Nobel Prize for Literature, 1950 (1872–1970)

A client of mine who was stuck in *endings* describes his feelings: "This transition into retirement broke up my old identity like a sledge hammer, destroying my familiar foundations and sending shock waves through my mind and body. I disliked my job and wasn't sorry to leave it behind. But now I actually miss my work. I'm feeling lost and frightened about what is next. I no longer know who I am or where I belong." (Renee L. Rosenberg, "Transitioning into Retirement", ICDC Conference, Sacramento, CA. 2003.)

Since *endings* is the stage where people have the most difficulty, I will focus mainly on its components in this chapter.

"No, your father has not lost his marbles.
He's just having a hard time grasping the concept of relaxation."

The Four Components of *Endings*

Bridges divides *endings* into four components: *disengagement, disidentification, disenchantment,* and *disorientation.* (*Transitions: Making Sense of Life's Changes.*) Based on Bridges' work and adapted from Helfand's work, the following section describes the significance of each of these components in their relationship to retirement transition.

1. *Disengagement*: giving up and breaking away from the functions of the job you retired from.

    Peter had been an insurance salesperson for over 25 years. He was conditioned to think of everything in terms of insurance policies. Although he was retired and no longer selling insurance, he confided in me that whenever he met someone new, "I can't help but wonder what their insurance needs are and what kind of advice I can offer them. It's very difficult for me to think differently. Insurance was a major part of my life; it's still in my blood."

Like Peter, when you disengage from your familiar work role, you may no longer have the opportunity to continue the functions of the role you previously performed. If you were a manager you may now have no one to manage (you may at this point be thinking of managing your significant other, probably not a very good idea.) (See Chapter Eight, for tips on handling your relationships during your retirement.)

If you were an executive salesperson or an account manager, you may have no products to sell or no accounts to handle. If you were a teacher, you have no students to teach. If you were an accountant, you may find yourself with no books to balance. In my case, I was a retirement career counselor for teachers in the New York City education system. When I retired, I no longer was in the role of counseling teachers before their retirement. I found myself however, still wanting to offer advice and suggestions regarding retirement and pension issues to every teacher I met. I was experiencing the difficulty of *disengagement*.

In the 1994 movie, *About Schmidt*, Jack Nicholson portrays a man who has had all his roles removed. He returns to his former office eager to help his young replacement learn the ropes, only to be politely rebuffed and made to feel irrelevant. In a sad moment, he realizes he must give up thinking he is still connected to the tasks of his old job. He is experiencing *disengagement*.

2. *Disidentification*: You can no longer define or identify yourself in your old role.

Do you introduce yourself to new acquaintances using your old job title? Or even worse are you unsure about how to identify yourself? Do you ask yourself, "Who am I now that I'm no longer who I was?" This was a problem for Schmidt, who suddenly lost his identity the moment he packed his belongings and left his office. Like Schmidt, you're now on your own and are in charge of developing a new role, a new identity to introduce to the world.

Betty Friedan in *The Fountain of Age* (B. Friedan, Simon & Schuster, New York, NY, 1993) writes, "Retirement marks the beginning of the 'roleless role,' older persons being forced to create their own roles in the absence of socially defined ones."

3. *Disenchantment*: separating from a job can cause confusion about how things really were. You may start to wonder, "What was real?" It may seem that your world has been turned upside down. You may feel let down and despondent. You may find yourself grieving over how good the old job was (even if it wasn't so good.) If you are stuck in *disenchantment*, look below the surface and ask yourself, "How true was all that? Was it really the perfect job? Were those people really my friends? Did I really enjoy working there?" When looking back at your work situation, you may see things through "rose-colored glasses." Try moving your perception closer to the real situation, not the glorified memory.

4. *Disorientation:* not knowing where you are; feeling that you are going nowhere. Letting go of the past can be both painful and overwhelming. A recently retired client exclaimed, "I keep wondering what's happening in the office. Who's working on my projects and how are my clients doing without me. I have to stop myself from calling in for an update. I keep forgetting they are not my projects or my clients anymore. I feel disoriented and wonder where I'm headed." Another stated, "I feel lost and confused and very uncertain about my meaning in the world. I used to have a schedule and knew exactly what was expected of me at work. Now I have to figure out what I'm supposed to do today and I'm not sure what that is."

The best way to deal with feelings of *disorientation* is to have a written schedule creating daily goals for yourself. Create your list the night before so that you have something to look forward to. Remember: The schedule isn't cut in stone. You can always change it. What's important is that you have taken the time to think about your goals; make a plan for the day and put it in writing.

The tragedy in life doesn't lie in not reaching your goal.
The tragedy lies in having no goal to reach.
   —Benjamin Mays, African-American minister and scholar (1894–1984)

If you are to be, you must begin by assuming responsibility.
You alone are responsible for every moment of your life, for every one of your acts.
   —Antoine de Saint-Exupery, French writer and aviator (1900–1944)

Are You Still in *Endings?*

Using the following scale, read the chart below to determine where you fall in regard to the four aspects of *endings*.

1 = not me at all
2 = describes me sometimes
3 = this is me frequently
4 = this describes me most of the time
5 = I always feel this way

Disengagement	1_____	2_____	3_____	4_____	5_____
Disidentification	1_____	2_____	3_____	4_____	5_____
Disenchantment	1_____	2_____	3_____	4_____	5_____
Disorientation	1_____	2_____	3_____	4_____	5_____

Scoring 3 or more in any one means that you are still working through *endings*. A score of 4 or 5 in all four means you may be stuck in *endings*. Don't be upset by this. After all this is the most difficult stage to work through. Being aware of where you stand is the first step toward acknowledging what you need to do. It may be a good time to consider working with a career coach to help you understand and move beyond your *endings* phase.

Why Is *Endings* so Difficult?

One of the most significant roles we play in life is that of worker. Nearly 1/3 of our life is spent working at one job or another. Whether you voluntarily gave up your job or were forced out, you may still find yourself struggling to give up your connection with the job you held. If you left on your own, you might initially feel relieved to be free of the stress of the work. However, unless you have some structure in your day, this initial sense of satisfaction may lead to feelings of low self-worth, boredom and depression.

Even though job-loss change may take place quickly—yesterday you were at work, today you are home wondering "what's next?"—the transition process may be long, stressful, and full of uncertainty and anxiety. Your retirement transition can actually take from months to years. Being patient with yourself and understanding that this is a normal process will help you to remain calm while you explore your new roles.

He, who lacks time to mourn, lacks the time to mend.
—Shakespeare, playwright (1564–1616)

After *endings* comes the second phase of Bridges' transition process, *the neutral zone.* This is a time suspended between what was familiar and the next and hopefully best phase of life, *new beginnings.* This is the "time out" phase. Take the time to enjoy and explore where you are in your life. You may feel eager to move through this phase quickly, eager to find a new role, a new identity, a new place to feel comfortable again. Instead, I recommend that you use it as a time of renewal, and reflection, of building self-confidence, and developing greater courage. I have seen clients move too quickly through this phase and become discontent and unhappy with their lives after experiencing an initial sense of comfort. Treat yourself by taking time to learn who you are and what you want next. Try out new things before you commit to something. Experiment and experience, explore new challenges, see things differently from the past, tap into your subconscious. Use the chapters in Part Two as your guide toward self-evaluation, self-discovery and envisioning your ideal retirement life.

The real voyage of discovery consists not in the seeking new landscapes, but in having new eyes.
　　　　—Marcel Proust, French novelist, essayist and critic (1871–1922)

It's not so much that we are afraid of change or so in love with the old ways, but it's that place in between that we fear . . . It's like being in between trapezes . . . There's nothing to hold onto.
　　　　—Marilyn Ferguson, American contemporary writer and poet

By patiently moving through *the neutral zone* the next and last stage in the transition process, *new beginnings,* will become a place for new skills and goals, happiness, fulfillment and meaning for your 30-plus years ahead.

Decide that you will not try to do everything at once.
That is why time is spread out.
　　　　—Norman Vincent Peale, Christian preacher and author (1898–1993)

Nine Questions about Retirement Transition

Review the list, checking the ones that cause you concern. Then read the strategies and suggestions to help you work through your fears and worries.

1. Who am I once I leave my job?
2. How will I spend my time?
3. How can I travel without a traveling companion?
4. Will my relationship with my spouse/significant other change?
5. Will I have enough money to live?
6. With whom will I socialize?
7. Should I relocate to be near my grandchildren?
8. I had respect and status in my job. How can I recreate that?
9. I want to continue working but I'm too old. Who will hire me?

Strategies and Suggestions

1. Who Am I Once I Leave My Job?

Loss of a job can lead to loss of identity. Try *reframing*: a different way of looking at the event by changing your language. Introduce yourself by where you are headed next, not where you have come from: For example, instead of, "I used to be the manager of the Sales Department for a national retail store," try, "I'm exploring becoming a sales consultant for several start-up computer companies." Or replace "I was a legal analyst working for a major firm," with "I had a long and successful career; now I'm changing direction and pursuing my life-long passion in (fill in the blank)." One client exclaimed succinctly, "I may be old but I'm not dead. Now that I'm finished with my career of 30-plus years, I've got a lot of new ideas and projects I want to explore. Call me a new man with a new career path called adventure. I'm moving forward not backwards." Using new language to describe your situation will help you break the mental pattern you have established of identifying yourself with a certain role.

A client who used this technique told me, "Using this strategy has given me the opportunity to disconnect mentally from my old identifying role and to experience the freedom to see myself in an entirely different role. I love it."

2. How Will I Spend My Time?

If you didn't think about it before you retired, try to develop a daily schedule now. It doesn't have to be set in stone. Be flexible. Your schedule should include an activity that will keep you involved and connected to others. One client, Phil, created a schedule, but it only involved him, and within four months he was feeling depressed and looking for something else to fill his time. Sign up for classes at the library, or a lecture series at your community center or local college. Join a book group, an ongoing exercise or yoga class, or volunteer in an organization that you support. Try something different, take a risk, and see how it feels. Michael, another client, started attending a local painting class. He'd always liked colors but never thought of himself as a painter. Today he shares a painting studio with two other artists and spends several hours painting each day.

This is your time to explore. Pursue your passion, don't be afraid to treat yourself and try out something you always wanted to do.

3. With Whom Will I Socialize?

It may take some time to develop new friendships or rekindle old ones. The only way to build a friendship is to start. Join a writers group, enroll in classes and make an effort to get to know your classmates and group members better. Take the time to visit and chat with neighbors you never had time to converse with before. Keep in touch with former colleagues who have also retired. Plan more frequent family visits. With the age of technology many people are turning to computer chat rooms or blogs to share ideas with similar minded folks. One good chat room source is www.seniorNet.org. Click on Discussion and Chat at the top of the page. If you have a special area of interest you may consider starting or joining a blog. (For information about blogs, go to ww.blogger.com.) Most importantly—get involved and stay connected. Don't isolate yourself.

4. How Can I Travel Without a Traveling Companion?

There are endless options available to you. Many companies specialize in group travel for individuals traveling alone. You will find quite a number of interesting volunteer vacation and travel references in Chapter Fifteen.

5. Will My Relationship With My Significant Other Change?

Yes, it may. So it is best to be prepared and plan how you intend to spend your time. If you relied on office camaraderie for your social life, then you need to explore how you can develop friendships and connections outside the office. Don't rely on your husband, wife or significant other to help you occupy your time. Instead develop your own friends and interests. One client shared with me that her husband would wake up each morning and ask, "What are 'we' doing today?" instead of making his own plans.

At the 1999 American Psychological Association annual meeting, sociologists Phyllis Moen and Jungmeen Kim presented their study of how retirement affects one's mental and physical health and well-being. They focused specifically on the differences in retirement attitudes in husbands and wives. They found "various levels of marital satisfaction and depression for different combinations of employment and retirement." Newly retired women were more depressed than long-term retired, especially if their husbands were still employed. Recently retired men, if their wives were still employed, experienced more marital conflict than non-retired men. They also found that men, who retired and then went back to work while their wives were not employed, had a higher morale than couples where neither spouse was working. Their conclusions support the effectiveness of getting involved in an activity different from your spouse. Take classes, volunteer in an organization whose cause you believe in, or find an enjoyable part-time job or a hobby.

That said remember that each of you will be approaching retirement differently depending on your life experiences and family relationships. You may be planning to spend more time with your spouse. In Chapter Five, you will read about George and his wife. He handles the retail customers; she bakes the cookies and cakes they sell in their store. Talk with your spouse and work out a plan that will keep you both busy, either together or independently. The key is communication and planning with your spouse or significant other. (Read more about this topic in Chapter Eight.)

6. Will I Have Enough Money to Live?

This is a financial planning question. There are many ways to make sure you have enough to survive on after you retire. Refer back to Chapter Three for suggestions and resources.

7. Should I Relocate? To a Warmer Climate? To Be Closer to Grandchildren? To Smaller or More Affordable Housing?

Retirement is already imposing major changes on your life situation; don't try to overload yourself with more major changes too quickly. Take your time to investigate and explore all your possible options. If you have been thinking about relocating, do your research first before you make any final decisions. Here are some suggestions for gathering information about a potential move:

- Speak to people who have lived in the area for some time as well as people who have just moved there.
- Do research on the Internet. Read local newspapers for stories about the area. Read both the good and bad.
- Visit the location you are interested in and stay awhile. George and his wife, mentioned in Chapter Five, sublet their apartment and rented another in Arizona for 6 months before they decided to make the move permanently.
- If you are relocating to be close to grandchildren, have a good heart-to-heart talk with your children. Find out what they think about your move. Don't expect them to be as available as they were when you were visiting for holidays or summer vacation. Your children may be busy with work. Your grandchildren may be occupied with school, homework, sports, etc. Don't make assumptions about their availability.
- Research the community. Are there activities that will enable you to live a rich life without depending on your children? Are there good transportation facilities? Will you need a car?

Don't walk into a situation that will become uncomfortable for everyone. James and his wife, decided several years ago, that they wanted to live closer to their daughter and her family (husband, two children, eight and ten, and a dog.) They sold their home in New York and relocated to California. Unfamiliar with the area, they soon realized they needed to drive everywhere, which became quite exhausting for them. They also discovered that they couldn't rely on their daughter as heavily as they had expected and would see the grandchildren only occasionally on the weekends when they weren't busy studying or playing sports. Things didn't work out the way they expected and when I last spoke with James, he and his wife were planning to return to New York.

8. I Had Respect and Status in My Job. How Can I Recreate That?

You were a manager, a CEO, a director. People looked up to you. You were a leader who made major decisions. What now? Get active and stay connected. You are still a leader. Become a decision-maker in your community; take over a responsible position as a volunteer organizer in a major organization; or become involved in a political campaign. Some specific ideas:

- Join an association related to your interests and expertise. Seek to be involved, volunteer to head a committee, become a governing board member.
- Join your local block or neighborhood association. Volunteer to head up a fundraiser, block party, a speaker's bureau. Run for office.
- Give speeches at your local library on a subject you are an expert in or feel passionate about.
- Become a mentor in your area of expertise and assist others to become knowledgeable in that field.
- Tutor a child.
- Become actively involved in a senior volunteer service organization, where you will be able to socialize with like-minded people, and also be involved in meaningful activities. One interesting organization to explore is Senior Service, whose website is www.joinseniorservice.org. There are many interesting opportunities available for you to discover and research (See Chapter Twelve and Chapter Fifteen for additional suggestions and resources.)

9. I Want to Continue Working but I'm Too Old. Who Will Hire Me?

This is your perception. If you believe it, then others will also believe it about you. (See Chapters Twelve, Thirteen and Fourteen for ideas on how to conduct a job search when you are over 50.)

Focus on the Seven P's as You Move Through Your Retirement Transition

- *Purpose*: Inspires you to focus and create your plan.
- *Planning*: A thought-out plan will give you direction and help you set your goals.
- *Place*: Structure your day so that you will have a place to go to each day. You need a destination.
- *Positive Attitude:* How you look at things will influence your actions and your daily activities (more about this in Chapter Six and Chapter Seven).
- *Preparation*: Try things out before you make a long-term commitment. This can help to avoid a possible future surprise or upset.
- *Practice:* Motivation and persistence will get you where you want to be.
- *Patience*: Most things take longer than you think they should.

Not in his goals but in his transitions man is great.

—Ralph Waldo Emerson, American author,
poet, philosopher (1803–1882)

Two Transition Stories That Illustrate the Need to Be Flexible in Your Retirement Plan

Bob's Story

When I met Bob, 62, he was five months into retirement and knew he needed to speak to a career coach. By the time he retired, after 25 years in the same job at a stock brokerage house, he had a plan that he felt good about. Four months into retirement he described his original plan to me. "I would get up in the morning and attend a morning men's group at my religious organization. I would then go to the gym, come home, eat lunch, take the dog for a long walk. When I came home my wife would be there, back from her job. We would have dinner and either do something together, or, if she was busy that evening, I would read or watch television.

I asked him how he felt about his plan now. He told me, "At first it was OK. I was exhausted from working hard at my job. I felt I should take care of myself, while at the same time keep busy. This plan is what I thought I really needed. Now, however, I see it was a rationalization. I actually stopped getting up early and attending the group. I spent more time at the gym, wanting to make friends and meet men I could talk to. This seemed the only place I could find other people who weren't working, but the same people were not always there. I guess I really miss my male friends from work. Retirement has not been easy for me. Transitioning from work to life at this moment has not been very fulfilling. I know now that I need a better schedule of how I will spend my time each day. I need to have a more structured plan to keep busy."

Glen's Story

Glen, 61, who retired four years ago, also had a plan he set into motion before retiring. He planned to work as a part-time consultant in the same organization he was retiring from. He had spoken with the hiring manager of his department and had a job lined up, or so he thought. He waited three months. Changes took place within the organization—the job never materialized. He became upset, but not despondent. "I had a lot of time on my hands and wasn't sure where to go. Although I didn't have to get up at 7 a.m. anymore, in three months I was tired of not having structure." He re-evaluated and developed a new plan with new goals. "I decided to look at other possibilities, and developed three different goals that included things I've never done before. I was energized and excited and looking forward to trying them out." Today, Glen is singing in a choir for the first time, learning woodworking, and working part-time teaching computers at a neighborhood youth center. He is also in the process of re-evaluating his plan to include more family time with his wife, who will be retiring soon.

Like Bob and Glen, it is important to be flexible and re-evaluate your plan frequently so that you can modify it to meet your needs, which will continue to change over time. Take action and formulate a plan that is both current and meaningful. (Read about creating a plan that works for you in Chapter Eleven and Appendix III.) Why not plan for a long future? Chances are, according to the latest reports, you will be around for many more years—I recently saw several 90- and 100-year-old birthday cards on the shelves of a local card store.

In this chapter, you learned about transitioning into retirement. When they are planned and managed, transitions are much less stressful. You can even learn to enjoy the process! Transition involves change. In the next chapter, I will address change and how to manage it.

5

•••

Learning to Manage Change

To exist is to change, to change is to mature, to mature is to go on creating oneself.
—Henri Bergson, French philosopher (1859–1941)

The Meaning of Change

All things change, nothing is extinguished . . .
There is nothing in the whole world which is permanent.
Everything flows onward; all things are brought into being with a changing nature;
the ages themselves glide by in constant movement.

—Ovid, Roman poet (43 BC–17 AD)

One thing that is a constant in our lives is change. As Tom Hanks so succinctly states in the 1994 movie, *Forrest Gump,* "Change happens."

Change happens anywhere and everywhere. Change can be temporary or permanent. You can plan for it, expecting and wanting it, or it can appear suddenly, taking you by surprise, uncomfortable, and unwanted. A client once told me, "I don't know how it happened, but everything in my life seems different, unfamiliar and chaotic since I retired." Retirement is one of life's major changes. How you choose to adapt to it is up to you.

Nothing endures but change.

—Heraclitus, Greek philosopher (540 BC–480 BC)

"I appreciate the goodbye party. But I wasn't aware I was going anywhere."

> *Webster's Dictionary* defines change as, "to make different in form; to transform; to give and take reciprocally; to transfer from one to another; to become different; to alter; to remove and replace coverings; to pass from one phase to another; a variation or deviation; to alternate between two tasks; to give or make smaller money, the substitution of one thing for another."
>
> All of these definitions resonate with the changes that happen during retirement. Even the definition "to give or make smaller money" can be looked at as a metaphor for changing from a multi-responsible, full-time job to a part-time job with lesser responsibilities and less money.

Are You Resisting Change?

Change, even good change, results in stress. The loss of a job, planned or unplanned, and the consequent retirement, welcome or forced, too soon or too late, ranks as high in stress as other changes in your life: the loss of a loved one, marriage, divorce, parenthood, relocation. You can make the decision to learn from and grow with change, to develop new attitudes and perceptions, and to plan new activities and move forward. Or you can say, "What is happening to me? I'm not ready for this."

Most of us are about as eager to be changed as we were to be born, and go through our changes in a similar state of shock.

—James Baldwin, American author (1924–1987)

People naturally resist retirement change when it disturbs their routine, takes them out of their comfort zone and makes them feel they have lost control of their lives

People Resist Retirement Change Because They:

- Want to keep the status quo—still dreaming of how things were:
  "I miss my old job even though it wasn't very stimulating anymore; I wish I were still there."
- Don't feel ready:
  "Why couldn't this have happened five years from now? I'm just not prepared to deal with this downsizing now."
- Are stuck in old habits or routines:
  "I've been going back to the office every week to check up on how 'my staff is handling my project."
- Fear the unknown:
  "I can't imagine doing something different. I've done this work for most of my life. I don't have any idea what I can do next. I feel unsure and frightened about the future."
- Want to hold on to tradition:
  "I've always done it like this. I'm used to being in charge. How can I change now?"
- Are worried about taking a risk and are concerned about what others will think:
  "I'm really not comfortable using a computer. I tried learning it once and made a real fool of myself. I'm not going back to that class."

To Overcome Resistance and Move Forward:

1. Identify and loosen the ties that bind you.
2. Confront and challenge the problems and barriers that are preventing you from taking action.
3. Work on developing a realistic plan of action.

The risk of not doing so is to find yourself falling headfirst into a downward spiral of depression, anxiety and fear.

We must become the change we want to see.
— Mahatma Gandhi, Indian spiritual, political leader (1869–1948)

Change Can Be Inspiring

Change can inspire a passion to learn new things, to expand your circle of acquaintances, to grow in your personal life, and to take risks that may push you where you have never been before but have always dreamed of going.

Accepting the challenge of change can provide you with renewed energy. It can create previously undreamed of opportunities for new adventure and learning. You might want to go back to school, develop new skills, take on new responsibilities, redefine yourself, relocate or reorganize your life to spend more time with significant others.

George, a VP at a fortune 500 company, had begun his career as a clerk and worked his way up the ladder. When his company downsized George, he decided to retire. Suddenly faced with a major life change, he was forced to restructure his life, find a new role, and make new plans for the future. George related his story: "After working at the same company for 35 years, you develop a certain pattern in your life. I felt pretty lost when I left. I lost my prestige and stature and gave up doing what I knew very well. Over the years I developed a supportive network of friends. We ate lunch or dinner together two or three times a week. Sometimes we even socialized on weekends. That feeling of belonging and camaraderie was gone.

My initial plan was to stay busy. I went job hunting. Everywhere I went I was told, 'I could hire three guys for what I will pay you, and they will work harder and longer.' I was 59 and it seemed like the doors were closing around me. I told myself that I should do something else, so I started consulting. I worked on a couple of projects over the space of a year and half. I realized it was not for me. I drove a limo for a neighbor's car service for a while, and then looked into starting a small business with a friend, who had also retired, but that fell through. I felt somewhat at lose ends when a cousin invited me to Arizona. I looked at my wife, and we said, 'Why not?' We sublet our apartment for six months, and off we went to explore possibilities in a new environment. Once in Arizona, I found several opportunities. I met some people who made sweets and cakes. I worked in their store for a while. I became inspired and opened my own sweets and cakes store. That was 10 years ago. Today I'm doing great. I'm really enjoying it. I realize I was made for retail. Ask me how I feel? It was rocky at first but now I'm really happy about my new life."

George's sudden change in employment status inspired him to try new venues and explore many options. He was willing to take risks, and at the same time didn't immediately jump into something new. (He sublet his apartment for six months, leaving the door open to return to New York if things didn't work out in Arizona). George spent time in the neutral zone experimenting with different options before he made any major life moves.

Lessons Learned from George

- Don't reject an idea until you have tried it.
- Explore options that appeal to you even if they seem unusual and off the beaten track.
- Take risks.
- Retirement is a time to find your authentic self.

You see things: and say 'why?' But I dream things that never were: and say 'why not?'

—George Bernard Shaw, in *Back to Methuselah,* Irish playwright, Nobel Prize for Literature, 1925 (1856–1950)

A dream is your creative vision for your life in the future. You must break out of your current comfort zone and become comfortable with the unfamiliar and the unknown.

—Denis Waitley, contemporary author

Change Can Be Uncomfortable

Many people are content to live their lives by playing it safe, opting to stay away from situations that may create change. In retirement, however, that option has been taken away. Fear and the unknown have replaced the familiar and the comfortable. It's easy to understand the resistance that accompanies change. If you've been reacting negatively to change, consider modifying your attitude and your behavior before it's too late. Holding onto negative emotional reactions can damage both your immediate and long-term well-being. For some people, thinking positively is easier said than done. (Tips on how to change your attitude can be found in Chapter Six and Chapter Seven.)

Are you still dreaming of the comfortably familiar? The status quo? The good old days? FORGET IT! And move on!

> *Nothing will ever be attempted if all possible objections must first be overcome.*
> —Samuel Johnson, English writer (1709–1784)

Before Tackling Change Learn More About Yourself

To take responsibility for your life and deal successfully with change, become aware of who you are: your experiences, skills, assumptions, influences as well as your self-perceptions. Below are basic questions to help you understand who you are. The questions are divided into four categories: **Personal-Awareness**, **Support from Others**, **Self-Accountability**, and **Proactive Action**.

Along with the questions are suggestions for reflecting on the answers. Don't be upset or worried if you are unable to answer affirmatively to some or all of the questions. Rather, use them as a guide to help you to begin to think about and incorporate, by degrees, some of these suggestions into your life.

Personal-Awareness

> *I think self-awareness is probably the most important thing towards being a champion.*
> —Billie Jean King, considered to be one of the
> greatest female tennis players in history, (1943–)

- How aware am I of my skills, interests and abilities?
- Do I know what I'm good at doing and enjoy as well?
- Have I taken the time to assess myself to discover what I do well?

Find out about your skills, interests, and abilities by using the Five O'Clock Club assessment inventories found in, *Targeting A Great Career* by Kate Wendleton. The assessments exercises include:

- The Five O'Clock Club Seven Stories Exercise (Read about The Seven Stories Exercise in Chapter Ten and Appendix III.)
- The Five O'Clock Club Fifteen-Year Vision and Forty-Year Vision (Read Chapter Eleven and Appendix IV to discover and plan your vision.)

- The Ideal Scene Worksheet/Looking into the Future
- Job Satisfiers /Job Dissatisfiers
- Looking into the Future Assessment

You will find additional self-assessment exercises in Chapters Ten, Eleven, Twelve and Thirteen.

Support from Others

When we share . . . that is poetry in the prose of life.
> —Sigmund Freud, the "father of psychoanalysis" (1856–1939)

I realized that what I needed was someone to talk to who could give me some feedback . . . And if I needed it others needed it just as much.
> —Jean Nidetch, founder, Weight Watchers (1923–)

- Do I have a good support system?
- Am I able to talk with family, friends, or a support group about how I feel?
- Do I choose influencers who are positive and support my ideas and plans for my future?
- Do I regularly attend groups such as the Five O'Clock Club to assist me in staying focused and on track?

The sociologist Charles Horton Cooley theorized in his "looking glass self" theory that our behavior is based on a reflection of how others see us. He wrote, "Other people's views build, change and maintain our self-image . . . If we sense that people agree with what we perceive . . . our behavior is likely to continue. If we sense that other people disagree . . . our self-concept will diminish and our behavior is likely to alter." (C. H. Cooley, *Human Nature and the Social Order*, Scribner's, New York, NY, 1902.)

Self-Accountability

Accountability breeds response-ability.
> —Stephen R. Covey, contemporary author

- Do I share what I have learned with someone else?
- Do I have a buddy?
- Do I have a system to keep myself accountable? Do I keep a journal?

- Do I set daily, weekly, and long-term goals?
- Do I create a written plan and develop possible targets to explore?
- Do I let negative thoughts control me or do I challenge them and turn them into something more positive?

Proactive Action

The person who gets the farthest is generally the one who is willing to do and dare. The sure-thing boat never gets far from shore.
> —Dale Carnegie, self-improvement writer (1888–1953)

- How committed am I to creating a positive action plan for moving forward?
- Do I react negatively or positively to events I can't control?
- Can I to identify the steps needed to take control over my attitude?
- Can I recognize the difference between worries I can change and worries I can't change? Am I willing and able to change what I can? (Read about how to deal with worry in Chapter Ten.)

God grant me the serenity to accept the things I cannot change, courage to change the things I can, and wisdom to know the difference.
> —*Serenity Prayer*, Reinhold Niebuhr, Protestant theologian (1892–1971)

Change has a considerable psychological impact on the human mind.
To the fearful it is threatening because it means that things may get worse.
To the hopeful it is encouraging because things may get better.
To the confident it is inspiring because the challenge exists to make things better.
> —King Whitney Jr., contemporary American writer

Review Your Past to Take Charge of Changes in the Present

Begin by thinking of times in your life when you experienced a major change. Pick three events as examples of when you chose to handle the event by using strong, productive behavior. Answer the questions below for each event:

- What was the event?
- Describe the situation as it occurred.
- What was the fear or difficulty you faced?

- What was your response to the event initially?
- What initiative did you take? What methods did you employ?
- What was the change that happened because of your actions?
- Did it work out in the end?
- What do you remember most about this event?
- What lessons did you learn from this event?
- How can you use these lessons today to help manage the changes you are presently experiencing in retirement?

Review your answers.

Looking back over your experiences in dealing with change can present you with a well-traveled road map to help you deal with your present concerns about retirement change. If you have adjusted to change before, survived, and even came out ahead, then you can do it again.

Success is never final. Failure is never fatal. Courage is what counts.
—Sir Winston Churchill, British Prime Minister (1874–1965)

Live and Rejoice in the Present Moment

Though no one can go back and make a brand new start, anyone can start from now and make a brand new ending.

—Anonymous

Here is a short poem by an anonymous author who undoubtedly knew how to look at change in a positive way.

The past is history
The future is a mystery
Today is a gift
That is why it is called the present.

In the words of Buddha, "the present is the only moment we have." Choose to begin to take control of the changes in your life today. Learn from past history, live in the now, and create for yourself a meaningful, rich, fulfilled life for the future.

The real contest is always between what you've done and what you're capable of doing. You measure yourself against yourself and nobody else.
                          —Geoffrey Gaberino, Olympic gold medal swimmer (1962–)

Life lived for tomorrow will always be just a day away from being realized.
                          —Leo Buscaglia, inspirational Author (1924–1998)

6
···

Developing Positive Thinking

It is not easy to find happiness in ourselves, and it is not possible to find it elsewhere.
> —Agnes Repplier, essayist (1855–1950)

A healthy attitude is contagious, but don't wait to catch it from others.
Be a carrier.
> —Tom Stoppard, Czechoslovakian born, British playwright (1939–)

Positive Thinking Contributes to a Successful Retirement

Studies show that people who adjust quickly and successfully to retirement have three attributes in common:

1. They are positive thinkers, high in optimism, who stay focused despite obstacles and are able to mobilize and focus themselves even when their retirement is brought on by unexpected events.

2. They prepare for and gather information about important retirement issues *before* retiring. (To learn more about gathering financial information see Chapter Three. For retirement transitioning information see Chapter Four, and for personal assessment information see Chapters Ten, Eleven, Twelve and Thirteen.)

3. They develop a retirement plan *before* they retire, consisting of realistic short-term and long-term goals. (For help planning an goal setting see Chapter Eleven and Appendix IV)

This chapter will focus on the combined attributes listed in #1, positive thinking and optimism. (The other two attributes, gathering information, planning and goal setting, will be discussed, as noted, in later chapters.)

Why Is Positive Thinking So Important?

According to Martin Seligman, author of *Learned Optimism,* people who possess a positive attitude are more "successful in life and are more likely to get better results achieving their goals." (M. Seligman, *Learned Optimism*, Alfred A Knopf, New York, NY, 1990.)

The stories of Jim and Sam, both 61 and recently retired, are a good example of this point. Jim and Sam had similar credentials and experience and were both seeking consulting work in the pharmaceutical industry. However, Jim had low self-esteem and feared he would be perceived as too old and no longer competent to handle the job. He worried his skills weren't up-to-date and that he would not be able to keep up with the younger workers on the team. Even though he had 26 years' experience in the field, he believed younger candidates would be more knowledgeable. Considering himself a long shot, his pessimistic beliefs created negative self-fulfilling behaviors. Jim didn't bother to update his résumé or prepare for his interview. During the interview he remained nervous and fidgety and even failed to make eye contact with the interviewer.

Sam, on the other hand, had a positive attitude; he was confident in his ability and believed he would land the consulting position. He updating his résumé and prepared for his interview by researching the current needs of the organization. During the interview, he remained relaxed and comfortable and was able to effectively address the hiring manager's concerns. He believed his 26 years' experience coupled with his strong knowledge of the industry, made him the best candidate to be added to the consulting team. He also saw himself as a role model and mentor to the younger workers. Who would you hire, Jim or Sam? Why?

The answer seems apparent. However, in a similar situation who would you be, Jim or Sam?

Are You a Pessimist or an Optimist?

If you are optimistic about your future, you'll find this chapter interesting and reaffirming. If you are pessimistic, this chapter and the next will be of great value to you by providing information on how you can you learn to change your attitude.

Napoleon certainly thought he could control negative events when he proclaimed, "Circumstances—what are circumstances? I make circumstances." You may not be as sure of being able to control your circumstances as was Napoleon but you can be in control of your attitude. First Lady Martha Washington knew that attitude is a matter of our choosing. She declared, "I am still determined to be cheerful and happy no matter what the situation I may be in; for I have also learned from experience that the greater part of our happiness or misery depends upon our disposition, not upon our circumstances."

To be happy, drop the words 'if only' and substitute instead the words 'what if'.
—Smiley Blanton, American psychiatrist (1882–1966)

Two Approaches to Create a Positive, Optimistic Attitude

Psychologist, Albert Ellis, founder of Rational Emotive Behavior Therapy, theorizes that people can control their emotions and be more successful in life if they can learn to confront and alter their irrational beliefs. (A. Ellis, Ph.D., W. Dryden, Ph.D., *The Practice of Rational Emotive Behavior Therapy*, Springer Publishing, New York, NY, 1997.)

To understand this better, let's look at Jean, 61, who was forced into retirement after working 22 years for the same publishing company. Jean searched for another job for over seven months. She got interviews but was never called back after her first interview.

This frustrating experience produced in Jean an irrational, self-defeating belief, which sounded like this: "I'm too old and probably too expensive. Why hire me when they can get a younger, less experienced person for less money? I may as well give up and forget about getting another job."

Ellis explains that if a person thinks frequently about an upsetting event without first trying to understand or explore why it happened, he or she will develop a negative belief about the event, which will lead to a negative consequence. Jean lost her sense of objectivity and control over her job search because she didn't take the time to examine the reasons behind her negative beliefs.

Jean became angry, depressed and unmotivated. She no longer felt she was employable. According to Ellis, a person needs to examine and dispute negative beliefs *frequently* to keep from losing focus and making faulty assumptions. In Jean's case, her negative and irrational beliefs became habitual. She wasn't aware she had them, even though they were controlling her life and influencing her job search.

In our work together, she was finally able to pause and examine her beliefs. She realized it wasn't her age or her salary requirements that were getting in her way but rather her inability to research and gather information about the needs of her target industry. With this new insight, Jean learned to dispute her old way of thinking by repeating frequently the following statements: "My skills and experience are valuable and needed in the industry." "Other people my age were able to find work and so will I." She challenged her negative beliefs by using words that represented a successful and desired outcome. She renewed her search with added energy. She began conducting informational interviews, networking and gathering information from people who worked in her target industry. Equipped with this information, she followed up with a Five O'Clock Club targeted-mailing approach. Jean renewed her search with enthusiasm and vigor. Jean obtained several interviews and call-backs and shortly landed a job researching documents for a privately-owned-security company.

Take some time to stop and conduct a mental check on your attitude. Are you focusing on irrational beliefs stemming from an unpleasant or frustrating event? How can you dispute these beliefs to keep harmony and optimism in your life?

> *The thing always happens that you really believe in; and the belief in a thing makes it happen.*
>
> —Frank Lloyd Wright, American architect (1869–1959)

Using *Learned Optimism* in Dealing with Retirement Issues

> *When you know how to choose the power of optimism, you'll gain an essential new freedom to build a life of real rewards and lasting fulfillment.*
>
> —Martin Seligman, American psychologist, writer (1942–)

Cognitive psychologist, Martin E.P. Seligman, Ph.D., expanded on Ellis' theory by conducting research in the area of optimistic thinking. He concluded that people who viewed setbacks as transitory and internal and were able to bounce back and continue forward in their lives after experiencing an upsetting event were *optimists*. Other individuals who saw negative events as permanent and external problems over which they had no control he labeled *pessimists*. Seligman found that even a moderate level of pessimism could pull you down, affecting all major areas of your life: your health, your productivity, your work, your relationships and your feelings of self-worth. Seligman's studies report that optimism is a trait comprised of a set of skills, and therefore, like all skills, it can be learned. (*Learned Optimism*, Alfred A Knopf, New York, NY, 1990.)

This theory can be helpful in learning to deal with challenging retirement situations. If you are experiencing thoughts of discouragement, disappointment, frustration, feelings of failure, or inability to create a plan for yourself, you can learn how to dispute these negative thoughts by:

1. listening to your inner thoughts and arguing against self-limiting and negative ideas,

2. avoiding sharing your ideas with people (including friends and relatives) who may discourage you or give negative feedback when you are thinking about exploring and moving out of your comfort zone into new and uncharted waters.

Alice was discouraged and disillusioned after her job was suddenly downsized. She realized she needed to take care of herself emotionally and psychologically by stepping out of her comfort zone and doing something completely different with her life. She decided to volunteer for two months at a self-help retreat located in the Berkshire Mountains in Massachusetts. She would be doing things she had never done before: camping in a tent by herself, working on an unfamiliar project, learning new skills in an environment with people she had never met before. She was dealing with her transition by attempting to explore *the neutral zone*. (See Chapter Four to review.) When Alice's closest friend heard her plan, she said, "I'd be very surprised if you lasted two weeks." Another said, "Why are you doing this? You are running away from your reality. You need to stay home, face your feelings and do something constructive with your life." Some people may care about you very much, but just don't understand the process of retirement transition. They may inadvertently hold you back from moving forward and exploring your dreams. These people are called "toxic people." If you know this type of person, who will not be supportive of your attempts to step out of the familiar, don't share your ideas with them. They will only further encourage negative thinking.

Nothing is good or bad. It is thinking that makes it so.
—Shakespeare, playwright (1564–1616)

Seligman in his book, *Learned Optimism,* asks the reader, "Is it possible to be happier, to feel more satisfied be more engaged in life, to find more meaning, and laugh and smile more, regardless of one's circumstances?" His answer and mine as well—*Absolutely!*

I have witnessed clients who have unconsciously short-circuited their ability to be successful and happy. I have also witnessed clients who moved from a negative state by practicing and incorporating Seligman's "learned optimism" strategies into their daily thinking pattern.

Juliette, for example, disputed negative thoughts and became optimistic about her future. At 59, she was planning to retire after thirty years of teaching. When I first met her, she was very pessimistic about her future and was convinced that she would be unable to do anything more in her life. Juliette told me, "All I know is teaching. How can I ever convince anyone that I can do anything else?" As we worked together, she learned to listen to her inner thoughts, which centered on her insecurity about leaving a place where she was known, acknowledged and respected for many years. She realized that she was afraid of retiring because she needed a place to go each day where she felt wanted, necessary and connected. Completing The Five O'Clock Club's Seven Stories Exercise and Self-Assessment Inventory helped her identify skills, interests and hidden qualities that she enjoyed and she could transfer to other environments. She realized that she had skills relating to infant care, and that holding and comforting babies gave her deep satisfaction. Once Juliette identified her concerns and her skills she was able to dispute her negative thoughts of; "Who would want me; I'm only a teacher." While she was still employed we worked together researching places where she could work with babies in need. She visited hospital centers developing connections with their volunteer departments. She realized she was capable of creating "a new and meaningful life after teaching 30 years." Soon after she retired, she was hired as a volunteer holding and nurturing AIDS babies in a community hospital.

The best way to break the spell of inertia and frustration is this: Act as if it were impossible to fail.

—Dorthea Brande, contemporary American author

Optimism is your choice. Even if you are pessimistic by nature, remember that *optimism can be learned.*

Two Wolves

One evening an old Cherokee told his grandson about a battle that goes on inside people. He said, "My son, the battle is between two "wolves" inside us all.

One is Evil. It is anger, envy, jealousy, sorrow, regret, greed, arrogance, self-pity, guilt, resentment, inferiority, lies, false pride, superiority, and ego.

The other is good. It is joy, peace, love, hope, serenity, humility, kindness, benevolence, empathy, generosity, truth, compassion and faith." The grandson thought about it for a minute and then asked his grandfather:

"Which wolf wins?"

The old Cherokee simply replied, "The one you feed."

—Author unknown

Which wolf do you feed?

What Does Positive Thinking Mean to You?

Scott W. Ventrella, (*The Power of Positive Thinking in Business*, Simon and Schuster, New York, NY, 2001) identifies ten qualities, based on the work of Dr. Norman Vincent Peale, which need to be present to create positive thinking. (N. V. Peale *The Power of Positive Thinking*, Fawcette Crest, New York, NY, 1952.)

They are:

- Optimism
- Enthusiasm
- Belief

- Patience
- Integrity
- Determination
- Calmness
- Confidence
- Focus
- Courage

How positive are you? How many of these attributes do you use on a daily basis? In which one of the attributes are you strongest? Which do you need to focus on and spend more time developing? Work on developing your weaker traits but don't worry too much about the results. If you focus only on accomplishing a task, and you don't accomplish it, you'll feel like a failure. Positive thinking is about the path and the process. So enjoy the journey.

Far away there in the sunshine are my highest aspirations.
I may not reach them, but I can look up and see their beauty, believe in them and try to follow them.

—Louisa May Alcott, American author (1855–1888)

In Chapter Seven, you will be introduced to some simple, tried and true strategies to help you stay on the road to positive thinking and optimism.

7

•••

Five Strategies for Positive Thinking

Chapter Six outlined the importance of thinking positively about changes you will face in retirement. Now that you understand the value of positive thinking, here are five simple strategies to help you reframe your attitude. Even if you're already a positive person, use these exercises to strengthen your skills, or pass these strategies along to others who need a better outlook.

1. Use Positive Affirmations

Change your thoughts and you change your world.
        —Norman Vincent Peale, Christian minister, author (1898–1993)

To stay positive we must begin somewhere. What better place than with affirmations? Affirmations are positive self-scripts you can use to help counteract negative beliefs that may hold you back from enjoying your retirement and your life. When I recommend affirmations to my clients, I'm occasionally met with skepticism. Clients even told me they thought the affirmations were too simple to be effective. Some of their comments were:

- "Why should I bother with them? I *know* I can't get a job anyway."
- "How can they help me change my attitude? I've *always* been like this?"
- "I really *can't waste* my time on something that doesn't work I want to focus on more important strategies."

The reality couldn't be further from the truth. So to the skeptics among you, I say: Try a positive affirmation, and see how it can work for you.

Affirmations are like prescriptions for certain aspects of yourself you want to change.
> —Jerry Frankhauser, American author (1980–)

Why Are People Skeptical About Affirmations?

Many of us are conditioned from a young age to think and even talk negatively about ourselves, our potential, our ability to succeed in a desired task and our view of the future.

- "I'll *never* get that job."
- "I'll *never* get good enough on computers to be considered competent."
- "I'm *too old* and not able to keep up with younger workers."
- "I'll *never* be able to achieve my goal."

Without even realizing it, people rehearse daily to create failure and discord in their lives. Negative thoughts can keep you from fulfilling your dreams and make you feel miserable along the way.

As you read in the previous chapter, if you want to create positive changes in your life, start by thinking positive thoughts about yourself and your future. These thoughts are positive affirmations, a simple group of words expressing something you want to change about yourself or something you want to achieve. Used in a regular, systematic approach, they can be a powerful tool for creating positive, life-affirming thoughts and actions.

As we think . . . So we become.
> —William James, American philosopher, psychologist (1842–1910)

Is there something you have been thinking about but are afraid you can't do successfully? Is there behavior or an attitude you would like to change? Why not try using a positive affirmation to help reach your goal?

Its minds, not muscles that win games.
> —Dr. Rob Gilbert, contemporary sports psychologist

Three Basic Rules to Create Your Affirmation

Affirmations should:

1. Describe the ideal situation or goal you want to achieve, not the behaviors you want to eliminate:
   - "I am active, excited and full of energy." *not* "I am no longer tired, depressed and lethargic."
   - "I am in control." *not* "I am no longer influenced by others' opinions of me."
2. Be brief, powerful, clear and specific.
3. Begin with either "I" or your name.

Three Ways to State Your Affirmations

1. Use "*I am*" to describe your desired state. State your message of something you want to achieve as if you have already achieved it.
   - "*I am* relaxed in my retirement."
   - "*I am* able to achieve my goal."
   - "*I am* ready to move ahead and accept my new life."
   - "*I am* positive about the future."
2. Use "*I can*" to state your desired goal or potential.
   - "*I can* organize my papers."
   - "*I can* take risks."
   - "*I can* change."
   - "*I can* enjoy my retirement."
   - "*I can* handle my problems as they occur."
   - "*I can* control my fear of the unknown."
3. Use "*I will*" to state a positive change you want in your life.
   - "*I will* create an action plan and set timely goals."
   - "*I will* take responsibility for behavior."
   - "*I will* succeed in building a great new life after I retire."

Create your affirmation following the above rules, but most important: *Don't forget to put your affirmation in writing.*

Practice Your Affirmations

In the last analysis our only freedom is the freedom to discipline ourselves.
—Bernard Baruch, American statesmen (1870–1965)

The best way to get an affirmation to work is to repeat it over and over again at the same time each day. Repeat your affirmation first thing in the morning, immediately after you wake up, and at night, before you go to sleep. Don't stop there; repeat your affirmation as often as you can during the day. The more you repeat it, the more it will influence you to create behavior to achieve your goal. Repeat it silently if you are around others or out loud if you are alone. It's the repetition that counts.

Write your affirmation on five or six 3 × 5 index cards and put these cards in prominent places in your home: the bathroom mirror, the refrigerator door, the inside of your front door, the bedroom mirror—anywhere you will see it daily and frequently. Carry one card with you at all times.

Each time you look at the card, *repeat the affirmation several times.*

Why Does This Work?

As studies on learning have shown, repeatedly telling yourself the same thing can program your subconscious mind to believe it without question and believing it will cause you to take the actions needed to make it happen.

Since we think negatively more often than positively, positive affirmations require work if they are to make a difference for you.

"Johnson, if you're going to have negative thoughts,
I suggest you get rid of that thought balloon."

The universe is change; our life is what our thoughts make it.
—Marcus Aurelius Antoninus, Roman Emperor (121–180 AD)

2. Use Visualization

Losers visualize the penalties of failures. Winners visualize the rewards of success.
—Dr. Rob Gilbert, American contemporary sports psychologist

Ordinary people believe only in the possible. Extraordinary people visualize not what is possible or probable, but rather what is impossible. And by visualizing the impossible, they begin to see it as possible.
—Les Brown, American contemporary writer

When an idea forms in your mind, it actually takes place in pictures not words. For example, think of a vacation on a warm sunny Caribbean island and what immediately comes into your mind? The words of the ad that says "relax and soak up the beauty of our white sandy beaches?" Or does your mind begin to focus on a visual image of you lying on a chaise lounge surrounded by white sand, palm trees and aqua water?

Pictures Have Been Around a Long Time

Our brain's image-making ability evolved long before written language developed. Cro-Magnon man in Lascaux, France communicated by drawing pictures on cave walls long before written language existed.

Visualization can be a powerful tool since visual images actually go deeper than language and appeal directly to our feelings and our emotions. You can increase your chances of obtaining a desired goal if you first imagine it as real and create a picture in your mind of achieving the goal.

Many athletes use visualization to create an image of a successful win before the game begins.

You must see your goals clearly and specifically before you can set out for them.
Hold them in your mind until they become second nature.
—Les Brown

To understand the power of both affirmation and visualization, let me tell you about Martin, an active, energetic man of 63, who had a retirement dream to traveling throughout Asia three to five months a year, exploring and photographing workers in rural environments. He had been planning his first trip for many years before his retirement. He eagerly looked forward to his retirement so that he could begin his travels and use his new digital camera.

Several days after he retired, his children began commenting that they needed him and wanted him to stay home, even though they were grown with families of their own. He worried that his children disapproved of his plan and that his friends thought him reckless and fool-hardy. Influenced by their attitude he canceled his trip and let his dream slide away. When I met Martin, he was feeling discouraged, listless and bored. He talked about wishing he could exchange his camera for a new television. Most days he either took long walks to occupy himself or he stayed home watching travel videos. "I never should have retired; I have nothing in my life now, nothing to look forward to," he shared with me.

We worked together on creating an affirmation to help him refocus his attitude and get back on track. The affirmation he chose was, "I can fulfill my retirement dream of traveling to unfamiliar places." He wrote his affirmation on index cards and posted them in visible places around his home. He developed a routine of repeating it in the morning before he got out of bed and again at night just before he went to sleep. This schedule was important because it brought the affirmation into his life on a daily basis at an expected time, making the affirmation an important part of his day.

I asked him to picture the affirmation as an image and then to describe the image verbally and in writing. Martin described a picture of himself walking in a lush green valley of rice fields. He described farmers with straw hats and bamboo tools working the fields. I encouraged Martin to draw the image or look for representations of it in magazines. He found pictures that resembled his earlier dream. He placed them around his house so that he could view them frequently. He revised his affirmation, making it more specific: "I am planning my trip to China." He visualized his trip until it became real and doable. He was ready to take the risk, despite what others thought. He became energized and focused and began planning again for his trip.

Martin has now taken three trips visiting six different Asian countries. He has presented a slide show of his photographs at a community college, has sold several photographs and is in the process of planning a larger exhibit in the near future when he returns from his next trip

Let's examine what happened to Martin. Daily repetition of his positive affirmation created a visual image sending a message to his mind letting him see the best possible outcome. He became open to taking a risk and was able to program his subconscious mind to accept the fact he could fulfill his dream and control any negative influences that were standing in the way of his dreams.

The future belongs to those who believe in the beauty of their dreams.
—Eleanor Roosevelt, U. S. first lady (1884–1962)

The Process of Visualizing: Two Short Exercises

Exercise A

1. Start with an affirmation of a specific goal you want to achieve. For example, "I am organizing my desk."
2. Ask yourself, "What does an organized desk look like?"
3. Picture the image of an organized desk. How are items arranged on the desk? Are the papers in neatly-stacked folders? Are they filed in multi-colored folders on a rack? Are the pencils in a holder or not visible at all? Is the new organizer you saw advertised in the Sunday paper now sitting on your desk?
4. Repeat your affirmation.
5. Then create a picture in your mind of achieving your goal. The mind will believe it is real. It will remember the image and say to you, "you've done it before, you can do it again." It's that simple.

Want to Practice?

Try the following:

- Choose a quiet, comfortable place to sit. Close your eyes and take several deep breaths to quiet and relax your mind. Repeat the affirmation several times, "I am successful in my retirement." Say it with strong conviction, really believing it to be true. Repeat it out loud at least five times.
- Sit quietly and observe what images come to mind. What does your successful retirement look like? Don't censor your thoughts; just let the images flow through your consciousness.
- Focus on one image. Remember; this is your personal visualization. Your pic-

ture will be different from anyone else's, determined by your values, personal goals and aspirations.

- Engage as many senses as possible in your visualization. Feel the carpet beneath your feet, smell the paint on the canvas, hear the doorbell ring, etc.
- Visualize others in the picture responding positively to you.
- Replay the visualization until it feels exactly just right.
- You can now choose to sit quietly with your visualization or you can draw a picture of your visualization including as many details as possible. It doesn't matter if you use stick figures or a realistic rendering. You may wish to cut pictures from a magazine creating a collage that portrays your successful retirement visualization.
- Repeat your affirmation whenever you look at your picture.

Exercise B

- List the three things you want to achieve this week
- Describe how they will look when finished.
- Look through magazines for pictures that symbolize the image you described.
- Place these pictures where you will see them daily.

Remember: create or visualize an image of an object that represents a desired goal and then place it in your mind with repetition. This exercise will help make that thought real and will help to make you goal attainable.

3. Take Responsibility: Act Toward Yourself the Way You Want to Be Treated by Others

The course of human history is determined, not by what happens in the skies, but what takes place in our hearts.
—Sir Arthur Keith, British anthropologist (1866–1955)

While you were working, you may have been too preoccupied with the demands of the job to think about yourself. If you had problems, you may have blamed them on work, co-workers, the environment or your boss. Now that you are retired, you have time to indulge in negative thoughts, which are a product of your past experiences. You may feel you are no longer in a position to receive respect or acknowledgement. The more you think this way, the more you will believe it. Ask yourself, "How do I want to be treated by others?" Empower yourself. Take charge and give to yourself what you want to receive from others. The more you give to yourself, the more others will be attracted to you, and the more you will get what you need. Janet's story demonstrates this concept.

Janet retired at 60, ending a teaching career of 30 years. She had no immediate plans except to "take it easy and relax." At first she felt relieved and happy. Then, three months into retirement, her world collapsed. She felt lonely and no longer acknowledged or needed. She began to believe that she had lost her status in the world and that people weren't interested in her or her expertise. Basing her sense of self-worth and happiness on others' opinions, she became depressed and reclusive.

As we worked together, Janet acknowledged that she missed feeling wanted, valued and respected. I asked her, "If *you* were meeting Janet, what advice would you give her to help her get what she needed?"

Janet responded, "I would tell her to stop sitting home feeling sorry for herself and go out and find a job—a new environment where she could feel acknowledged and supported." She was motivated to take action when she realized she needed to find a productive activity where she could commit both her time and energy. Even though Janet didn't have pressing financial concerns, she knew she wasn't interested in volunteering. Financial remuneration for work was important to her.

After completing the personal assessments, she knew she wanted to remain in education. Janet contacted hospitals, community agencies and local schools. Through the AARP Job Hub, a service that assists people over 50 who are seeking employment, she was hired at a private school as a part-time reading tutor. The students liked her, their reading scores improved, and she developed several new friendships with the staff. She quickly became respected for her knowledge and expertise and was soon assigned additional hours and a higher-level position.

The lesson? Janet needed to take control and find for herself what she needed; no one else could do it.

You are your own best friend. Be Bold. Take Action. Counter your negative thoughts with positive antidotes and positive suggestions. Take responsibility. Push yourself forward using constructive thoughts, helpful suggestions and visualizations of desired outcomes.

If a stranger came up to you and said, "You will never be able to do that" your reaction might be, "How do you know? You don't know anything about me and what I can do. Who are you to tell me what I can do and can't do?" Pretend you are the stranger and talk back to yourself the same way. Tell yourself you are capable, energetic and worthy of enjoying life to it's fullest. Don't sit home bemoaning what you could have done. Get out and do it.

> *Whatever you do, or dream you can, begin it.*
> *Boldness has genius, power, and magic in it.*
> —Johann Goethe, German writer (1749–1832)

> *The world belongs to the energetic.*
> —Ralph Waldo Emerson, American essayist (1803–1882)

4. Have Compassion: Help Others

> *A man's true wealth is the good he does in the world.*
> *Beauty is eternity gazing at itself in a mirror.*
> *But you are eternity and you are the mirror.*
> —Kahlil Gibran, Lebanese-American poet (1883–1931)

Explore ways to contribute to others. Helping other people is a wonderful way to also help yourself. Rather than focusing energy worrying about your problems, procrastinating or simply sitting around feeling unproductive, try to think of ways you can rechannel your energy by giving to others. Many retirees volunteer at hospitals, religious schools, community centers, non-profit organizations and the like. It gives them a sense of purpose and adds meaning to their lives.

You may not be interested in volunteering. That's fine; there are many other ways you can show compassion and assist others. Do you have a neighbor who is elderly and needs help shopping or going to the doctor? Does a friend, who just had surgery, home alone, need some assistance or perhaps a visit? Is there a teenager who needs help writing an essay for college? Does you block association need someone to design a flyer, review a financial statement or present a workshop in an area that is within your expertise? Even the simple act of noticing a person and greeting him or her with a warm, friendly smile can brighten up their day as well as yours.

Look around and recognize people who may need help. Look for ways you can contribute to make them feel better. Care about others and they will make your life much richer and fuller in return.

To those who see with loving eyes, life is beautiful.
To those who speak with tender voices, life is peaceful.
To those who help with gentle hands, life is full.
And to those who care with compassionate hearts, life is good beyond all measure.
—Author Unknown

5. Eliminate Personal Barriers by Reframing Your Negative Self Talk

The greatest thing in this world is not so much where we are, but in what direction we are moving.
—Oliver Wendell Holmes, U.S. Supreme Court justice (1841–1935)

"That's the difference between you and I: You see a giant, angry gorilla outside our window.
I see a giant t-shirt on him with out Web address on it.

Negative thoughts are always lurking, ready to jump out and short circuit your plans and dreams. Don't let them take control of your thinking. Be aware of influencing circumstances that may produce negative thoughts.

Review the list below. Do you indulge in any of these behaviors or attitudes?
Rate them as follows:
1=Never feel/behave this way
2=occasionally feel/behave this way
3=frequently feel/behave this way

- Thinking life has let you down _____
- Feeling hurt and deflated _____
- Feeling sorry for yourself _____
- Feeling alone and isolated _____
- Thinking that you are not in control of your life situation _____
- Feeling dependent on others for approval of your actions _____
- Feeling you are a victim _____
- Feeling depressed frequently _____
- Thinking you are unable to change your life _____

If you scored 3 in any of the above, try to give some attention to how that thought or feeling may be controlling your actions and negatively affecting your well-being.

To change a negative thought, reexamine the words you use when you talk to yourself. Self-talk can be subtle, automatic and unconscious, making it difficult to recognize how it influences your actions. Negative self-talk can have a negative affect on your mood or feelings before you even realize what is happening and before you can determine how irrational your thoughts may be.

Juliette, who we met in Chapter Six, was completely under the influence of her negative "what-if" self-talk. "What-if they think I'm too old to hire?" "What-if I can't keep up with the work?" "What-if I can't handle the interview?" "What-if there is really no job out there for me?"

Without realizing it, she created a negative belief system, which interfered with her ability to seek and obtain meaningful work. She accepted her irrational self-talk as the truth and consequently expected the worst outcome from her search. By slowing down, gathering the facts, and carefully examining the validity of her self-talk, Juliette was able to see her situation more clearly and change accordingly.

Don't limit yourself by being a "what-if-er." Change your language by reframing negative self talk. Use the strategies in this chapter to move forward, boldly, fearlessly, positively, to accomplish your dreams.

It's choice—not chance—that determines your destiny.
    —Jean Nidetch, Founder of Weight Watchers (1923–)

Don't wind up like John Babbit in the Sinclair Lewis novel, *Babbitt*, who states at the end of the book, "I've never done a single thing I've wanted to in my whole life! I don't know's I've accomplished anything except just get along. I figure out I've made about a quarter of an inch out of a possible hundred rods." (S. Lewis, *Babbitt*, Harcourt Brace, New York, NY, 1922.)

The only limit to our realization of tomorrow will be our doubts of today.
Let us move forward with strong and active faith.
    —Franklin D. Roosevelt, U.S. President (1882–1945)

Part Two

······················

Moving Forward
Discovering Who You Are, What You Want and How to Find It

8

•••

Together at Last: *Where Do We Go from Here?*

by Marjorie Hendrickson, M.S., in collaboration with her husband, Allen Hendrickson

Retirement is a time most people look forward to. We dream about the opportunity to relax and spend time with spouse and family—and finally get to do "what we want to do" once we are no longer driven by work's demands, structure and scheduling. There might be a tendency, however, to idealize retirement.

Similar to dreams of happily-ever-after wedded bliss, the retirement dream will usually require many adjustments. Here are a couple of scenarios to consider: Evelyn and George, Joan and Joe.

Under One Roof: Whose Space Is It?

"Honey, I'm home." These are nice words to hear, yes. But what if your honey is home all the time? Even if both partners have been looking forward to the time when they can have more time together, friction can develop over unforeseen issues related to space and the invasion of space.

Evelyn retired a few years before George did. Initially, she had to make adjustments to not working, but she developed patterns of life that she enjoyed. She savored starting her day quietly, alone with a cup of coffee and the crossword puzzle. This was her time to gather her thoughts and plan the day that often involved activities with her friends—some of them old, some new. She had made volunteer commitments to a local organization, first doing clerical work but then taking on more important responsibilities. Her week had developed a pattern that she enjoyed.

Then George retired. Although Evelyn and George had a close relationship and had enjoyed many activities together over the years, having him home was more difficult that she had anticipated. His biorhythms were different: he liked to charge into the day; eager to do all the things he had waited so long to do. Gone was her "quiet time" approach to the morning. For a while she tried to get up before he did, but she found she really couldn't manage it.

So she and George faced the day together: for Evelyn the chattering about the news or future activities—which had been enjoyable in the evenings—was now an irritant. Although George was usually a patient man, he expected her to come promptly to look at what he was doing, or he spontaneously would read something aloud. These constant interruptions were also an irritant. In addition, he didn't seem to understand that her volunteer commitments to the community organization couldn't just be swept away at the last moment. The "relaxed" time together that they had so looked forward to—during the hectic work years of their life—was not turning out as planned.

Joan and Joe encountered similar difficulties. Joan reached retirement two years before Joe was scheduled to retire. She was looking forward to some time to get projects done and generally catch up with items on her own agenda. But then Joe was offered a retirement package that was too good not to accept. "Their time" had finally come. Traveling had always been a dream, but they never had enough time off together to do more than an occasional short trip. Now they eagerly planned a month-long trip with stops to see friends in different parts of the country. What fun it would be! But neither had anticipated that retirement requires considerable adjustment individually and as a couple. As they talked about what to do and how to do it on the trip, it was clear that they had very different ideas. On top of this, there would be the additional adjustment of traveling together on a long road trip. Even in the best of circumstances, being together in the same small space, 24/7 requires skills that can test the relationship of the most compatible couple.

Avoiding Retirement Strains and Stresses

What can a couple beginning, or approaching, retirement do to ease the transition?

Communication is a key factor in resolving tensions in life. Lack of communication can lead to misunderstandings that can leave both parties with the impression that their feelings and concerns have not been considered. Harboring resentments often leads to silent wars with small unpleasant skirmishes that only escalate the resentment. To keep the idyllic time of retirement from turning sour a couple not only needs to communicate, but also needs to mediate and negotiate.

The following is a formal problem-solving technique that may work for some couples. To resolve an issue each party needs to:

- Define the problem as he or she sees it. Once there is agreement as to the problem they are trying to resolve, each person needs to:
- Have uninterrupted time to voice his/her views on the issue while the other party really listens.
- Together they need to:
  Define and list possible solutions, with each person being allowed time to voice and include on the list his/her feelings on each potential option.

These feelings should be acknowledged as valid even if the other person does not agree with them.

The next step is to:

- Note areas of agreement and disagreement, continuing the discussion until they have narrowed down the possible solutions.

At this point, they can consider the following questions, "What is most important to you and why?" and "What is most important to me and why?" Again, each partner needs to really listen to the other person. They should continue this process of eliminating options until they have come to a resolution of the problem.

While this process may seem to be too stilted or formal, the structure may provide a way to discuss issues that will affect how the couple builds a life together that they both will love and find fulfilling.

George and Evelyn Work It Out

When George and Evelyn sat down to discuss what was important to each one, they found that, even though each one decided to give up something, it was not a loss.

George decided to start the day playing golf, an activity that he had always enjoyed. After a few weeks, he found that he enjoyed the opportunity to play when the course was less crowded. This allowed Evelyn to continue the quiet time that was so important to her. When George came home with news of his game and conversations he had had, she was eager to listen and let him show her how he had improved his swing. In time, by the way, George found that one can only golf so much and he decided to take a part-time job an industry that intrigued him. But he had stopped treating retirement as if it were a work activity where productivity was important.

In other words, attitudes and patterns of daily life in retirement continue to evolve. Although he was still active, he started to gradually slow down, relax, and take time to smell the flowers before his body forced him to slow down.

Joan and Joe: Postponing the Big Trip

As they were planning their month-long trip, it became apparent to Joan and Joe that they each had different expectations of a vacation. Joan felt that it was time to chill out and take time to renew herself. Joe, on the other hand, wanted to see and do as much as was humanly possible in each new location that they planned to visit. He felt that, since he was now retired, he could rest when they got home.

After much discussion, they decided to put off the month-long trip for a year. Instead they signed up for several short group trips and took some weeklong excursions. By the next year, when they had had time to adapt to retirement, they had eased into a more compatible traveling style.

Learning to Live Together—Again!

Past experience, work habits and attitude about both relaxation and work can complicate the complex task of learning to live together again. When both partners were together only evenings and weekends, it may have been a very workable combination to have a goal-oriented partner paired with someone more relaxed; it may be another story altogether when they are under the same roof day after day.

Relaxing can be a *learned activity*. There are no classes for "Relaxation 101," but perhaps there should be. A newly retired person may have to learn how to let go of the goal-oriented behavior that had ruled his/her life and had been useful in keeping it all together with a busy work and home life.

What if the newly retired partner was a manager? What if both partners were managers? When Philip finally retired, he continued doing what he had done for years, i.e., managing and overseeing the activities of people in his area—which now meant his wife, Barbara! She had always kept an immaculate house, but suddenly found herself being managed. It took some negotiation and adjustment for Philip to realize that the house had been well run before he was there to manage it. He had to cultivate activities and projects that helped him to stop managing and overseeing activities at home.

When Will My Time Come?

Alex was semi-retired, working at a part-time job near home. Each day as his wife Maureen was rushing to her job, she wondered when her time would come. It was hard to go to work when her other half could plan his day with the activities of choice. She had always enjoyed her job, but nonetheless started to feel jealous that she didn't have time for herself and the activities she enjoyed. It had been many years of saying, "Well, not this year" to the numerous projects she wanted to accomplish. Her frustration was building.

Alex helped ease the problem by agreeing to take on additional household chores, freeing up quality time for Maureen. She created a list of "satisfaction activities" that would decrease her feelings of frustration. This approach allowed her to celebrate each completed goal, rather than just surveying the many postponed projects that had been simmering in her mind for years.

Both party's feelings need to be considered in situations like this. The person still working may resent doing the usual chores and errands if the retired partner has more time and choice of activities during the day. However, the retired partner may feel that this is his/her time that has been earned through years of hard work, and feel it is unfair to now be burdened with the housecleaning and other chores. Again, communication about the division of labor is the key to resolving these issues.

Together at Last: Who Does What?

The division of labor is different in each household. Some couples openly discuss the division of household tasks; others just drift into patterns. Patterns frequently evolve over the years as the composition of the family changes. In some households the person who is best at a task becomes responsible for it; in other homes tasks are divided by who is available or who hates that chore the least.

When one or both partners are retired, the assignment of tasks—or the burden of tasks by default!—can cause difficulties and resentment if functions and responsibilities are not negotiated. Develop a list of chores as a guide to opening a discussion on a new division of labor.

A reminder for partners switching chores: each person needs to consider the standards of the previous owner of that chore, while the previous owner needs to allow for a learning curve and perhaps a relaxed standard of performance. Grocery shopping is one example of this concept. Time and schedules probably dictated how this was done before retirement but now there are more options to completing this task. Does this task switch hands? Do partners do it together? What is each person's style of shopping? For years Mary did the shopping, stocking up on sale and coupon items so she could save money—in addition to not having to make as many trips to the store. Then Andrew retired and took over this task. However, he preferred to get a few things each day and didn't like to bother with coupons or price comparisons. This was an irritant to Mary who saw it as wasteful of their reduced financial resources. The solution: a little bit of training in the "science of shopping" and a more relaxed attitude toward couponing!

And whatever division of labor is decided upon, cross training is a good idea. While it is always a difficult topic, it is a fact of life that one person may die or be disabled and the other person will need to carry the whole load. It will be easier for that person if he or she does not need to learn new skills while also dealing with the feelings of grief. This applies especially in areas much more serious than grocery shopping, e.g., paying bills and liaising with the family lawyer and accountant.

Relocation: Double Trouble or a Solution?

After retirement, many couples decide to relocate to a better climate or to be nearer to family. For some this works fantastically, but for others it can be a rocky road. Let's look at a positive example:

Ellen and Gerald made a major move from a large metropolitan city to a semi-rural setting after Gerald retired. Ellen had a very portable career in the healthcare industry, so she took some time off to get over burnout. She enjoyed setting up their new home and getting to know the new community. Eventually, she found a part-time job, because she wanted the stimulation of working. Gerald also found a part-time job and enjoyed finally having more time to spend with his stamp-collecting and other hobbies.

However, relocation may be difficult if one partner is not enthusiastic about the move, not adventurous or finds it difficult to make friends easily. Some people prefer to preview the location—and possible lifestyle change—before pulling up stakes and cutting ties. Others decide to have the best of both worlds and stay in one climate in the winter and another in the summer. With this last scenario the couples need to realize that at some point in the future limiting physical resources may make it necessary to choose one location.

This Wasn't the Way I Planned It

Many people idealize retirement as the time to escape the demands of work—and finally enjoy life—often forgetting the reality that physical abilities change, usually for the worse. As we have heard so often, if you have your health you have everything. You can still be basically healthy, but age may have changed your physical capacity. The dreams you and your partner had may not be possible. The realization that you cannot complete the plans that you waited so long to accomplish is difficult for each partner, and the spousal relationships can suffer. Health issues may bring greater dependence of one partner and less freedom for the other partner. Dreams may have to be mourned or restructured, but remember that they can sometimes be rebuilt; life may be different than planned but it can still be enjoyable. As always, communication is the key to both partners' enjoying a life that is different than what had been planned.

Dollars and Retirement: Adjusting to Less Income

Retirement usually means a reduced income. If the retirement is voluntary and planned, the couple has had time to prepare for the reduction in income. Some aspects of a retirement lifestyle can reduce financial burdens. For example, if one or both partners commuted each day, transportation expenses will be less and there may no longer be a need for two cars. The same is true of wardrobe expenses.

However, there still is a need to look at spending patterns and goals to assure that the dollars are being used in a way that will provide for both retirees' activities and a lifestyle they enjoy. Communication and negotiation can help establish appropriate spending patterns.

Most of us have grown up with the word *retirement* meaning no longer working or intending to work. In fact just a generation ago, people could not work past 65. However, these days people can work far beyond 65 because they want to or need to, and sometimes early retirement simply means that there has been a premature push out the door (because of mergers, downsizings, etc.). Because there may not have been time to accumulate enough cash for retirement, the newly retired person may find his/her self conflicted between two thoughts, "I am retired, time to relax and enjoy myself" and "I'm retired, but I really need to find another well-paying job—and soon." Extended family members may not understand this situation and further complicate matters with their comments and expectations.

I Love My Spouse—But I Need My Friends, Too

Most people spend more time with people at work than they do with their families, so it is natural for a retiree to feel a sense of loss and miss the camaraderie of his/her work family. It is important to remember that even in the early days of wedded bliss, each person had other associations at work or in the community to fill his/her social needs.

Today's retirees are healthier and can expect to be retired for many years. Taking up the life of a hermit and expecting one person to fill all of one's need for affiliation can put a strain on a relationship. The prospect of being together 24/7 will probably heighten the need and desire for outside friendships! So this is the time to form new social connections in the community. Many retirees volunteer as a couple or individually. Some retirees enjoy learning new skills; others use their current skills to help others and give something back.

The Space Issue

In discussing the space issue with retirees, it appears that the kitchen is a critical territory. One man told his wife that he planned to redo the kitchen to be more efficient. Although he had never cooked more than breakfast on the weekends, now that he was retired he planned to do more of the cooking. This was vetoed and he was told emphatically, "No, this is my space." One woman, nearing 90, remarked as her husband of 60 plus years eased her and a visitor out of the kitchen, "Next time I get married, I am going to marry a man who will let me in the kitchen."

Most partners have weathered many challenges and changes in a lifetime together. Retirement can be one of these, but it is also an opportunity for a couple to build a new life together—to love the life that they have carved out together. So communicate, negotiate and enjoy!

Chores Chart

Chores	Partner Number 1				Partner Number 2			
	Expertise	Likes to Do	Willing to Do	Hates to Do	Expertise	Likes to Do	Willing to Do	Hates to Do
Meals								
Breakfast								
Lunch								
Dinner								
Clean up								
Dishes								
Cleaning								
Area # 1								
Area # 2								
Bathrooms								
Laundry								
Washing								
Folding								
Ironing								
Outdoors								
Grass								
Weeding								
Raking								
Watering								
Trimming								
Snow Removal								
Maintenance								
List tasks								

9
•••

Discovering Your Needs and Finding Your Purpose

When a man does not know what harbor he is making for, no wind is the right wind.

—Seneca, Roman playwright, (circa 4 BC–65 AD)

Now is your opportunity to open the book called *THIS IS MY LIFE*: to review your past accomplishments, and to contemplate and answer the question, "Who am I and what do I want my life to be as I move into the next stage?" Discovering your passion, vision, and purpose involves commitment, focus and time. The next four chapters will assist you in your exploration to find your new life path. Before moving into the assessment chapters, however, it will be helpful to make sure that your path toward understanding, passion and purpose isn't littered with barriers and obstacles that may detour and prevent you from moving forward.

Coming to Terms with Your Basic Needs

You can't always get what you want but you can get what you need.
—Mick Jagger and Keith Richards, Contemporary English rock stars

Over sixty years ago, psychologist Abraham Maslow developed *The Hierarchy of Needs,* a human motivation theory, in which he identified a hierarchy consisting of four basic levels of needs. He described the four basic needs in this order:

1. The need for survival—food, water, and shelter
2. The need for safety and security
3. The need for love and belonging
4. The need for ego fulfillment or esteem

Maslow believed that these basic needs must be met before you can address your wants. If they are not met, a person will remain stuck in place, non-self-actualized and unable to fulfill his or her potential. He further stated that if you have met a basic need but the need then reoccurs, you will find yourself regressing back to that need until it is again satisfied. (Abraham Maslow, edited by Richard Lowry, *Toward a Psychology of Being*, Wiley and Sons, New York, NY, 1991.)

> *Even God cannot talk to a hungry man except in terms of food.*
> —Mahatma Gandhi, Indian spiritual, political leader (1869–1948)

Maslow regarded the four basic needs as deficit needs, A person doesn't think about these needs until they are missing. In other words, when you miss or lack something, you develop a deficit or need for that thing and will focus your immediate attention and energy on trying to satisfy it. This brings to mind the words of an old saying I once heard, "I don't miss you honey 'til you're gone." Once the need is met, the deficit disappears—your focus shifts back toward higher-level needs as you move up the hierarchy.

During the stress of retirement transition, you may find yourself regressing back to the lower-level needs on Maslow's Hierarchy. Examining the four deficit needs in relation to your retirement transition goals can help you discover where you may be stuck and being prevented from fulfilling your potential.

A Description of the Basic Needs and Examples of Retirees Getting Stuck in a Deficit Need

Level 1:

Physiological needs are the basic survival needs: air, water, food and bodily comforts. If you lack air, you will soon die. If you are hungry, the only thing you will want to focus on will be finding food. Obviously, these needs must be met before you can move on. Disease and disability also fall within this need level. If you suddenly become ill or disabled, you will find yourself spending all your energy and time and even money on your physical well-being. Nothing else will seem as important or urgent to you.

Janet developed a hereditary disease shortly after she retired. She stopped attending classes and soon dropped out of her teaching certificate program. Her plan to become an ESL instructor was put on hold. She also withdrew from her volunteer job and spent most of her time researching and dealing with her disease. This became the total focus of her life. It was only when she felt she had the illness under control that she could think about continuing with her plan.

Level 2:

Safety and security needs may surface after physiological needs are met. In retirement, many people stagnate at this level. Lack of stability, fear about losing the protection and dependability of a job, or fears of financial insecurity can all prevent you from feeling safe and secure. This might help to explain why many retirees become solely focused on financial planning and are unable to deal with anything else.

Fred was so concerned about his savings being sufficient he was only able to focus on this one aspect of his life. He worried constantly if he would be able to pay the bills and provide for his family's financial needs. He attended financial seminars, met with financial planners and spent a good part of each day on the Internet researching ideas and strategies on how to grow his money. He put his future on hold and was unable to continue his plan to return to school until he felt secure about his finances.

Level 3:

Love and belonging needs can be addressed only after physiological and safety and security needs are satisfied. This need can be very deeply felt when you retire and experience the loss of community, friendship and meaningful relationships. No longer are you a member of a work team or an office lunch group. If this happens, you can expect to experience bouts of loneliness and feelings of isolation and detachment.

Susan, recently retired, told me she wasn't very close to, nor did she like, her former officemates, but, "Now that I don't see them every day, I'm beginning to really miss them. I have no one to talk to. No one challenges my ideas or disagrees and argues with me. Much to my surprise, I even miss the constant bickering about office politics." If you are experiencing this need, seek out new friendships. Build a new community by signing up for classes, or joining a group or an association with interests similar to yours.

When Stuart retired, at 64, he felt lonely and isolated. He knew he didn't make friends easily. His job of 32 years satisfied his need for connection by providing him with a network of acquaintances with whom he could communicate daily. After his retirement, he put aside the novel he had been writing and became depressed and lonely. A few months into his retirement, he discovered a small neighborhood coffee shop frequented by other retirees. During the next two years he visited the coffee shop for lunch two or three days a week and was able to develop several casual friendships, including one with the waitress. This activity satisfied his need for connections and friendship. He felt energized and content, and he resumed working on his novel.

When the coffee shop suddenly closed, Stuart again found himself feeling lonely, depressed and isolated. He was unable to locate a substitute for the coffee shop and was not able to identify any opportunities to build new friendships. He stopped writing and spent his days taking long solitary walks, looking for a new venue where he could establish new relationships.

Stuart is an example of a retiree struggling with the Level Three need for belonging and friendship. Initially he found a way to satisfy his need by building a community of friends within the restaurant. He began writing again and even started sharing his writing with some of his new friends in the restaurant, which met his Level Four need for ego satisfaction. When the restaurant closed, he reverted back to the level three need, connectedness. He felt lonely and lethargic, put his novel aside and developed what he called, "a writer's block."

Level 4:

Ego fulfillment or esteem need is the need for recognition, self-respect, and confidence in one's self. As mentioned in Chapter Four, when you lose a responsible or high-level role in an organization, you can lose status, recognition, and self-esteem. To satisfy this need for ego fulfillment, find other situations that provide you with status and recognition. Become active in your community; become a mentor in your area of expertise; join an association and spearhead a new committee. (See Chapter Four for additional suggestions.)

Ted was district manager for a large non-profit organization with over 300 employees when he retired at age 59. Ted had been a vibrant, well-liked, and highly respected manager. When he retired, his colleagues threw him a big retirement party and honored him with a plaque that read, "To the Boss: We don't know how you put up with us, juggle all your work, and still have plenty of time for a smile and a joke. Your appreciative staff, we will miss you."

Things have certainly changed for him. Now, at 64, Ted sits at home wondering why he's been forgotten. He spends his days reading newspapers, magazines and playing Internet word games. He rarely goes out, and when he does, it's to take long walks or go to the movies. His wife stays busy outside the house and is seldom home. He lamented to me, "When I first left my job, the phone rang all the time. They were calling me for assistance and information. I was asked on several occasions to come back into the main office to train new staff. I even spoke at several retirement functions. I was feeling pretty good in the beginning. Gradually, the phone rang less and less, and then stopped ringing altogether." What has happened to Ted in these last five years? He is stuck in Level Four, unable to satisfy his need for status and recognition. His ego is suffering; he is exhibiting a lack of confidence and low self-esteem and he can't move beyond these feelings.

Where Are You in the Hierarchy of Needs?

The challenge before you and the gift you give to yourself is discovering your inner needs that act as barriers to reaching a fulfilled life. This is not always an easy task because not only are you a complex human being but you also are influenced daily, consciously and unconsciously, by events and other people. These influences can act as shareholders in your mind telling you what to do and what not to do, and thereby clouding your needs and preventing you from knowing the real you. Review the list of basic needs and ask yourself, "Do any of these describe me? "Am I lacking a basic need in my life?"

And since you know you cannot see yourself, so well as by reflection, I, your glass,
will modestly discover you to yourself, that of yourself which you yet know not of.
—William Shakespeare, British playwright (1564–1616)

To help you discover which needs you have satisfied and which you still need to meet, start by asking yourself the following questions:

Level 1
- Can I put enough food on the table?
- Am I healthy or do I have medical concerns I need to take care of? Are my family members healthy or do they have medical concerns that need to be addressed?

Level 2

- Do I live in a secure and safe environment?
- Am I taking care of my family members and myself financially?

Level 3

- Do I have friends and/or relatives I can talk to about problems and concerns that are troubling me?
- Do I have friends I can socialize with? Go to the movies with? Go for walks with? Have a cup of coffee or tea with?

Level 4

- Am I respected and appreciated by others?
- Do people ask me for advice and do they acknowledge my contributions?

If you answered any of the above questions negatively, pause here and determine if you are stuck in a deficit need. Once you have identified your needs, you can work to address them, meet them and then move on to explore your potential and your purpose.

Identifying Your Purpose

Many people have a wrong idea of what constitutes true happiness. It is not attained through self-gratification, but through fidelity to a worthy purpose.
—Helen Keller, American author (1880–1968)

The consequence of forging life by purpose and resolution is a sense of inner harmony, a dynamic order in the contents of consciousness.
—Mihalyi Csikszentmihalyi, Hungarian born psychologist (1934–)

Mihalyi Csikszentmihalyi, in his book *Flow*, states that "purpose gives direction to one's efforts and each person must discover ultimate purpose on his or her own." (M. Csikszentmihalyi, *Flow The Psychology of Optimal Experience*, Harper Collins, New York, NY, 1990.)

Author Richard Leider defines purpose as "Your aim. Your reason for being. Your reason for getting up in the morning." And he adds, "Everyone needs a reason to get up in the morning." (R. Leider, *The Power of Purpose, Creating Meaning in Your Life and*

Work, Berret-Koehler Publishers, Inc, San Francisco, CA, 1997.) What is *your* reason for getting up in the morning?

One needs something to believe in, something for which one can have whole-hearted enthusiasm.
One needs to feel that one's life has meaning, that one is needed in this world.
> —Hannah Senesh, WW II, Jewish resistance fighter (1921–1944)

What better time than retirement transition, when the base of familiar reality shifts, for you to discover your purpose, the basic core that creates meaning in your life. For some of you, self-discovery may be very straightforward, with no surprises, since your purpose may already be consistent with your life values. For others, the process of introspective assessment and soul searching may open new pathways for you to redirect and refocus your life. Your goal is to discover your true self. (The assessment exercises in the following chapters will help you in your self-discovery process.)

I have learned that if one advances confidently in the direction of his dreams, and endeavors to live the life he has imagined, he will meet with a success unexpected in common hours.
> —Henry David Thoreau, author, naturalist (1817–1862)

Consider Exploring Experiences Off the Beaten Path

As many seniors start to question the current models for retirement and aging, they are seeking alternative options to assist them in exploring their passion and purpose. Two seniors Ted, 63, and Susan, 65, have turned to Native American rituals and Vision Quests. As Ted describes his experience, "I decided to partake in a vision quest to work on my personal rite of passage during my retirement transition. The experience was amazing. It helped me to clarify the vision and meaning of my life purpose and what being an "Elder" would mean to me. I discovered and strengthen the passion connected to my soul as well as the opportunity to explore my reason for being." (For information on Vision Quest sites, see Chapter Sixteen.)

Winners are people with definite purpose in life.

—Denis Waitley, American author (1933–)

Questions to Help You Define Your Purpose

Read the questions below and record your answers in your notebook:

- What would my ideal life or world look like?
- What turns me on? What inspires me?
- What kind of people do I admire?
- What do I consider meaningful?
- What kinds of relationships are important to me now and why: family, friends, professional connections?
- What types of activities give me a sense of fulfillment?
- Do I want more challenge in my life? If so, what kind?
- Do I want to immerse myself in something that is bigger than I am?
- Do I have a vision of something I have always wanted to accomplish or a life-long passion that I haven't realized?
- What makes me tick?

A Self-Actualized Retiree Who Has Discovered Her Purpose

Clare has clearly established her priorities and defined her purpose. She has spent time reflecting on her values and her needs. She knows how to get her needs met and is able to ask for what she wants.

Clare is enjoying her life.

She explained, "When I retired, I examined my life and decided to make two lists that I add to regularly. The first list was of things I didn't want to be bothered with anymore. Here it is:

- Not spending time with anyone I don't want to be with.
- No cell phone.
- No more shopping for clothes I really don't need.
- No call waiting.
- Clean up and throw out or give away things I no longer want or need.

My second list was things I wanted to include in my life:

- Take time out each day to nurture myself in some wonderful way.
- Surround myself with younger friends.
- Be honest with myself.
- Stay active and fit.
- Eat healthy, smaller meals.

I decided to reinvent myself. I went back to school to study painting. I get great satisfaction from creating art that makes me happy. I only do art for me. Going back to school has given me a new outlook on life. I'm the oldest student in my class and it's great. I learn from the others, they keep me informed and thinking about things I've never heard of before and, of course, they also learn from me.

I know I'm getting older but my age makes no difference to me. I'm taking care of myself. I walk three miles a day in the morning, rain snow or sleet. Even though I still enjoy cooking I eat less than I used to. When I can't sleep at night, I no longer get upset and wonder what's wrong with me, instead I read until I fall asleep again.

My motto? 'Onwards and upwards, there is nothing more fantastic.' "

Discover Your Purpose

Purpose includes many factors, the most important of which is self-discovery. What is your calling, your mission at this time in your life? What is your vision, your new path in life, your new reason to wake up in the morning? Only you can answer these questions.

Musicians must make music, artists must paint, poets must write if they are to be ultimately at peace with themselves.
What human beings can be, they must be.
They must be true to their own nature. This need we may call "self-actualization."
—Abraham Maslow, American humanistic psychologist (1908–1970)

Cherish your visions. Cherish your ideals. Cherish the music that stirs in your heart, the beauty that forms in your mind, the loveliness that drapes your purest

thoughts, for out of them will grow all delightful conditions, all heavenly environ-
ment; of these, if you but remain true to them, your world will at last be built.
> —James Allen, 19th century English writer

The next four chapters contain a variety of self-assessment inventories geared toward helping you discover who you are and what you want to do. Along the way I hope you will discover your passion and develop purpose for your new path.

10
. . . .

Assessment and Taking Action

Know thyself.

—Ancient Greek Aphorism inscribed at the lintel
of the entrance to the Temple of Apollo at Delphi

*To feel in control and actually be in control of your life, make choices based on
your inner direction. With so many changes swirling around, the only stabilizing
point must be inside of you. Nothing outside can be your anchor.*

—Kate Wendleton, President, The Five O'Clock Club

Discover Your Skills and Interests

Some of you have formulated a plan and are beginning to lay the groundwork for
your new life. Others may have some ideas, but need assistance to help clarify what's
next. Alternatively, you may feel that your routines, roles, relationships and assumptions have changed, and you're left a little lost, without a clue to what you want to do in
retirement. No matter what stage of the transition you are in, it is up to you to decide
how you will spend the next years of your life.

Before you can establish goals and set plans into action, you must discover your unique skills, talents, motivations and values and determine what role they will play in your retirement.

Answering the following questions will help you move toward that discovery:

- What am I good at?
- What motivates me?
- What do I want to accomplish?
- What were the activities I enjoyed when I was age 8? 15? 25? 35?
- What did I learn from them?
- What experiences and activities do I enjoy now? Are they similar to my earlier experiences or different?
- What did I learn from any of these experiences or activities?
- Would I like to include any of these experiences or activities in my future?
- Do I want to engage in different and new experiences and adventures?
- If I could do anything now regardless of money, skills or education, what would that be?
- How do I like to spend my time?
- With whom do I like to spend my time?

Even if you can easily answer these questions, I invite you to use the assessment exercises in this chapter and the next three chapters as tools to assist you in clarifying and refining your answers even further.

To know oneself is the first step toward making flow a part of one's entire life. But just as there is no free lunch in the material economy, nothing comes free in the psychic one. If one is not willing to invest psychic energy in the internal reality of consciousness, and instead squanders it in chasing external rewards, one loses mastery of one's life, and ends up becoming a puppet of circumstances.
—Mihalyi Csikszentmihalyi, Hungarian born psychologist (1934–)

The Five O'Clock Club Seven Stories Exercise

The Five O'Clock Club's Seven Stories Exercise presents you with an opportunity to explore your skills and interests by examining successful and satisfying experiences in your life. First brainstorm and write down 25 experiences that you did well and enjoyed doing. The key word is *enjoy*. This may take you awhile, so you may wish to carry the list with you and add to it as you remember accomplishments. Some people complete this exercise quickly; others take much longer. The idea is not to become stuck on any one event but to keep thinking of significant enjoyable accomplishments that may now be forgotten and remain buried deep within your memory. These accomplishments can be from any time in your life, childhood to adulthood. As we say in the Five O'Clock Club, "It doesn't matter what other people thought, whether or not you were paid, or when in your life the experience took place. All that matters is that you felt happy about doing whatever it was, thought you did it well, and experienced a sense of accomplishment. Just write down anything that occurs to you no matter how trivial it may seem. Try to think of concrete examples, situations and tasks, not generalized skills or abilities." (Kate Wendleton, *Targeting a Great Career,* Delmar-Thompson, Clifton Park, NY, 2003.)

Once you have identified and listed your accomplishments, pick seven that mean the most to you. Rank them in order of importance and then analyze them by writing a short story for each one. Describe in detail what took place, who was involved, your role, a description of the main accomplishment and, most importantly, what you enjoyed about this experience.

Even though the skills you identify may be connected to your previous work, they can be transferred to other areas of your life. These are the skills that motivate you to create, to learn, and to develop as a person. If you decide to continue to work, either paid or unpaid, The Seven Stories results will help you clarify your direction and set your goals. The Seven Stories Exercise, along with the skills check-off list, can be found in The Five O'Clock Club book, *Targeting a Great Career.*

> *Capacities clamor to be used, and cease their clamor only when they are well used . . . Not only is it fun to use our capacities, but it is necessary for growth. The unused skill or capacity or organ can become a disease center or else atrophy or disappear, thus diminishing the person.*
> —Abraham Maslow, American humanistic psychologist (1908–1970)

Michael's Seven Stories Helped Refocus His Life

Michael worked for a large insurance company. He was promoted for successfully bringing in new clients and consistently exceeding quotas. When we first met, he wasn't feeling happy about his recent promotion. He knew he was considered a star in the organization but he didn't feel any sense of satisfaction in performing his job. He was planning to retire shortly and continue working as a consultant in the industry. While reviewing his stories he was surprised to discover that not one of them was about his present work. He began to doubt his retirement plan and realized that despite being successful and acknowledged for his work, he didn't really *enjoy* his job. It became clear to him that he had outgrown the job and was doing it only for the financial rewards. After reviewing his stories, he noted that experiences he enjoyed and experiences where he was successful were not necessarily the same thing. Taking the time to reflect upon his stories helped to motivate Michael to think about what he *really* wanted to do with the rest of his life.

The thread that ran through Michael's stories centered on his long-term tutoring experience at the neighborhood youth organization where he taught and mentored teens. Michael discovered his real passion through the Seven Stories Exercise. At 59, he retired from the insurance industry, enrolled in Teach for America, and became a high school math teacher in an urban school setting.

> *Do you do it for the money, honey? The answer is no. Don't now and never did. Yes, I've made a great deal of dough from my fiction, but I never set a single word down on paper with the thought of being paid for it . . . I have written because it fulfilled me. Maybe it paid off the mortgage on the house and got the kids through college, but those things were on the side I did it for the buzz. I did it for the pure joy of the thing. And if you can do it for joy, you can do it forever.*
> —Stephen King, contemporary American author

True Enjoyment Is an *"Autotelic"* Experience

"*Autotelic*" is a term coined by Mihalyi Csikszentmihalyi, from the Greek word "*auto*" for self and "*telos*" for goal. According to Csikszentmihalyi, an "*autotelic*" experience describes a task whose "performance is not based on future benefits derived from completing the task, but rather provides a person with an inner reward or joy solely from performing the task." (M.Csikszentmihalyi, *Flow, The Psychology of Optimal Experience*, Harper and Row, New York, NY, 1990.) Even if you may not have had these experiences in your previous work life, take the time now to identify them and be sure to include them in your life plan when contemplating your retirement goals. "*Autotelic*" or enjoyable experiences are essential for a happy, fulfilled life.

The Seven Stories Exercise Redirected Vicki's Life

Vicki's life changed dramatically as a result of completing The Seven Stories Exercise. At 55, she considered retiring from her managerial position in the marketing department of a major telecommunications company. She had returned to graduate school in her 40's, received her MBA and landed her present position immediately. She was the first member of her extended family to earn a college degree as well as an advanced degree. She not only felt very proud of herself, she was also the "shining star" of her family. Vicki came to the Five O'Clock Club because she felt unhappy at work, despite the fact that she was good at her job and was well liked by everyone in her office. She didn't want to stop working but felt she needed to retire from her job.

"Something is missing," she said. "I wake up in the morning and feel no excitement about going into the office." When she started working on her seven top stories, she told me, "I'm the first member of my family to attend college, so that will be one of my stories. The next is about achieving my degree, another is about entering graduate school, and the fourth will be about finishing my MBA. Another story is about how I beat out the competition and obtained my current position."

As Vicki talked about her stories, she didn't appear to take delight in telling them. She related them rather matter-of-factly, with little enthusiasm or joy. I asked her to spend some quiet time contemplating what she enjoyed about these stories before she started writing about them. Vicki experienced a life altering "aha" when she realized that the initial stories she presented were actually not *her* stories; they belonged to others. She saw that she had been playing a role determined by the expectations of her culture and the influences of others in her life: family, friends, teachers. What she had considered her achievements were not things that really made *her* happy.

Vicki returned to the group with a *different* list of seven stories and a greater understanding of her real life dreams. Ever since she was a child, Vicki had loved to sew and design clothes for family and friends. All her new stories were related to some aspect of sewing: winning sewing contests, designing costumes for her high school and college drama productions, designing the bridesmaids' dresses for her sister's wedding party years ago, and more recently, for her niece's wedding party. Vicki told me that after she started college, she put her sewing machine away but was always sketching new fashion ideas whenever she had a spare minute. She realized her goal as a young girl was not to work in a corporation but to become a high-end, one-of-a-kind clothing designer. The Seven Stories Exercise provided Vicki with the insight to realize that she was living her life through the dreams of others. She refocused her direction, retired from her corporate job, signed up for several fashion-design courses at an art school and pursued the dream she had put on hold for many years. Today, she is happily working part-time, designing women's clothes for a small fashion house in California.

Exploring Your Values

Values are your personal preferences; they are neither right nor wrong, good nor bad. They are at the center of your belief system and play a large role in determining your behavior and how you make decisions. If you fail to incorporate your values into your retirement activities, you may create feelings of unrest in your life. On the other hand, living your values can provide you with deep feelings of satisfaction. Your values may remain unknown and hidden until they are challenged or confronted, and, if confronted, you may be surprised to find yourself taking extreme steps to defend them. John's story is an example of how values can influence decisions in your life.

John worked as a part time instructor in an after-school arts program. He and the students were building large, mixed-media sculptures that included glass, metal, newspapers, magazines and plastic. When he requested separate recycling bins to discard the unused materials he was told, "Just throw everything into the same can, it doesn't matter." John became upset about the school's attitude toward recycling and what he considered a lack of concern for the environment. He wrote a letter to the director requesting recycling bins. When he didn't receive a response, he sent letters home to the parents, urging them to send letters to the director. His campaign to secure recycling bins went unacknowledged. John told me that he never realized how much he valued protecting the environment until it became an issue he couldn't do anything about. The school's *laissez faire* reaction greatly disturbed him and he felt that he couldn't continue working in an establishment that didn't see "eye to eye" with his principles. He no longer enjoyed his job and shortly thereafter he decided to resign.

Identify Your Values

Read the entire list of 35 values before you begin, then cross out the values that are not important to you.

_____ personal growth	_____ family	_____ variety
_____ friendship	_____ spirituality	_____ helping others
_____ natural beauty	_____ power	_____ honesty
_____ security	_____ health	_____ protecting the environment

_____ love   _____ morality   _____ religion

_____ pleasure   _____ social justice   _____ challenge

_____ achievement   _____ money   _____ knowledge

_____ exciting life style   _____ status   _____ ambition

_____ skill   _____ creativity   _____ competition

_____ education   _____ leisure time   _____ working alone

_____ working with others   _____ independence   _____ challenge

_____ recognition   _____ social issues

From the remaining values pick your top five, rank them in order of importance and then answer these questions:

- If you were forced to compromise on any one which one would it be?
- Which would you be most reluctant to give up? Why?

Review your results. What have you discovered or reaffirmed about your values? Are your retirement plans consistent with your most highly ranked values?

Other Assessment Exercises

Additional assessment tools can be found in our book, _Targeting a Great Career._ They are: Interests, Satisfiers and Dissatisfiers, Special Interests, Looking into the Future, The Ideal Scene, My Ideal Job and My Ideal Work Environment. (K.Wendleton, _Targeting A Great Career_, Thompson Delmar Learning Press, Clifton Park, NY, 2003.)

By knowing your skills, interests, talents and values you will have clearer picture of the kind of life you want to live, allowing you to make informed decisions, set goals and create plans to reach those goal. See Chapter Eleven and Appendix III and Appendix IV for more in depth help to identify your skills, interests and goals.

Decision-Making

After you have gathered information about yourself, you'll be ready to focus on making decisions about your retirement goals and plans. Follow the seven-step process below to help you develop your decision-making muscle:

1. Identify your goal.
2. Brainstorm actions you need to take to reach your goal. Ignore the voices inside your head that may be saying to you, "Why bother, I am too old," "I

can't do that," or "I'll never be able to learn that, so I give up." Include all the solutions or actions you can think of—even if they seem silly.

3. Review the results of your brainstorm. Gather information through Internet research or speaking to people, and pick three viable actions or solutions.

4. Weigh each action and consider the risks and work for each alternative.

5. Choose one goal or solution. Create a written plan, which includes a time frame for both short-term and long-term goals.

6. Create a chart to track your progress.

7. Review frequently and keep reevaluating and redoing steps for each goal or solution you choose.

Become Goal-Focused

Elwood N. Chapman, in *Life is An Attitude* states, "Goal-oriented people are more positive than others . . . They are so involved in reaching their goals that they don't have time to dwell on negatives . . . Once they reach one challenge, they create another. A goal becomes a positive factor. A realistic, reachable goal motivates (you) to reach (your) potential." (E. N. Chapman, *Life is An Attitude,* Crisp Publications, Menlo Park, CA 1992.) Taking action toward achieving your goals will not only energize you but will provide you with a sense of control, accomplishment and satisfaction.

Inaction breeds doubt and fear. Action breeds confidence and courage.
If you want to conquer fear, do not sit home and think about it.
Go out and get busy.

—Dale Carnegie, American author (1888–1955)

If you find yourself feeling lethargic and stuck you may be under the influence of procrastination or worry.

Are You Procrastinating?

It's important to gain insight into what you choose to pursue, but insight without action is no help at all. Procrastination is not uncommon at this stage. Negative reactions such as fear, anxiety, apprehension, doubt and confusion can be very strong when you attempt to move out of your comfort zone and begin to take risks and explore new options. Procrastination occurs when you give in to your disabling thoughts. Negative thoughts create disabling actions, which leads to inertia and causes you to wonder, "Why am I so unfulfilled and unhappy?" or "What's the use, nothing is going to change?" Use the mnemonic **SARAT** to help you get from the planning stage to the doing stage.

S A R A T

S–Take *Small Steps*

Begin with a specific goal rather than a global goal. "I will organize one draw in my desk." not "I will organize all the papers I have been accumulating for the last year" or even more globally, "I will organize on Friday." Pick one small goal or task that can be reached in a short time and define it very specifically. This activity is called "chunking down." Imagine a big boulder at the mouth of a cave. With each task, you chip away a chunk of rock and the boulder gets smaller and smaller until you have nothing left. You have then cleared the entrance of the cave and your goal is achieved.

A–*Act* Now

Do something! Even a small step is better than no step all. You'll feel better and will likely be motivated to do more, once you get moving. Don't wait until you feel ready, just start!

R–*Record* Your Goals

Write your goal in your notebook. Don't just think about them. Putting your goals on paper will give you something to look forward to. (Don't worry if you don't get to all of them. Just the act of recording them will be helpful).

A–Are Your Goals *Achievable?*

Can your goal be accomplished? Is it reasonable and reachable? Do your research before deciding to put all your focus and energy toward a goal that may be unrealistic for you at this time in your life. For example, if you are the caregiver for an elderly parent(s), you may not have the time to go back to school and study full time.

T–*Take the Time* Needed to Complete the Goal

Determine how long it may take you to achieve your goal; one week, two months, six months, one year? Some goals are short range; others are long range. Know the difference and plan accordingly.

Five Tips to Get You Moving

1. Visualize a picture of yourself having completed the task. Your mind will become familiar with the end goal and it will be easier to achieve it.

2. Reframe your language to identify and discard your self-defeating and disabling behavior. Change from the victim language, "I can't be successful in that, and so why even begin?" to the empowering language, "I choose to take control and will start by taking the first step."

3. Set up a weekly schedule that includes both exercise and relaxation to help you stay focused toward your goal.

4. Acknowledge yourself each time you achieve a mini goal.

5. Reward yourself after achieving a major goal.

Review Chapter Seven for details on visualization, affirmations and reframing.

Don't sit around waiting to be motivated before you act. Taking action, no matter how small, will be your motivator.

Is Worry Getting in Your Way?

Worry never robs tomorrow of its sorrow, it only saps today of its joy.
> —Leo Buscaglia, American author (1924–1998)

If you can't sleep, then get up and do something instead of lying there worrying. It's the worry that gets you, not the lack of sleep.
> —Dale Carnegie, American inspirational writer (1888–1955)

Charlie Brown shares his advice about eliminating worry, "I've developed a new philosophy. . . . I only dread one day at a time." *You* may wish to be a little more proactive, however, and follow the tips below adapted from the work of Daralee Schulman, a stress management consultant.

Nine Tips for Managing Worry

1. Take an inventory of your worries and see what they accomplish. Did worrying about any of the items on your list ever alter their outcomes?

2. Realize you have a choice: to worry or not to worry. Think positively. Choose

not to worry. Label your worries as negative thinking and undeserving of your attention.

3. Find something constructive to do instead of sitting and indulging in worry.

4. Face your fear. What is the worst thing that can happen? What would you do if it happened? Consider the options you have. Make concrete plans of action.

5. If you catch yourself worrying, look in the mirror, put up your hand and tell yourself to stop. This is called "thought stopping."

6. Reward yourself for cutting short your worry and do something constructive that will bring you pleasure.

7. Practice relaxation breathing techniques.

8. Challenge irrational fears that are causing you to worry. Look at your irrational thoughts and substitute positive, rational thoughts in the form of positive self-talk. Example: Irrational worry: "This has always been a problem, how will I ever be able to handle it now? Rational thought: "I can handle this problem."

9. Recognize the wisdom of accepting life's uncertainties and confusion.

Drag your thoughts away from your troubles . . . by the ears, by the heels, or any other way you can manage it.
—Mark Twain, American writer (1835–1910)

Remember, behavior is influenced not by what happens to you but by your decisions and responses to the event. It's human nature to worry. The good news is that you have control over what you choose to worry about. There are aspects of your life over which you have little or no control. But there are many more that you can control. Change the things you can, and don't spend your time worrying about the rest.

Realizing our hopes and dreams, goals and aspirations—depends on having control . . . over events that we initiate ourselves and . . . that come into our lives unbidden—the . . . stresses, obstacles, and disappointments.

Without the conviction that we have some control, we have no way to negotiate the tides of life.
—Dr. Joan Borysenko, contemporary American writer

If things go wrong, don't go with them.
      —Roger Babson, American educator, philanthropist (1875–1967)

11
····

No Matter What Your Age:
The Value of Having a Long-Term Vision

by Kate Wendleton

We are living in a culture that emphasizes immediate gratification, does not value planning, and gives slight consideration to consequences. Hence, far too many people, young and old alike, are saddled with credit card debt and live as if there's no tomorrow. We are urged to live one day at a time especially in the face of adversity, and that may be all some people can handle. But this is not healthy for most, and one-day-at-a-time does not qualify as a goal.

Many of our favorite clichés are *wrong*. Tomorrow does not take care of itself. Not everyone learns from his or her mistakes. "Following your bliss" does not necessarily make you happier. And sometimes it doesn't "all work out." Instead, many people end up resigned to bad situations and "live with it." They say, "This is what fate had in store for us."

Ironically, Americans are action-oriented and like to think they'll figure things out as they go along. I've even heard very famous people brag that they don't have a plan, which adds to the mystique. But they *do* have a solid strategy, which they follow religiously. They may let someone else figure out their detailed plans, but they are not as haphazard as many would like to pretend.

For example, when I heard a successful children's book author give a speech, I was intrigued by her lack of candor. People in the audience were dying to know to what she attributed her success. She said it was pure luck, that she rarely got out of her pajamas, and the money kept pouring in. Yet, she wrote four or five books a year and had many deals for related items. I believe she was far more *planful* than she let on, and she simply didn't want to tell us any of her secrets.

I once appeared on the radio show of a major, nationally syndicated host. As we were waiting for the show to start, he asked about the contacts I might have at the prominent TV shows I had been on and what I thought of each. Then he bragged that he was lucky because he'd never had to job search in his life! He said things just happened to fall in his path. But that wasn't true: he was using me to network! He was actually job searching *continuously*, although not formally, *and* he had a plan for himself.

Many successful people don't like to admit that they plan. It ruins the aura. But most successful people are always aware and always planning—and modifying their plans depending on what they learn.

People are happy when they are working toward their goals. When they get diverted from their goals, they are unhappy. Businesses are the same. When they get diverted from their goals (for instance, because of major litigation or a threatened hostile takeover), tensions build and morale sinks. Life has a way of sneaking up and distracting both individuals and businesses. Many people are unhappy in their jobs because they don't *know* where they are going.

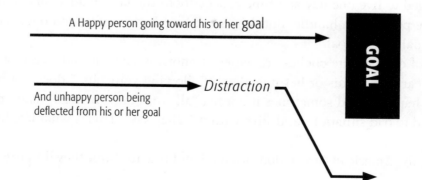

People without goals are more irked by petty everyday problems. Those with goals are less bothered because they have bigger plans. To control your life, you need at least a *tentative* vision of your future that encompasses your whole life.

Dreams and goals can be great driving forces in our lives. We feel satisfied when we are working toward them—even if we never reach them. People who have dreams or goals do better than people who don't.

Setting goals will make a difference in your life, and this makes sense. Every day we make dozens of choices. People guided by dreams make choices that advance them in the right direction. Dreams are the equivalent of the North Star. People without dreams also make choices—but their choices are strictly present oriented, with little thought of the future and are more likely to have bad consequences. When you are aware of your current situation, and you also know where you want to go, a natural tension (between what you face today and what you're trying to create!) leads you forward faster.

When you find a believable dream that excites you, don't forget it. Write it down. Look at it daily. It's less likely to slip out of your mind in the heat of day-to-day living. Happy people keep an eye on the future as well as on the present.

Lack of Vision and Depression

Herbert Rappaport, Ph.D., conducted extensive studies on the way people thought about time (temporal attitudes). His book, *Marking Time* (Simon and Schuster, 1990), is sub-titled "What our attitudes about time reveal about our personalities and conflicts." Dr. Rappaport asked various people to draw "timelines" of their lives: on a horizontal line representing a life span, make a dot to indicate the "NOW point" of life, noting your age. Then note your age at every significant event before NOW and every significant event after NOW.

In one poignant example, he notes the timelines drawn by two women in their early 70s. One, who was depressed, imagined *only two* significant events in her future. The second was fully engaged in life. She imagined almost as many events *after age* 72 as she had before that age, and she noted the end of the line—her death. "Death for this woman is a motivator rather than a suppressor of goals and objectives. The acceptance of death as a 'punctuation' point in the life cycle signals her to 'crowd' the future with the unfinished business of her life."

Rappaport points out that although the two women are approximately the same age, they view life quite differently. The first woman seems to have little in her future to look forward to. She spoke frequently about aging and was considering moving into a retirement community. The second woman had a sense of urgency and planned to "work until it hurt too much."

Having a vision is important *at every age and stage*. Without a vision, we are on a journey without navigation. We are taking day trips and not heading toward a significant destination.

Since I read his book, I, too, have noticed this temporal difference in individuals. One elderly couple, in their late 80s, still has goals and milestones. They are determined to crowd the years ahead with events. They look forward to the marriages of six of their grandchildren who happened to get engaged at about the same time. They also look forward to the renewal of their wedding vows on their 60th anniversary. And they also picked out the plot where they want to be buried—with great cheeriness.

A second couple, in their early 70s and 15 years younger, said they no longer wanted to have photographs taken of themselves because they weren't going to look any better than they now did! They are cheerful but full of nostalgia for the good old days. Their only anticipated event is the high school graduation of the youngest of their eight grandchildren, which will take place in four years. Otherwise, they plan events one day at a time.

Both couples are aware of their future deaths, but one couple takes great joy in the details of their future. The other has their feet planted firmly in the present and *past*.

When a person focuses mainly on the past, that person is often described as depressed. Depressed people, experts say, often have a hard time thinking about the future. The present and its immediate extension are all there is. Rappaport has an opposing and compelling point of view about depression:

> "Typically, it has been reasoned that the patient cannot relate to the future *because* he is depressed. . . . While some individuals clearly become depressed in response to problems such as divorce, death, job loss and natural calamities, there are also individuals who seem to be depressed without a clear precipitating cause . . .

> "Eugene Minkowski (1970), in his profound treatise on temporality and depression, suggested the opposite: 'Could we not, on the contrary, suppose the basic disorder is the distorted attitude toward the future.' The future and its possibilities are for Minkowski and a host of other existential theoreticians the force that energizes us and carries us forward in our lives."

Rappaport and others are suggesting that rather than being unable to relate to the future because he is depressed, **the person has become depressed** *because he is unable to relate to the future.*

And don't people know this intuitively? When a friend is having a down day, it comes naturally to encourage him or her to think about the future. We say that tomorrow is a new day and the possibility of a bright future is there. "This is just a bump in the road," we say. We all know to steer the person *away from the present and into the future.* "Things will get better." This applies, of course, only to those everyday "depressions" we all experience—not to clinical depression or depressions caused by a chemical imbalance.

An Ability to Move On

One interesting aspect of the Fifteen- and especially the Forty-Year Vision® is how it helps people to overcome being programmed by their past. A woman whose parents both died in their 50s cannot imagine a life for *herself* beyond 50. We urged her to push her imagination a little and see what her life *would* be like if she lives until 80—which is probably what *will* happen to her if she stops counting on dying at 50!

Some people *overcome* traumatic childhoods and others are *bound* by them. Some people overcome by re-writing the past. They *choose* to remember certain things or interpret the past in a certain way. Others may choose a negative interpretation. One may become proud of one's poverty-stricken roots rather than feel deprived by them. As Alfred Adler (a disciple of Freud) said, "What an individual seeks to *become* determines what he remembers of his *has been.* In this sense, the future determines the past." (R. May, E. Angel, and H.F. Ellenberger, *Existence,* New York, Simon & Schuster, 1958). A Fifteen- or Forty-Year Vision can help a person to create a new future, and re-frame a person's past so that it no longer disables.

People must move on. We are sad not just because of some traumatic experience, but because we feel *tied* to it. It controls us; We can't get over it. One of my aunts in her 90s lost her husband of 70 years. She doesn't want to go out; she says she wants to "spend the evening with Frank." Even at her advanced age, we are trying to help her move on, because the years she has left *can* be brighter.

We must replace lost loved ones—those who are no longer in our lives for various reasons. When my grandmother was in her 80s but still vibrant, she volunteered to rock babies at an orphanage. Those babies perked up the minute she walked into the room. She knew that her efforts were worthwhile, and the babies satisfied her need for the everyday caring of children after her own children and grandchildren were grown. That was *her* bright future, instead of sitting home thinking about the past.

Her daughter, my now 87-year-old mother, makes hundreds of rosaries for the missions and volunteers at her church, helping others and making friendships at the same time.

Ultimately, man should not ask what the meaning of his life is, but rather he must recognize that it is he who is asked.

—Viktor E. Frankl

"We stop growing when our human losses are no longer replaced," wrote George Vaillant in *Adaptation to Life*. "Letting go" and moving on—making the replacement—is a healthy response.

When one's life has become unsettled, such as through the death of a loved one, the loss of a job, and other situations, to thrive again one *must* envision a new future. It takes hard work, and sometimes it takes years to figure out what your new life should be like. But it's the same result at any age: You will have a more satisfying future if you put effort into analyzing yourself and also exploring your options.

Work alone does not do it. Without love for others and from others, it is hard to grow. It is the continuity of those important relationships that keep us going over the decades. If you don't have them, you must make them.

The Impact on Older People of Imagining a Future

We say your vision should push you past age 80 so you can see what can happen if you live that long. People are sometimes emotionally scripted for bad health or unhappiness. But all of us *can* break away from the script and re-write the future—as well as the past. We can re-write the way we see our past. We can decide to have very different lives from those we grew up with or now have. That different life requires a different vision of our future.

No matter what a person's age, the process of imagining a future is difficult and can provoke anxiety. We would all like to "go with the flow" and hope it will all work out. Rappaport noted: "More so than individuals who are in their forties, for example, those who are over sixty have a great deal of trouble extending into the future." Yes, those who are over 60 may feel that imagining a future is wishful thinking. Even some career coaches titter at the thought of a 60-year old doing a Fifteen- or Thirty-Year Vision.

When Rappaport met with older people who were simply living day-to-day, doing what needed to be done and essentially wasting time, he asked them: "If you learned at the beginning of a two-week trip to Alaska that the trip had to be shortened, would you forget about your itinerary and aimlessly wander around your room? Would you pick up and go home, or would you accelerate and get as much done as possible?" The reality of death can make us get more out of the time that we do have, including making our wills and putting our houses in order. We're all going to die. What matters is what we do *with the time we have*. It makes sense to accept our future deaths and *make the most of the time we have*.

When he asked someone over 60: "What would you do if you were told you had a few weeks left to live?," the question helped a person to explore his or her priorities. Rappaport found that, in most cases, people who had been wandering aimlessly became energized and focused on what was important to them.

Most of us *do* have a lot of time left. Being 60, 70, even 80 is not the end of the road. The average life expectancy today in the United States is 29 years longer than it was in 1900. Because of better health care, these years have been added to middle age, not old age. You have the time to learn and be productive for many, many years. You could have your greatest life accomplishments after the age of 50 or even older. Why give up now? You have plenty of time to make great progress toward whatever you plan. When Jean Calment of France was asked on her 120th birthday what kind of future she expected, she answered, "A short one"—but, guess what—she lived for two more years!

So, the after-retirement years may add up to 30 or more. We have plenty of time to make progress toward our vision of the future. Yet, people "retire" with no thought of how they will spend that time or how they will manage their lives through the decades. People may want to retire to get off the treadmill, but to do *what?* I have met too many retired people who are depressed and at a loss for what to do with their time. If a person was used to a vibrant career, this feeling of dislocation can go on for *decades*.

Often unplanned years are full of self-oriented pursuits: shopping, traveling, and keeping physically fit. But many don't *think through* what their lives will actually be like. Some decide that they want to live in an adult community where there are no children around, but later become sad at being around all these old people. They think, "I'll travel or play golf." But 30 years of self-indulgence is a long time. Where is the sense of momentum and purpose?

Self-oriented pursuits are not considered the healthiest for the long haul. If you have been working hard for years and deserve a break, take a break. Cut back. But stay involved with life, especially in pursuits that *help others*. Rappaport says that one of the common themes he sees among depressed adults in his practice is the deep sense of regret for not "stretching oneself" at different life stages. It is not too late to become deeply immersed in something that matters. Rappaport found that those who engage in meaningful activities are happier than those who engage only in self-indulgent activities.

Yet the evidence at hand suggests that ultimately life does not appear satisfying or socially valuable when approached as an opportunity to be free of responsibility.

—Herbert Rappaport, Ph.D.

All of those Years Ahead

People usually imagine retirement—if they imagine it at all—as one big lump of time. But 50 is *different* from 70, 80 and 90, just as 10 is very different from 30, 40 and 50. Each of the segments over 50 can be envisioned and planned for.

Let's take living arrangements, for example. You may want to continue to live where you do now until age 75, and then move to something smaller—say a two-bedroom apartment instead of a four-bedroom house. Then, at say age 85 or 90, you may have to move to a retirement home, and finally to a nursing home. If you don't like this vision for yourself, that's okay. Write your own! Where do you want to live geographically? What does your residence look like at each stage? If you live to be 90, your living arrangements will be worked out somehow, by someone. If *you* don't plan them, chances are, you won't be happy with how things work out. In the Fifteen- and Forty-Year Visions, you will plan this for each stage of life ahead.

Now, what about your preoccupations? Are you planning to travel when you retire? Thirty years is a long time to travel. How much time can you actually spend doing that? Many older people are depressed and bored. Life seems to drag. That's because the retirement dream was too vague and not well thought out, *i.e.,* "travel." They're not productive and contributing. More and more people are in great physical health and not as well off emotionally because they're *drifting*. They lack goals.

In the Fifteen- and Forty-Year Visions, we suggest that you push yourself to at least age 80 so you can see what can happen if you live that long. According to Kubler-Ross, while there is life, there is still potential for meaningful behavior. Rappaport, in a study of adults in a retirement community, found that those with an unstructured future ended up being present-centered, which is actually stagnation. For those in their 60s and 70s, there is a link between lack of purpose and death anxiety. Planning for the rest of life and retaining a sense of forward motion are at the core of mental health. "Once we get people over the bias that it is frivolous to [plan] at these ages, there is usually ample time, focus and financial resources to face these critically important issues."

What would you like your pursuits to be? If you are now 60, for example, why not now imagine what your pursuits will be like at age 70 and get started in those pursuits now. This may take a lot of thought and exploration, just as it would for a young person choosing a profession. Would you like to raise dogs, for example? Then join dog-related associations now.

When I retire, which is many years away, I envision myself continuing to teach in prisons and have already researched the prisons and their educational programs in the geographic area where I plan to live—just to make sure the vision is doable. I also envision having an active role as a grandparent and have had serious discussions with my children about living in the same community. If that doesn't work out, I imagine myself doing something with young children. I also imagine myself gardening, always my favorite hobby, and cooking more—although I do now cook just about every day. I also imagine myself writing another book, but probably not about careers. Working with children and inmates, gardening, cooking, writing books: I can research and plan now for all these activities, to assure that they don't remain pipe dreams, but can have real structure and content.

What kind of future would *you* like to imagine for yourself? You may have to work hard to make it happen, and you can plant the seeds now. The present is an opportunity to plan what we would like to do with the rest of our lives, but ironically that happens only when we accept that there is only so much time. Then we begin to worry that there is not enough time. Time becomes precious, not something to be squandered. We can still play bridge and go to the movies, but they become pastimes—just as they were during our "productive" years, and the foreground of our lives become areas of contribution.

Your Age: How Much Longer Do You Want to Work?

Age puzzles me. I thought it was a quiet time.
My seventies were interesting and fairly serene, but my eighties are passionate.
I grow more intense as I age.

—Florida Scott Maxwell

I started this business at age 40; my brother started his business at age 55. With the Fifteen- and Forty-Year Visions, you realize that you have the time to start and be successful in whatever your pursuits are. Would you like to make an impact on an environmental issue? Your family? Other families? A community issue? Or just on the quality of life? Would you like to learn new things (you still have time to become an expert in something new)? Actually work for a not-for-profit? Do consulting work?

Culinary expert Julia Child, for example, brought joy to millions when she was past 60. She died at age 91, and is a striking example of those who don't really hit their stride until they are older. She was forced to abandon her first career because she married a fellow civil servant, Paul Child. After several years of searching, she discovered French cooking when her husband was assigned to France as a USIA officer. Starting at about the age of 35, Julia trained as a chef, founded her own cooking school, and worked on a cookbook, *Mastering the Art of French Cooking*. In 1960, when she was almost 50, the couple moved back to the United States, where the book was published. A chance publicity appearance on television led to her famous TV series.

At one point, by the way, after a double mastectomy, Julia was convinced that her life was ruined. But after many weeks of grieving and weeping, she snapped out of it. "After all, I could be six feet under," she said, "but I'm not." She résuméd her forward motion. She had a new lease on life and decided to make the most of it.

Any why not? At age 40, 50, 60, you will find that you are now using everything you have ever learned in your life and bringing it all together. You don't have the pressure of putting the kids through school. You can afford to take risks. Some fields, such as consulting, often favor the older folks. Who wants a twenty-year-old financial advisor?

The trouble with the future is that it usually arrives before we're ready for it.
—Arnold H. Glasow

The Fifteen and Forty-Year Visions®

Our business is about helping people with their careers, but we have always urged our clients to do the Forty-Year Vision—or at least a fifteen-year version of it. You can't consider one part of your life without also considering its impact on the rest of your life: where you want to live, your relationship with your family, and so on. Write down, in the present tense, the way your life is right now, and the way you see yourself five years from now and fifteen years from now, using the questions below.

When you have finished the exercise, ask yourself how you feel about your life as you laid it out in your vision. Some people feel depressed when they see on paper how their lives are going, and they cannot think of a way out. But they feel better when a good friend or a Five O'Clock Club coach helps them think of a better future to work toward. If you don't like your vision, change it—it's your life.

Start the exercise with the way things are now so you will be realistic about your future. Don't think too hard. See where you wind up. You have plenty of time to get things done.

The fifteen-year mark proves to be the most important for most people. It's far enough away from the present to allow you to dream. Here are the questions to ask yourself:

- What is your life like right now?
  (Say anything you want about your life.)
- Who are your friends? What do they do for a living?
- What is your relationship with your family, however you define "family"?
- Are you married? Single? Children? (List ages.)
- Where are you living? What does it look like?
- What are your hobbies and interests?
- What do you do for exercise?
- How is your health?
- How do you take care of your spiritual needs?
- What kind of work or work-substitute are you doing?
- What else would you like to note about your life right now?

We know that engaging in the Fifteen-Year Vision (at least) has energized many people to turn their lives in exciting new directions.

We are prone to judge success by the index of our salaries or the size of our automobiles, rather than by the quality of our service relationship to humanity.
—Rev. Dr. Martin Luther King, Jr.

12
• • • •

Want to Retire to Something? Will It Be Working for Pay or Volunteering?

People say that what we're all seeking is a meaning for life. I think that what we're really seeking is an experience of being alive, so that our life experiences on the purely physical plane will have resonance within our innermost being and reality, so that we can actually feel the rapture of being alive.

> —Joseph Campbell, American writer (1904–1987)

Real joy comes not from ease of vibes or from the praise of men, but from doing something worthwhile.

> —Sir Winfred Grenfell, medical missionary (1865–1940)

Do you want to retire but still be involved in meaningful work? What will it be? Another career? Part-time or full-time employment? Paid or volunteer?

A client described his thoughts, "When I retired I thought I would be entering another phase of life where I would be seen as wiser but less active. I saw myself becoming a mentor to the younger generation. I realize now that I want to continue to work, to stay active and be involved. I want to participate and not be relegated to the sidelines. I want to use my knowledge and experience to make a difference, if not in the world, then at least in the work environment. I guess I'm just not ready to hang up the towel, but what will I do? That's the question."

A recent AARP study showed that two out of three individuals over 50 view retirement as a new chapter in life, a time to start new activities and develop new goals. The study reports that people in their 60s, 70s, 80s, 90s, and even a growing number of centenarians are making decisions about staying involved and active by continuing to work in their current jobs or finding new jobs.

Another AARP study has shown that 80% of boomers, 45 and older, want to continue working either full- or part-time past 65, for either money or enjoyment. When Horace B. Deets, the AARP executive director, was retiring in 2002, after 26 years with the organization, he remarked, "I'm looking forward to an opportunity where I can control more of my time, but I'm going to keep working at something . . . since . . . I don't play golf and I don't own a rocking chair." He went on to say that he planned to work on several small projects. "You could call it 'phased' retirement," he explained. "The worst thing I think I could do would be to withdraw from all work. I think it would be detrimental to my health and well being." (*AARP Magazine*, June 2001.)

"See? I told you it was possible to mix business with pleasure."

Ken Dychtwald, author of *The Power Years: A User's Guide to the Rest of Your Life*, sums it up nicely. He declares that as the baby boomers start to turn 60, "They don't want to fade into obscurity. They want to trade success for satisfaction . . . It's time to retire retirement."

Most of the people I interviewed for this book wanted to stay involved and connected, work at something, and at the same time have the freedom to do the things that they want to do. The problem they faced, however, was that many of them weren't clear on how to proceed. Marie, a client, confided, "Retire? No way. Financially I can't. I need the money. I need to keep working for at least three to five more years. My plan was to work until I reached 67. Now that I have been downsized I have to find another job. Will it be full time or part time? I need to see, I'm just not sure what to do next." Another retiree, Sam, expressed his confusion, "Right now perhaps I should supplement my income, with a part-time job that would give me the freedom to visit my grandchildren, travel a little, and tackle repairs around the house. On the other hand, maybe I should volunteer my time and run for office on our community board. I have so many thoughts in my brain, how do I choose?"

What to Do Next

Start by asking yourself these questions:

- What would I like to do?
- Do I have a hobby I can turn into a job?
- What activities make me happy?
- Do I have skills that I would enjoy continuing to use?
- Do I need to upgrade my skills to make myself more marketable?
- Is there something I've always been curious about?
- What do friends and family come to me for help with?

Today's retirees are approaching work in a variety of ways. Some people are continuing on the path they chose at the beginning of their careers, but doing it a bit differently. Others are exploring new ways to create enjoyment in their lives by altering old work patterns. Still others are taking major risks trying things they dreamed of but never dared to engage in before. Which is your path? It's up to you. This is your journey. The road may be bumpy and curvy, and may even have detours, but the path is yours. The journey is your life.

To be as successful as you would like to be, develop a plan: set goals, stay focused and, most, importantly, *take action*. In the previous chapter, you read about the importance of having a vision and creating a plan to meet your present needs. Remember, things will change in your first year after retirement, in your fifth year, in your tenth year, and so on. As you change, and as your circumstances change, so will your plan. However, it is never too early to start thinking about and planning for your retirement, whatever shape it may take.

The assessments in Chapter Ten provided you with information about your interests, talents, skills, and values. The Fifteen-Year Vision and Forty-Year Vision exercises in Appendix IV present you with the steps to create your plan.

Three More Assessment Exercises

The three short self-assessment exercises in this chapter will guide you toward tapping into your thoughts below the conscious mind: your imagination, your instincts and your intuition. You may at first resist these exercises because they seem too simple. I invite you to reframe your language (See Chapter Seven, for a review on reframing language) and regard them as tools to help you open your mind and explore what's next. If you are experiencing boredom, inertia and confusion—what do you have to lose? But you do have a lot to gain. You may discover new possibilities that may be different from your previous career or you may reinforce the direction in which you are already headed. Most importantly, they may help redirect you away from thinking, "I'm doing it this way because I always did it this way."

The first assessment exercise **My Fantasy Day in the Not-So-Distant Future** presents you with an opportunity to fantasize what the future (work) day of your dreams will look like. **Finding My Inspiring Role Models** exercise will help you to connect your values with those of real-life people over 50 whose retirement strategies inspire you. Finally, **Where Do I Fit in the Future?** exercise will open your mind to thinking about the types of work that you would find motivating, enjoyable and satisfying. I have been using variations of these assessments, adapted from various sources, with my clients over the last 20 years. The versions below specifically address retirement issues.

Exercise: My Fantasy Day in the Not-So-Distant Future

Your task is to create a visualization—a mental picture that is as detailed as possible using the open-ended questions below. This is your personal fantasy: your dream of your future. Shake out the shareholders who live inside your brain—the voices that tell you what *they* think you should be doing. Free yourself from these influences and enjoy your dream.

Before you begin, find a comfortable chair, where you will be undisturbed and can sit quietly and relax.

Tips to Enhance Your Ability to Think More Deeply

Visualization is most effective when your mind and body are relaxed. Before you begin your visualization exercise, try one of these suggestions:

- Take a walk in nature: visit a park, walk by the water, walk down tree-lined streets with little traffic and observe the beauty of nature.
- Sit quietly and listen to music that inspires and motivates you. There is evidence that Baroque music is good for influencing your brain to relax and concentrate. Why not try a little Vivaldi or Mozart?
- Spend some time playing with a pet. Don't have a pet? Watch birds in flight or spend some time observing people walking their dogs. It can really be quite amusing and very relaxing.
- Take a long, warm bath or shower.

You may have another favorite activity that soothes and relaxes your mind—add it to the list, and enjoy.

Once you feel relaxed you are ready to begin. Close your eyes and take a few deep breaths. When you open your eyes, write down the answers to the questions below. Don't spend too much time thinking about the answers. Jot down the first thought that comes to your mind and move on to the next question.

In Your Fantasy Day:

- What time is it when you wake up?
- What do you do after you wake up and before breakfast? Immediately after breakfast?
- When you get dressed, describe the type of clothing you wear.
- Where do you live? In a rural setting or in a city? In an apartment or a house?
- At what time do you leave your home, or do you stay home and get involved in an activity?

- If you leave home, do you take the subway, bus, or train, or do you walk, drive, or ride your bike to your destination?
- To where do you travel: the city, country, or suburbs?
- How long did it take to get there?
- What type of building do you enter?
- What time is it when you arrive? What time do you finish?
- Are the hours and activities the same every day or do they vary? If they vary, how?
- How is the space you have entered arranged?
- Are there others in the space or are you alone?
- If there are others, what are they doing?
- Are you working with them? If so, are you in charge or is someone supervising you?
- Are you involved in doing something that you have done before or is it new to you?
- Are you using skills from your previous work or hobby? Or are you using new skills?
- Do you need to learn more to do this work better? What additional skills would you like to learn?
- Are you getting paid or are you doing the activity solely because you enjoy it?
- What three things do you like most about what you are doing?
- Is there any additional information would you like to add?

Look over your answers to determine what your fantasy has told you. Any surprises, or does it all fit together? Try to determine which aspects were most important to you and which you consider least important. How much of this fantasy can be put into your real life? Is any of it in your life now? What can you do to translate the fantasy into reality? To keep this vision fresh in your mind, you may find it useful to turn your answers into a paragraph and record it in your notebook. Since retirement transition can be a long-term process, you may think of additional resources and insights when you review your notes at a later date.

Exercise: Finding My Inspiring Role Models

This exercise will help you imagine your future through the lives of your heroes. Pick three people your age or older who you consider a role model. Each person should be someone who inspires you and whose life and/or retirement strategies you admire.

The person can be a famous one from the present or past, or someone from within your circle of friends, family, or acquaintances. Try to include at least two retired persons.

Now, record in your notebook why you admire each person. Do you admire his or her character, beliefs, courage, achievements, values, or integrity? Do you respect his or her ability to lead and inspire, to succeed in business, to create art, to take risks, to teach others? List any other reasons that come to mind. Note whether each is working as a volunteer, as a paid employee or as a business owner. Describe the ways in which you would like to be similar to them.

Having trouble finding a retired role model? Look around; speak with people who have been retired for several years. Look for people who are accessible and still active and working at 70, 80, and 90 years of age. Interview them. Listen to their stories. Connecting with a positive role model can inspire you and give you new insights into creating your personal future plan. Work on developing a long-term relationship with one of your role models by keeping in touch on a regular basis. Make this person your mentor. Be accountable. Give him or her feedback on how you are progressing and how you have incorporated his or her suggestions. Remember, a mentor could be a major force in helping you to shape your retirement plan and your life.

Exercise: Where Do I Fit in the Future?

This is another paper and pencil exercise designed to help you open your mind to discovering new possibilities. Before you begin, make sure you are again sitting in a quiet, comfortable place. Close your eyes, take a few deep, calming breaths, and relax. When you are ready, begin thinking of things you would like to do that would satisfy you, challenge you, and make you happy. Don't try to understand the meaning behind what you are thinking; simply record whatever comes to mind.

For example:

- Are you around children?
- Are you in a school or sitting in an office with one child?
- Do you see yourself in the company of the elderly, in a senior center or senior housing facility, or a church or synagogue?
- Do you see yourself in a park or garden surrounded by nature, or in a large modern office with windows high above the city?
- Do you see yourself walking by the seashore or in a boat, standing on top of a mountain?
- Are you standing in front of a painting?

List whatever comes into focus. Review your list and ask yourself: What will I be doing in these places? You could be teaching, tutoring, training, working on charitable endeavors, working on saving the environment, writing grants, researching information, soliciting money, creating beautiful objects, learning to sail, or leading a tour group, among many other possibilities. Record your answers. You don't have to immediately give each action a name. Just describe the activity. You can find out what it is called later. Look over your list and rank your choices in order of most exciting prospect.

Look to Your Hobbies as a Source of Inspiration

You may also want to explore skills you have developed in your non-work life. The skills and talents you developed in your hobbies can play an important role in determining your future direction.

Denise's, David's and Jane's stories, below, each illustrate how to launch a retirement future based on hobbies and interests. Denise loved building small-scale model dioramas in her spare time. She became quite skilled in arranging miniature nature scenes. When she applied for a volunteer position at a museum her unique hobby was noticed by one of the curators. Instead of being assigned a position as a docent she was assigned to the restoration department where she happily repaints and restores miniature figures.

David loved the water and boats. He always wanted to "go to sea" as a boy and later as a young man. He realized his dream after he retired by working on a cruise ship as an entertainment coach, organizing games and events for the passengers.

Jane's story is an example of how a life-long hobby and passion can be turned into a second career. Jane retired at 55 "because I could," she explained. "I realized that the one thing you can't buy is time." For two years she traveled, met friends for lunch and wondered what she would do next. When she realized that she always loved yarn and knitting, she was encouraged by her supportive significant other to open a retail yarn store. Worried about her limited business knowledge, she enrolled in classes and spoke with other knit-store owners. She carefully researched locations. Jane opened her store and today has grown it into a successful business. She also started a wholesale yarn business, importing cashmere yarn from China, hand dyeing it and selling to yarn shops though out the U.S. "It is a wonderful feeling to have fulfilled one of my life's dreams," she stated. "It makes me feel as though anything is possible. Life is good when your work and your passion are one and the same."

The way to find out about your happiness is to keep your mind on those moments when you feel most happy, when you are really happy—not excited, not just thrilled, but deeply happy.

—Joseph Campbell, American writer (1904–1987)

Combine the information you gathered from the assessments in the previous chapters and in Appendix III and Appendix IV with the information from the three exercises in this chapter. Examining this new self-knowledge will assist you in answering the following questions, "What's next? What are my expectations for my years ahead? What should I do now?" This may also be a good time to consult with and share your assessment results with a career coach and remember: your goals and expectation will change, so revisit these assessment exercises every few years.

Choosing Between a Paid Position and a Volunteer Position

Now that you have identified what you may want to pursue, you need to determine if it will be paid work or volunteer work. The deciding factor will probably be the numbers connected to your financial situation. At this point, a revisit to Chapter Three may be in order, as well as a review of your finances and a meeting with a financial advisor. To help you with your decision consider answering the following questions while reviewing Chapter Three. Only you can answer these questions—be honest with yourself.

- What are my financial needs? (Remember, your financial plan will change over the years.)
- Do I need to work to supplement my income, or are my savings, investments and pension sufficient?
- Do I plan to work only until I can collect social security?
- Do I want to work for enjoyment and involvement first or do I feel it is important to be paid for my work?

The challenge now is to focus and direct your energy toward exploring and researching your options. The work you choose—whether it be paid or volunteer—will be most gratifying if it brings you happiness, fulfillment, social stimulation and challenge. Volunteering or paid employment are discussed separately below. Each is followed by a selection of resources to get you started. (Since information becomes obsolete so quickly, always double-check websites and phone numbers for the most recent listing.)

Volunteering

Make yourself necessary to somebody.
> —Ralph Waldo Emerson, American essayist (1803–1882)

Some people give time, some money, some their skills and connections, some literally give their life's blood. But everybody has something to give.
> —Barbara Bush, former U.S. First Lady (1925–)

Almost 44% of those over 55 volunteer at least once a year. 26.4 million senior volunteers gave approximately 5.6 billion hours, to non-profits and other causes . . .

> —"America's Senior Volunteers,"
> *Independent Sector*, updated June, 2006.

It's not enough to have lived. We should be determined to live for something. May I suggest that it be creating joy for others, sharing what we have for the betterment of person kind, bringing hope to the lost and love to the lonely.
> —Leo Buscaglia, inspirational author (1924–1998)

Volunteering Offers Many Benefits

Volunteering can add focus, structure, discipline and energy to your life, as well as a sense of purpose and involvement. Giving to others is also giving to yourself: engaging in activity and interacting with others helps to maintain your intellectual and social capabilities.

Volunteering Will Help You:

- Keep connected to others through social networks and support systems.
- Make new contacts, build friendships, and become part of a new community. (Staying connected is one of the key factors in fighting depression and promoting healthy aging.)
- Boost your self-esteem, recognition, self-respect, and confidence (see Chapter Nine, for more about meeting your basic needs.)

And most importantly,

- Improve your health and prolong your life.

A study in 2004 of older adult volunteers in Experience Corps, a volunteer urban education program in Baltimore, Maryland found that while volunteering in the schools the subjects showed improvement in both their mental and physical health. "Giving back to the community may slow the aging process in ways that lead to a higher quality of life in older adults." (Linda P. Fried, M.D., director of the Center on Aging and Health at Johns Hopkins, *Journal of Urban Health: Bulletin of the New York Academy of Medicine*, Vol. 81, No. 1, March 2004.)

Seeking a Volunteer Position Is Similar to Seeking a Paid Position

In the Five O'Clock Club job-search methodology, you are asked to identify a target, which consists of the industry (or specialty area), the position and the geographic location of the position. In seeking volunteer work, the process is the same. Do you know what your target field is? Do you know what position you are targeting, and where you want to work?

Some Volunteer Activities Could Include:

- tutoring children or adults in either basic education skills or English as a second language,
- training,
- advocacy for political or environmental issues,
- fundraising for a local theater group,
- reading to the blind,
- working with unwed mothers,
- organizing community events,
- mentoring a child,
- delivering meals to the homebound,
- caring for animals in a shelter,
- answering questions and guiding the public at your local library or visitors bureau,
- conducting tours in museums or public buildings,

- helping out in a school, hospital prison or religious organization.

Ask yourself: What is really important to me? What do I care about? What industry or organization really interests and excites me—healthcare, children's rights, gay activism, the environment, women's issues, education, the elderly, animal rights, community service, the homeless, the arts, tourism, cultural institutions, politics?

Next, consider the environment you prefer: indoors or outdoors, sedentary or on the go? Would you like to work on independent assignments or work with a team, be behind the scenes or in the front office dealing with the public? These are only suggestions. Use them to figure out what matters to you. The choices are many and the decision is yours.

Locating Volunteer Positions

- Identify organizations in your area that serve the causes you are interested in and find out whether they use volunteers.
- Research and investigate resources by contacting your local congress person's office.
- Look up resources online. Begin with the suggestions at the end of this chapter.
- Talk to other volunteers to learn about the organization you are targeting.

Questions to Ask After Identifying an Organization

- What is the interview process?
- How many hours, how many days, is the commitment?
- Do they require a résumé?
- Will you need references?
- Is there training? If so, what kind and how long will it be?
- Is there a waiting list?
- Can you change assignments?
- How many volunteers do they have? How many do they need?
- How does the organization support and acknowledge its volunteers? Certificates? Luncheons? Training opportunities? Discounts?

Don't take it for granted that you can walk right into a volunteer opportunity. If the organization is well known, the chances are that there may be a wait list for hiring and training. In popular cultural institutions, the process could be long and time-consuming. At New York's Metropolitan Museum of Art, for instance, competition is so fierce that several of my clients waited a year to be accepted into the docent-training program. Other cities are far less competitive however.

While the bottom line is your motivation and commitment to help the organization, don't ignore your strengths and talents when identifying appropriate assignments. Volunteering is work—just not paid work. You should explore possibilities and research options as if you were seeking paid employment.

Intergenerational Programs

While researching volunteer opportunities, you may want to consider intergenerational programs that focus on promoting interaction between seniors and youth. These programs strive to eliminate age segregation and encourage the young and the not so young to respect and learn from each other. As the senior participant, you have the opportunity to learn what's up-to-date: computers, technology, language, ideas on politics, dress, and so on. The younger participant can learn from your wisdom and experience of what's "tried and true." Your conversations and your experiences are different, and so the way you view the world may also be different. You learn about life from a different perspective when you interact with a younger person, creating energy and a different or new way to view the world. It's a great way keep your mind alert and your brain challenged and growing. In fact, you may even decide to broaden your social circle by developing friendships with younger people rather than surrounding yourself only with contemporaries.

Not Interested in Volunteering?

Some people who would benefit from volunteer work feel negatively about working without pay. Why is that? I asked some of my recently retired clients, who were in supervisory and executive managerial positions, to answer the following questions:

- How much time am I willing to commit to volunteering?
- How can the organization benefit from my skills and experience?
- What type of work would I like to do?
- What kind of environment would I feel comfortable working in?
- Do I know anyone doing this kind of work?
- Do I know anyone who can introduce me to someone who is doing this kind of work?

- What can I hope to personally gain from volunteering?
- How do I really feel about volunteering?

The responses I received surprised me. They answered questions one to six easily but hesitated at question number 7, "What can I hope to personally gain from volunteering?" and question number 8, "How do you really feel about volunteering?" Some of their responses were:

- "It's not work if you're not paid for it."
- "I don't feel I will benefit at all."
- "I'm not really too excited about doing it."

They explained that they felt they should work only if they were paid, regardless of whether they needed the money or not.

I was taken aback. I've worked with retirees for some years and have witnessed first hand the positive influence volunteering has on a person's physical, spiritual, and emotional life. In trying to understand why they felt this way, I decided to explore a little further.

Authors John W. Rowe and Robert L. Kahn write about this phenomenon in their book, *Successful Aging*. They explain, "Seeing paid employment as productive while seeing unpaid as unproductive is a notion that is promulgated by our national statistics as defined by the Gross Domestic Product." (J. W. Rowe, and R. L. Kahn, *Successful Aging*, Bantam Dell Publishing, New York, NY, 1998.) They concluded, "Counting only paid work as productive creates a strong bias against the substantial contributions of older (unpaid) workers in hospitals, religious organizations, schools, and other organizations. It also seems to create a feeling of low self-worth and even anger for persons who had high status, powerful jobs managing large staffs."

Does this resonate with you? If so, you may wish to speak to someone who really enjoys his or her volunteer experience to gain another perspective.

Do You Want to Continue Working for Pay?

Perhaps you've taken a closer look at your finances and realize you need to supplement your income to fill the gap between what you will receive and what you will need to cover rising expenses such as health care costs, inflation, housing, gasoline, etc. Or perhaps you just want to continue earning a salary.

If you are planning to work past the traditional retirement age, you're not alone. The AARP study, *Staying Ahead of the Curve: Working in Retirement*, AARP, 2003, reports that 80% of baby boomers planned to work after retirement or beyond their retirement age. In 2001, a *New York Times* article entitled, "To Be Old, Gifted and Employed is No Longer Rare," chronicled the work of several persons, all over 85, who continued to work well into their 90s and beyond. Nearly 70% of those over 55 expect to work for pay once they have retired (Employee Benefit Research Institute). While 20% say they will never retire (AARP study, 2005.)

Retirees Are Choosing to Work

Jackie retired from two concurrent careers: public school teacher and real estate agent. Because she had been extremely active her entire life, she didn't want to "just sit down and relax." She chose to keep working but in an entirely different venue. She obtained a paid position as a part-time sales representative at Home Depot. "I love being around people and being helpful. I'm really having fun doing what I want to do with very little stress and making some extra money as well."

Rather than withdraw from the working world, retirement, for many, has become a time to shift focus toward even more fun or fulfilling work.

Marie, 68, was a waitress in a hotel restaurant for over 30 years. She was surprised and upset when the hotel was suddenly sold and she was out of work. Marie was given two weeks' notice and six weeks' severance pay. She loved her job, having missed only a few days in her 30-year stint. "I enjoy being busy," she said. "I like being active and talking to people. I had many regular customers, who were retired and lonely. I became their family and they became mine. I felt a little lost and lonely now."

Marie discovered that volunteering in her local senior center at first helped her deal with her job loss. She wasn't satisfied however, until she also found a part-time position working three days a week, as a lunch shift waitress at a neighborhood diner. Her new employer was delighted with Marie's ability to deal with his customers and was equally thrilled when her old customers followed her to the new restaurant. Marie explained to me, "Although I was distraught and worried at first when I lost my job, I am happier now and feel I have more balance in my life than when I was working full-time."

Working seniors are more and more in the public eye and are being looked upon as role models for those who want to continue in the workforce. Anthony Quinn was still acting at 85, Julia Child was still demonstrating her culinary skills at 88, Dr. Spock was still actively involved in medicine at 95, Grandma Moses was painting up until her death at age 104 and Strom Thurmond served in the U.S. Senate until he decided not to run for reelection at age 99. Studs Terkel, when interviewed at 93—one month after undergoing heart surgery, talked about his plan to continue writing. He exclaimed, "I still have a memoir I want to do . . . so I have that to look forward to." Daniel Schorr, who covered the world for more than 60 years as a journalist, now works, at 90, as the senior news analyst for National Public Radio (NPR). And the list goes on and on.

Why Do People Choose to Keep Working After They Retire?

There are many reasons to keep working for pay after you retire. Perhaps you were offered an early retirement package that you couldn't resist, but you really wanted to remain in the workforce. Or maybe the choice wasn't yours. Did your company close, relocate, or downsize? There you are at 50, 60 or older, thinking, "I guess I'll retire now, but boy, I'm not ready. If only they had waited two more years, then I would be ready."

After Robert, 64, lost his job of 29 years, he became extremely angry when his friends called him "retired." He lamented, "Yes, they took away my job and gave me a good severance package, but I don't feel 'retired.' I see it as losing a job, but why do I *have* to retire? I'm not ready and I don't want to! But guess I have no choice now but to retire."

Actually, Robert *did* have a choice. After some career coaching sessions, he learned to channel his anger and redirect his energy. Robert formulated a plan and began reconnecting with people in his network. Within just five months, he landed a position at a research company through connections he had made in his professional association.

Sometimes the bottom line is not only about finances. Jack, 82, has no plans to stop working. He offers this advice: "You need to keep working. It keeps you busy and connected, which makes your life work better. Your body and your mind stay young, you think clearly, you have friends and interests, and you never get bored. Don't retire, continue working and enjoying your work."

A Tip on Job Longevity

Arthur Winton, 100, retired from the Los Angeles Metro Transit Authority (where his last job was supervising a maintenance crew), after 75 years of service. When asked the secret of his longevity, he replied, "Don't smoke and don't drink and stay away from credit cards."

"I've called this meeting to inform you that I'm resigning my position as CEO. I've landed a sweet role on a very popular TV sitcom."

Finding Your Place in the Changing Job Market

If you want to continue working and are involved in a job search, you may occasionally feel discouraged. Sometimes you may find yourself saying "There may be nothing out there for me at my age." In some industries, this is true, but in most cases, this may be a faulty perception on your part. It is difficult to resist the stereotype of aging and often it can become, without your realizing it, a self-fulfilling prophecy. This topic will be dealt with in greater detail in Chapter Fourteen.

Let's look at what Kate Wendleton has to say about this in her article, "The Old Gray Mares They're Better Than They Used To Be", reprinted from the *Five O'Clock Club News:*

Fifty isn't as old as it used to be. . . . The average American today is living 29 years longer than the average American did a century ago—but those years are being tacked on to middle age, not old age. Middle-aged people today are in better health and are planning to work longer. Many have whole new careers in front of them!

Lydia Bronte, author of *The Longevity Factor*, conducted a study of the careers of people over 50. Almost half of the study participants had a major career peak after age 50.

About 1/3 of the study participants had major career peaks after the age of 65!

Those over 50 experience job searches that take just a few weeks longer than the searches of those under 50. If a person wants to work, what can he or she do?

1. Decide how many more years you want to work. If it's only 5 years, you can try to stay in your current field. But if you want to work for 20 more years—as many do—develop a plan that you find exciting.

2. Think about how you want to live those years. Here are a few examples:
    *   Steve had done what others wanted all his life, and now he thought it was time to do what he wanted. He just didn't know what that was.
        At age 61, it took him six months of planning to start his own consulting business. He's having more fun than he ever thought possible. And he has flexible hours so he can spend time with his grandchildren and run marathons in Bermuda!
    *   Gerry, at age 55, decided to move from his banking job to private banking, which is a growth field and one where age is a plus. He became a certified financial planner, and is now targeting 14 companies, trying to decide which would be best for him.
    *   Janet, at age 52, wanted to get into the hospitality field. She got a job in events planning at Arthur Anderson through Advantage Human Resourcing—a temporary placement firm. She's full-time in the field she wanted.
    *   Art had been a general manager of top radio stations. He now helps a major company set up new radio affiliates—and is moving towards ownership.

3. Pay attention to image—get new clothes, if need be.

4. Appear energetic—talk about going skiing or hang-gliding (just kidding).

5. Be willing to pitch in—don't see anything as beneath you.

6. Exploit your age and experience! "I hope you want a mature person: someone who's been around the block . . ." Many companies overrun with kids want a few gray heads around to call on the big corporate clients and help the company avoid the big mistakes.

7. Don't confuse age prejudice with salary prejudice. If people don't want you because you cost too much, then don't moan about being too old. Address the salary issue and intensify your search to find someone who is willing to pay you what you are worth.

8. Look to organizations with fewer than 1,000 employees. They need people who can hit the ground running.

9. Learn new skills now. Don't think, "I'll learn after they hire me." Take courses. Join associations. Consider consulting or part-time work to learn more.

10. Don't use your age as an excuse. Maybe the problem is something else. Try to figure out what it is.

11. Don't give up!

Other positive news for the older worker is that some fields are beginning to see a talent shortage. According to the Towers Perrin study conducted for AARP, "The Business Case for Workers 50+; Planning for Tomorrow's Talent Needs in Today's Competitive Environment: A Report," the fields of healthcare, engineering, finance and retail are beginning to experience a labor shortage because they are unable to attract qualified younger workers to fill their openings. The study concludes that with this anticipated growing shortage of workers, "companies will have to rely more on the older worker and will start offering them incentives such as reduced workloads, flexible hours and telecommuting."

Be Current in Your Research

It may have been a number of years since you last looked for a job. If so, it would be useful to gather information concerning your career search.

This will help you:

- Determine if the field you are interested in is growing or declining.
- Discover what new opportunities are available in booming industries.
- Leverage your experience and skills in a new way. For example, you might be able to train or mentor others in your area of expertise, or you may bring your past experiences and skills to a new industry.

Be sure to also checkout the annual hot list complied by AARP for "Best Employers for Workers Over 50."

You could return to school and study a specialty where you can combine your new studies with your previous work experience. Jeannie's story, in Chapter Sixteen is an example of using additional education to build a second career on the experience and skills of your first career.

To stay educated about the changing job market, frequently review online employment resources. (See the resources listed at the end of this chapter. But remember websites change, so continue to do your own research to make sure the information is current and accurate.) The resources will provide you with information about employers' needs and salary standards. Read the listings carefully, paying close attention to the industry-specific language. Include this language in your résumé and during your interview. Your attitudes and beliefs about the job market can profoundly affect your actions. Once you educate yourself about your options, you are more likely to notice job possibilities, become more confident, and promote yourself more effectively to potential employers.

If you are under 65, obtain information from the Social Security Administration (www.socialsecurity.gov or call 1-800-772-1213) or a financial planner on earning restrictions before you accept employment. If you are going back to work, you will need to decide whether to delay receiving Social Security benefits until you are eligible to collect your full benefits at age 70. Waiting until you are 70 to collect can be a gamble. Why? Depending on your age it may take you many years to break even and make up for the amount of social security money you will have lost by waiting until 70. To make an informed decision consult with the Social Security Administration for help in calculating the numbers based on your personal factors.

If you decide to keep working, I invite you to read the Five O'Clock Club job-search books listed at the back of this book. These books will provide you with a researched methodology and proven strategies on how to search for and land a job. After completing the assessments in this chapter and reviewing the assessments in Chapters Ten and Eleven, you will have a better understanding of what you would like to do next. Whatever you choose, keep your mind open to new experiences and you will enjoy the journey.

When you follow your bliss . . . doors will open where you would not have thought there would be doors, and where there wouldn't be a door for anyone else.
—Joseph Campbell, American writer (1904–1987)

Resources for Volunteer Opportunites

Listings in schools, hospitals, prisons, religious and community organizations provided online byHelpguide.org:

American Red Cross, National Headquarters
2025 E Street, NW, Washington, DC 20006
www.redcross.org/donate/volunteer or redcross.volunteermatch.org
202-303-4498
Opportunities in staffing, health services, client casework, feeding, transportation, facilities, supply, and sheltering, teaching first aid and CPR, helping out during times of emergency, and much more.

Experience Corps® National Office
2120 L Street, NW, Washington, DC 20037
www.experiencecorps.org/join_us/index
1-202-478-6190
Work on parent involvement campaigns and library book drives Located in Baltimore, MD; Boston, MA; Chicago, IL; Cleveland, OH; Indianapolis, IN; Minneapolis, MN; New York, NY; Oakland, CA; Philadelphia, PA; Port Arthur, TX; Portland, OR; San Francisco, CA; and Washington, DC.

Senior Corps
1201 New York Avenue, NW, Washington, DC 20525

help@joinseniorservice.org
1-800-424-8867
Foster grandparent program, mentoring children
Senior companion program, assisting adults with activities of daily living.

RSVP—Retired and Senior Volunteer Program

1201 New York Avenue NW, Washington, DC 20525
www.seniorcorps.org
1-707-462-2596 x 110
Service local community organizations. Matches interests, skills and life experiences of volunteer to the needs of the organization.

SCORE Association (Service Corps of Retired Executives)

www.score.org
1-800-634-0245
Mentor small business entrepreneurs by providing confidential, one-on-one management and technical advice. Provide team business counseling, conduct training workshops and seminars.

The Global Greeter Network

Association of worldwide "welcome visitor" programs. Introduce visitors to your city one on one or in groups. Contact local tourism office or city council office for information in your area. Programs include:

> **Big Apple Greeter**
> 1 Centre Street New York, NY 10007
> www.bigapplegreeter.org
> 212-669-7308
> Other programs available: Chicago Greeter, Houston Greeter, Golden Heart Greeter (Fairbanks, AK), Tap into TO (Toronto, Canada), Melbourne Greeters and Adelaide Greeters (Australia), and Cicerones (Buenos Aires, Argentina).

Big Brothers Big Sisters

www.bbbsa.org
Mentor youth from single-parent families.

Seniors Coalition

4401 Fair Lakes Court, Suite 210 Fairfax, VA

www.senior.org

1-800-325-9891

Serve as an advocate for the concerns of senior citizens at state and federal levels.

Corporation for National and Community Service

1201 New York Avenue, NW

Washington, DC 2052

www.nationalservice.org

1-202-606-5000

Provides information about three major service initiatives: AmeriCorps, Learn and Serve America, and the National Senior Service Corps. Offers fellowships and internships.

Peace Corps

1111 20th Street, NW, Washington, D.C. 20526

www.peacecorps.gov

1-800-424-8580

Volunteer areas include education, youth outreach, community development, health and HIV/AIDS, agriculture and the environment, business development, and information technology.

Teach for America

315 West 36th Street, 6th Floor, New York, NY 10018

www.teachforamerica.org

1-800-832-1230

Teach two years in under-resourced urban or rural public schools.

SeniorNet

900 Lafayette Street, Suite 604, Santa Clara, CA. 95050

www.SeniorNet.org

1-408-615-0699

Teach computer classes to adults in nonprofit organizations

VolunteerMatch

385 Grove Street, San Francisco, CA 94102

www.volunteermatch.org

1-415-241-6868

Matches volunteers within specific area of interest.

World Wide Opportunities on Organic Farms (WWOOF)

wwoof.org

Offers opportunities to work on organic farms in 24 countries worldwide.

Craigs List

www.craigslist.org

Provides listings for volunteer opportunities by location.

AARP

601 E Street NW, Washington, DC 20049

1-888-OUR-AARP (1-888-687-2277)

Opportunities in community-based programs:

- Tax-Aide Program; assist with estate planning and tax returns; www.aarp. org/money/taxaide/
- Driver Safety Program: teach defensive driving; www.aarp. org/families/driversafety
- Money Management Program: assist low-income seniors or disabled persons with budgeting and simple financial concerns; www.aarpmmp.org

Benefits Outreach Program

www.aarp.org/money/lowincomehelp

Help people apply for public health and financial assistance.

Ombudsman Volunteer

seniors-site.com/retiremt/budsman

Contact state Agency on Aging for local information on how to become an advocate for institutionalized elders in long-term care facilities.

CanSupport Visitor Program

seniors-site.com/retiremt/cancer

Contact local chapter of the American Cancer Society.

Visit isolated cancer patients in their homes.

Environmental Alliance for Senior Involvement—(EASI)

PO Box 250, 9292, Old Damfries Road, Catlett, Virginia, 20119

www.easi.org

Offers opportunities to work in programs to protect and improve the environment.

Resources for Intergenerational Programs

Generations United

1333 H Street NW, Suite 500 W, Washington, DC 2000

www.gu.org

1-202-289-3979

Provides a database for locating intergenerational programs.

The OASIS Institute

7710 Carondelet Avenue, St. Louis, MO 63105

www.oasisnet.org/volunteer/science

Matches older adults with youth.

Generations of Hope

1530 Fairway Drive Rantoul, IL 61866

www.generationsofhope.org

1-217-893-4673

Neighborhood complex where surrogate grandparents receive apartments and reduced rent in return for spending six hours a week volunteering with foster children who live in the complex.

Employment Resources

The AARP Resources Senior Community Service Employment Program

601 E Street NW, Washington, DC 20049

www.aarp.org/money/careers/findingajob/jobseekers

Work-training program for low-income persons 55 and older. Provides information about job retraining and job placement.

Cool Works

www.coolworks.com

Features summer and seasonal jobs for "older and bolder" seniors in national parks, ski resorts, ranches, camps, cruise ships and other interesting places.

Wetfeet

www.Wetfeet.comMonster.com

Lists job openings nationally and locally. Provides information on salaries, companies and industries.

Monster.com

www.monster.com

1-800-MONSTER (1-800-666-7837)

Online resource offering lists of job opportunities in all fields at all levels enabling you to make your résumé available to thousands of potential employers, research specific companies, and access the latest salary information.

CareerSite

www.careersite.com

Lists openings locally, regionally and nationally.

Careerbuilder

www.Careerbuilder.com

Large site lists daily job openings nationally and locally.

New York State Department of Labor Homepage

www.labor.state.ny.us

Job listings updated daily. Also provides information on community service centers, labor market, unemployment insurance, and links to other NYS government agencies.

Small Business Administration

www.sbaonline.sba.gov

Helps small business owners find information and resources to start, maintain and operate a businesses.

Senior Community Service Employment Program (SCSEP)

www.doleta.gov/seniors

National network of service providers with partnerships in public and higher education, national and local businesses and community, and religious organizations.

America's Job Bank—Job Search

www.ajb.dni.us/job.search/index

Nationwide listings of jobs linked to state Employment Services offices

Best Jobs in the USA Today

www.bestjobsusa.com

Contains employment ads from USA Today newspaper.

Job Hunting Guides

The Best Companies for Older Workers

www.aarpmagazine.org/lifestyle/Articles/a2003-09-17-bestemployers

Lists the Top 15 Companies for older workers.

Career Journal.com

Job database with 100,000 job listings updated daily also contains salary information

Newspaper/Magazine

The New York Times

www.nytimes.com

Wall Street Journal Online

www.wsj.com

Non Profit Opportunities (National and International)

Idealist

www.idealist.org

Information about nonprofit volunteer opportunities and job listings. Offers a free email service; sign up for announcements of jobs that meet your criteria.

New York Regional Association of Grantmakers

www.nyrag.org

Lists jobs and resources in nonprofits.

Opportunity Knocks: Non-Profit Organization Classifieds

www.opportunityknocks.org

Lists jobs and career resources.

The Nonprofit Times online

www.nptjobs.com

Lists all levels of non-profit jobs.

For additional resources see the comprehensive career and job-search bibliography in the Five O'Clock Club's book, *Shortcut Your Job Search*.

13
....

Easing the Transition into Your Retirement Career

by Harvey Kaplan, Ph.D.

I'd always had a childhood ambition to go into the investment capital business, and spent twenty-odd years in it. But the thought of spending the second half of my career in the same business was boring, so I looked around for other opportunities.
—Chris Corrigan, contemporary, Australian businessman

If you've read very much of this book already, you know what we mean by 'retirement career.' Millions of retirees continue working because they want to keep busy and to contribute to the common good—and because they need the money. Sometimes a retirement career means *trying something new* after completing a career of full-time work for pay. There might be a better chance of balancing work for pay and work for *psychic income*, that is, getting more satisfaction from work. The balance, of course, depends on the realities of an individual's situation when the time comes to forge the retirement career. And it depends on doing proper assessment and planning. The Club's Forty-Year Vision exercise might seem unrealistic if you're 50 or 60—but we won't let anyone get away with skipping the *Fifteen*-Year Vision.

Emphasis Your Motivated Skills

If you didn't fully enjoy much of your work in your earlier career(s), you can attempt to achieve a retirement career that will be more pleasing and satisfying. The key is to use your *motivated skills* during your retirement career. For years you may have been using other skills that you certainly possess, but these may not have been the skills that *motivate* you and get you excited about going to work. It can be comforting to realize that, from now on, you'll fall back on non-motivating skills only if your life depends on your doing so!

Your *motivated skills* are the skills that you *enjoy* using. These are skills that enable you to make a contribution and feel that your work is important and meaningful. So when you think about your retirement career, we want you to keep your Fifteen-Year Vision in mind, be aware of the skills that you hated using, and limit your focus and energies to the application of your *motivated* skills.

Assessment for Planning and Implementing Your Second Career

Think not of yourself as the architect of your career but as the sculptor. Expect to have to do a lot of hard hammering and chiseling and scraping and polishing.
—Bertie Charles Forbes, Financial journalist (1880–1954)

The proper assessment that I just mentioned includes the Club's Seven Stories Exercise. It is the key tool for identifying your motivated skills—and it works because it is based on *accomplishments*—your *own* accomplishments. The Fifteen-Year Vision enables you to visualize clearly your life roadmap. If you don't have a long-term vision, you won't make the right decisions as you put your retirement career together. Instead, you'll make choices and decisions that lead you astray from what you really desire for your future.

Research to Remain Grounded in Reality

No matter what your dream may be, a retirement career must be based on what is possible. Research will help you discover what is possible and plan the transition into a retirement career. There are two kinds of research:

Primary Research

This is simple: you talk to people—usually the people who *do* what you want to do. It is important to establish, nurture and maintain long-term relationships with them. You trade the commodity that is important in the decision-making process, namely *information*. You give and get advice, contacts or referrals and support. This all commonly takes place in the context of *networking or informational interviews*.

Secondary Research

We used to say, "Go to the library," because secondary research means reading about your targeted retirement career(s). Now we just as commonly say, "Use the Internet." There are thousands of publications and resources, and a good place to start on your secondary research is the Five O'Clock Club book, *Shortcut Your Research: the Best Ways to Get Meetings.* Part V is the 80-page "Career and Job-Search Bibliography."

Make the List: What Do You Want Your Life and Work to Be Like?

With your targeted position in mind, try to identify the environmental factors that are really important to you from now on. For years you may have spent many hours a day driving to work or riding a bus or train. So you may resolve: "From now on, I don't want that exhausting commute." That's one of the negatives you want to eliminate in your retirement career. On the other hand, you may be looking for elements that were *missing* in a career that you pursued for many years, such as recognition for work accomplished. What particular kind of recognition are you seeking? What do you need as *psychic income*? If this factor is important to you, make certain to include *recognition* on your list of environmental elements for your future work environment.

The table below lists some of the most common elements that people identify when they think about retirement careers. You may think of things that are not the list—so don't limit yourself, but do remember that you need to identify elements that you want to be *present* in your work environment as well as those that you want to be *absent*.

When you've compiled your list, perhaps of 8 or 10 or 12 items, it's vital to *rank them*. Of course, they're all important to you since they're on your list, but putting them into priority order will help with strategy later. When the time comes to make decisions, you'll need to review your *prioritized* list of factors. If your new role is not perfect in every way (i.e., it doesn't matches all of your listed factors) and if there's any trading off to be done, reviewing the priorities will be extremely important. Don't trade off the items at the top of the list! If *independence* is at the top of your list, and *challenging work* is second, be careful about yielding on these. If *variety* in your work is Number 8 and *job security* is at the bottom, these are elements on which you may consider compromising.

Ideal Characteristics for a Retirement Career

In order of priority, list the factors that are important in choosing a retirement career.

1. _____   6. _____
2. _____   7. _____
3. _____   8. _____
4. _____   9. _____
5. _____   10. _____

Examples of Elements/Factors:

Ability to do some/all work at home
Being in control
Benefits (general, specific)
Challenging work
Helping others (as a key part of the role)
Independence
Job security
Location: cost of living
Location: home town or other area
Location: proximity to home
Location: accessibility to public transportation
Location: living conditions/surroundings
Location: working conditions
Location: public schools, colleges

Mgmt/supervisory responsibilities
Opportunity for advancement
Opportunity for creativity
Opportunities for continued learning
Participation in a developing
    organization's plans/direction
Personal satisfaction
Prestige/recognition for achievements
Salary
Stability of work routine and duties
Variety of work
Work schedule (including flexibility)

(This exercise is similar to the values exercise in Chapter Ten. When you complete this exercise compare your responses with those on the values exercise. Are they consistent? Any surprises?)

Types of Employment: Many Options for Your Retirement Career

It may also be helpful to think in terms of how you can work for another person or organization—in contrast to the ways in which you can work for yourself. The accompanying table illustrates the most common possibilities. Many people who've worked for a paycheck their whole lives, or who have been with a single organization (or two or three at most) often have difficulty appreciating that there are other options open to them as they step away. But assessment and hammering out a fresh vision can be the keys to realizing that there are *options* in retirement careers.

Each type of employment listed on the table has its own obligations, constraints and rewards. It is possible for people to work for someone else on a part-time basis while operating his or her own business as well—depending on the business. In other words, the table suggests that there can be a lot of flexibility: you have options. For example, the franchise possibilities (three variations are listed) fall somewhere between the traditional arrangement where you work for another and the entrepreneurial situation, in which you're working for yourself.

Types of Employment: Many Options for Your Retirement Career

Work for Another

[Traditional Arrangement]
Regular full-time
Part-time (with one or more employers)
Per day/per week/etc.
Temporary
Block of time (e.g., seasonal)
[Not applicable]
[Not applicable]
[Not applicable]

Work for Yourself

[Entrepreneurial Situation]
Full time (contract)
Part-time (contract for one or more roles)
Per day/per week/etc. (contract)
Temporary (contract)
Block of time (contract)
Buy a business/"silent" (others manage)
Buy a business/"active" (self-manage)
Start/operate your own business

Franchise

[Some characteristics of both columns]
Buy and operate a franchise (or set of franchises)

Manage a franchise territory/subset (usually a geographic area)

Sell franchise opportunities, etc.

Retirement Career Transition Takes Time

At the Five O'Clock Club we usually advise members that career *continuation* should take a matter of weeks, but career change usually takes longer. And that's very much the case when you're working to create a new retirement career. It may even take a year or two, but if you're planning ahead—based on your Fifteen-Year Vision—you can take it all in stride, and methodically do what you have to do to make it happen.

Over the past 15 years, I have coached many people transitioning out of government and the military. I know that many of these people are told by their agencies and organizations that they should plan their transitions, which include the establishment of milestones, up to two years before they actually step away from their government roles. Transition takes time and energy and, if you try to ignore or shortcut the process, you're setting yourself up for a lot of frustration and stress.

Realistically, you cannot decide today that you want to retire next month and expect it to happen and be happy with the results, in terms of finding a *satisfying* role. Give yourself ample time to conduct the necessary research, do the appropriate networking, figure out the milestones and the schedules, and accomplish the objectives that you've set for yourself. This approach will minimize stress on you and other members of your family, who are in the transition process right along with you.

The Importance of Self-Promotion

Getting into your retirement career will require the same kind of self-marketing that any job hunter faces. Expand your network and talk about your plans and areas of interest to as many people as possible. You'll need well-targeted résumés and cover letter, as well as a detailed market plan to show on networking and informational interviews. If you're working on an entrepreneurial venture, a brochure will also be necessary.

You must prepare for interviews very meticulously, as any other job hunter would. Be sure to study the Five O'Clock Club book, *Mastering the Job Interview and Winning the Money Game.*

The Three Aspects of a Thorough Marketing Campaign

1. You are the product to be promoted. Understand your strengths, skills and achievements and be able to articulate them powerfully.

2. You are the marketing manager, with oversight of all your marketing resources (résumé, cover letter, Two-Minute Pitch) and the appropriate positioning. You also must be a time manager for the marketing efforts. Even while you're still working in your primary career—and preparing for transition—you need to allocate and manage the time spent on your marketing campaign. Critical resources, such as money (for travel and research), need to be managed as well.

3. You are the research manager. You are responsible for planning and conducting both primary and secondary research throughout your exploration. Sometimes a lot of research will be required to end up in the role that you will find ideal.

Pitfalls to Avoid While Exploring Your Retirement Career

- Don't try to go it alone. For many people this can be a time of major stress. Talk to your family and friends—and to people who have been through it. Above all, *work with a career coach* who has expertise on retirement career planning.

- Don't assume that everybody knows what you're looking for. Tell people clearly—which means *you* must know very clearly. Even if you've provided people with a résumé and cover letter, have your Two-Minute Pitch ready for face-to-face meetings.

- Don't expect things to happen overnight. Remember that hiring managers operate on their time-tables, not yours. Yes, you're responsible for thoughtful follow-up, but be prepared for delays.

- Don't get demoralized by delays and rejections—learn from them, but don't take such setbacks personally. Be polite and move along to develop more opportunities.

- Don't take your references and your network for granted. Remember to thank people, and protect your references from getting too many calls.

- Don't prepare a résumé in a rush or *without assessment*. Figure out *precisely* what you're targeting before you write your résumé, especially the summary or positioning statement at the top. Prepare all of your marketing documents very carefully. Be sure to consult the Club's book, *Packaging Yourself—The Targeted Resume.*

- Never do anything unethical. Conduct yourself as a professional in every respect.

- Don't assume that you will be defeated by age discrimination. Many employers value people with decades of experience.

- But don't assume that your seniority and seasoning will have people falling over themselves to hire you. You must be able to articulate your skills, position yourself appropriately, and demonstrate your knowledge and understanding of your targeted industry.

- Don't confuse getting interviews with getting offers! Turning interviews into offers is what matters, so be prepared to continue influencing decision-makers after you've met with them.

- Don't leave things hanging. Be imaginative and creative with follow-up; be assertive or even aggressive, but don't badger. That will never win you any points!

You May Be Rusty: Practice Your Skills

- You may be a specialist in your field, but don't assume you know everything about interviewing, especially if it's been years since you went on a job interview. You may need a lot of preparation and practice.

- Don't attempt to *wing* anything, whether it's getting ready for an interview, following up on an interview—or putting a résumé together. Get help, especially from others who are savvy about the job market.

- As you're presenting yourself in the market, don't use unique terminology, professional jargon or acronyms unless you're absolutely certain that expressions from your prior career are recognized and understood by the people with whom you're speaking.

Additional Tips for Transitioning into Your Retirement Career

- Track everything: keep careful records and notes. With whom did you speak and when? What did they suggest, what follow-up is required? But don't just count volume. Measure the effectiveness and impact of your efforts. See *Mastering the Job Interview and Winning the Money Game* for information about Stages 1, 2 and 3, the Five O'Clock Club tool for assessing your job search.

- Be honest with yourself and with others. If a targeted field or industry turns out to have too many drawbacks, change course. Don't delude yourself about a possible role if it's not realistic or appropriate one for you.

- Associate with positive, successful people as you plan your retirement career. Negative or pessimistic associates can drag you down—and keep you from seeing and seizing opportunities.

- And be a positive person yourself! Maintain energy and enthusiasm in your dealings with other people.

- Be flexible, remembering that circumstances change as you proceed in implementing a transition.

- Always be polite, courteous, thoughtful and tactful. The impressions that you make definitely do matter.

- Try your best to be a superior communicator. Be an active listener and ask meaningful questions.

- Be professional in your appearance at all times, even in informal setting. Your posture, demeanor and grooming send messages about you.

- Work hard at fashioning your retirement career, but schedule time for fun and relaxation. You'll come across as a normal, healthy human being if you pay attention to all your needs during the very demanding and stressful transition process.

It's your right to look forward to your retirement career. It should be a time to be thoroughly involved in activities that you wholeheartedly enjoy. If you've planned well, then you've selected wisely and you're looking forward to the change. As you proceed through the transition process, recognize that the period of stress will come to an end and that, very soon, you'll be where you want to be in your retirement career—and *enjoying* work, perhaps as never before.

14

. . . .

Age Discrimination—
Or Is It?

Aging is not 'lost youth' but a new stage of opportunity and strength.
— Betty Friedan, American author (1921–2006)

Age is only a number, a cipher for the records. A man can't retire his experience.
He must use it. Experience achieves more with less energy and time.
— Bernard Baruch, American financier, statesman (1870–1965)

Are you over 50 and want to continue to work after you retire? Are you afraid to look for work? Do you think finding work will be difficult because employers want to hire younger people? Charles, 62 sadly lamented, "I feel discouraged because of my age. I'm not going to bother to look for work anymore. I've decided to give in and give up. I'll just collect my social security check at an earlier age than I planned."

It is projected that the total U.S. workforce population over 55 will rise to 20% in 2012 from 13% in 2000. (Mitra Toossi, "Labor Force Projections to 2012: The Graying of the U.S. Workforce," *Monthly Labor Review*, February, 2004.) This will mean more employment opportunities for the mature worker in the years ahead. At the same time, age discrimination remains a strong "ism" beginning even as early as 40 in some youth oriented industries. Given that age discrimination does exist, will you be included in the over 55 and still working statistic? Or are you giving up like Charles and giving in to age discrimination by telling yourself, "Employers don't want to hire people my age. Why bother?"

Most of the job hunters who attend the Five O'Clock Club are in their 40's, 50's, and 60's. Some are in their 70's. The average, regularly attending member has a new job within ten weekly sessions.

Twelve Suggestions to Combat Age Discrimination

If you feel discouraged and fear employers will discriminate against you because of your age, empower yourself by following these twelve suggestions:

1. See yourself as capable to succeed and not as a victim. You can choose how you want others to see you.
2. Value the depth of resources, strengths and talents you bring to the table.
3. Present your unique strengths effectively while doing your best to overcome barriers standing in your way.
4. Avoid falling prey to the myths about older workers. Review Chapter Two, "Dispelling the Myths of Aging."
5. Identify and study inspirational models to encourage you. Read stories and/ or watch videos describing mature persons who peaked in their later years. Find contemporary mentors actively involved in living full, rich lives.
6. Be flexible and adaptable toward change. Prepare and practice a positioning statement that demonstrates you are a person who is successful in learning new skills.
7. Answer the question, "What am I passionate about?" and go for it.
8. Have confidence you will succeed. Visualize your success.
9. Create a targeted résumé that draws attention to your strengths and experiences. Read *Positioning Yourself: The Targeted Résumé* by Kate Wendleton and seek the assistance of a career coach to help you position your résumé correctly.
10. Keep enthusiasm and energy levels high by maintaining a sense of humor.
11. Remain current: read trade magazines in your field, enroll in classes, attend conferences, and join associations. Sign-up for Google Alerts and request

specific email updates of the latest relevant Google results of a topic you are interested in. Go to www.google.com/alerts for more information.

And most importantly:

12. Accept the fact there are some organizations that won't hire you because you're older. You can fight them, but why waste your energy? It's more useful to be proactive and to redirect your energy toward discovering people and companies that welcome mature workers.

"I know you're good with computers, Johnson, but can you play the drums. A couple of us got a band together and we're hitting the road with Kid Rock next month."

What is important is not what happens to us, but how we respond to what happens to us.

—Jean-Paul Sartre, French existentialist writer (1905–1980)

Courage is resistance to fear, mastery of fear, not absence of fear.
—Mark Twain, American writer (1835–1910)

Countering Negative Thoughts

Don't let negative thoughts about age discrimination sidetrack you. You are not a stereotype. Don't give others permission to make you feel discouraged. You might have heard well-intentioned friends or relatives say to you, "You're too old, why bother looking for work?" Or perhaps, "What! You're going on an interview? You're wasting your time; they only hire young people." Don't let these people's perspective squelch your passion and throw you off your course.

Those who danced were thought to be quite insane by those who could not hear the music.
—attributed to Angela Monet

The best way to counter age discrimination is to develop strong networks and to maintain a positive attitude. Credentials open doors but more important are motivation, energy, courage, optimism, enthusiasm, confidence and persistence. If you're thinking, "Easier said than done," then you may want to review Chapter Six, "Creating a Positive Attitude" and Chapter Seven, "Five Strategies for Positive Thinking."

He who has lost confidence can lose nothing more.
—Pierre-Claude-Victor Boiste, French lexicographer (1765–1824)

Optimists usually expect the best outcome, so they're generally more motivated to bring it into reality.
—Norman Vincent Peale, Christian preacher, author (1898–1993)

Create a Positive Affirmation

As mentioned elsewhere in this book, negative words lead to negative thoughts, leading to negative actions. Create an affirmation specifically geared toward handling negative age discrimination thoughts.

Some examples are:

- "I am a unique, experienced person who is worth hiring."
- "I can find the right job to match my skills; my age is irrelevant."
- "I can capitalize on my knowledge and expertise to help me obtain meaningful work."
- "Other people my age are getting hired. I can too."
- "I can identify many opportunities for meaningful part-time employment."
- "I am smart, capable and dependable and will be an asset to any company."

Use one of the above or create your own personal affirmation. Be sure to put it in *writing* and *repeat* it often.

If you believe you can, you probably can. If you believe you won't, you most assuredly won't. Belief is the ignition switch that gets you off the launch pad.
                    —Denis Waitley, contemporary American author

Negative Stereotypes of "Old" Are Disappearing

The 50+ boomer generation is redefining what aging represents. Its members are declaring that they want to remain engaged, active, and productive into their 60s, 70s, 80s, 90s and, increasingly, 100s.

I am an old man, but in many senses a very young man. And this is what I want you to be, young, young all your life.
                    —Pablo Casals, virtuoso Catalan cellist (1876–1973)

Retire at sixty-five is ridiculous. At sixty-five I still had pimples.
                    —George Burns, American comedian (1886–1996)

There is a steady rise in the proportion of older Americans remaining in the workforce. A federal government study shows that rates for men 65 to 69 grew to 34 percent while for women 65 to 69 rates increased to 24 percent. The report points out that work force participation rates for individuals 70 and over have increasing markedly in the last decade. ("Older Americans Update 2006: Key Indicators of Well-Being," produced by the Federal Interagency Forum, 13 federal departments and agencies that collect, provide, and use data on aging.)

A Doctorate at Age 56

"I went back to graduate school at age 48, and got my doctorate in adult education at 56." If Barbara Plasker was intimidated by the thought of age discrimination, she didn't let it stop her. She strategized how to get into a new field, and devoted a lot of thought to the issue of positioning. "The challenge for me is to find the right fit, and get potential employers to see what I can do, to see my potential. I don't see age as a factor—I may be in denial, but I tend not to look at it in that way, although that does creep into my fears as I go through the process." Barbara found the Five O'Clock Club assessment exercises especially helpful in defining her goals and positioning herself to get into training and development.

Even before finding The Five O'Clock Club, Barbara knew that getting experience that she lacked would help her to move ahead. While in a counseling role at a university, she volunteered for staff development and faculty training projects. "These efforts were outside the purview of my job, but gave me experience towards my long-range goal."

Barbara feels that it also helps to position herself as a person with energy; age discrimination, after all, may be largely a fear about people over 50 keeping up. When applying for a job that would require her to learn educational software and work with a different population, "I told the president of the company that I had the energy and ambition of a 27-year old." She positioned her herself so well in fact—and with such enthusiasm—that she was offered $12,000 more than the job was advertised for. "The Five O'Clock Club methodology helped me negotiate the job first and then the salary."

Barbara says that she can't recall a time when she actually felt that age discrimination has held her back, but she notes that it can be hard to read. Is it there or not? She recalls one interview in which she might have been at a disadvantage simply because of the youth of the interviewer, who was a recent MBA grad. "He was a delightful young man, but I don't think he knew what he was doing. He asked me lots of questions, but I don't know that he heard the answers."

Barbara is not necessarily focused on retirement. "I love what I do. I want to continue doing it. I'm the breadwinner in my family. I'd like to work without the pressure of having to do it. In 10 or 15 years, I'd like to feel like I'm making a contribution to the world by using my gifts and talents, and I'm looking forward to enjoying my children and grandchildren."

Story excerpted from, *Report From The Front Lines* by the Five O'Clock Club's David Madison, (D. Madison, Delmar Thompson, Clifton Park, NY, 2006.)

I have enjoyed greatly the second blooming . . . suddenly you find—at the age of 50, say—that a whole new life has opened before you.
—Agatha Christie, English mystery author (1890–1976)

Focus on the Unique Skills You Have to Offer

Believe in yourself! Have faith in your abilities! Without a humble but reasonable confidence in your own powers you cannot be successful or happy.
—Norman Vincent Peale, American
Christian preacher, author (1898–1993)

The Towers Perrin, study for AARP, (see Chapter Twelve,) along with other major studies, identified favorable attributes older workers bring to the work environment. If you start to think negatively and begin to feel discouraged about your age, focus on the following list of attributes to remind you how capable you and your boomer cohorts are. Be sure to use these attributes when describing yourself to others.

Favorable Attributes of Older Workers

- Experienced
- Dedicated
- Possess a sense of strategic focus
- Loyal
- Attend to task and stay motivated
- Exceed expectations
- Dependable and stable
- Exhibit high levels of productivity
- Use common sense, insight and wisdom to develop innovative solutions

- Long standing knowledge of the industry
- Able to process complex information
- A strong sense of motivation and perseverance to succeed at the job
- High levels of engagement
- Communicate with older customer base
- Results-driven

The universe is change; our life is what our thoughts make it.
—Marcus Aurelius Antoninus, Roman emperor (121 AD–180 AD)

Joan Changed Her Attitude and Got the Job

When Joan, 64, was downsized, she felt no one would hire her because of her age. She didn't realize that she was buying into the stereotype of aging by undervaluing both her skills and the knowledge and experience she had gained in her many years of employment. We worked together to reestablish her self-esteem and ego-strength by discussing her skills and achievements from her Seven Stories Exercise. (See Chapter Nine to review the importance of meeting your needs.) She created a list of her talents, skills and accomplishments. She then crafted her positioning statement: "I have 19 years' experience dealing with client requests, as well as researching and cataloging legal documents. I am a dedicated, loyal employee known for exceeding expectations in developing new client markets and completing assigned tasks ahead of schedule. My experience has taught me the importance of: being open to change, being able to work under pressure, and being able to effectively and quickly deal with client problems and concerns."

She wrote her statement on an index card and carried it with her, practicing it several times a day. Joan was able to clearly articulate her skills and experience and gave very little thought to her age during her interviews. She felt confident about her abilities and optimistic about her opportunities for employment. Within six months after she left her job, she was hired by a legal support company to work three days a week as a customer service researcher, contacting clients and researching reports and data.

Joan was hired because she realized she had the skills and experience that employers are seeking. She did her research, knew the needs of the company and was able to sell her skills to the hiring manager.

During Your Job Search Follow These Five Steps:

1. Research and network.
2. Lead with a positive attitude.
3. Develop and practice a positioning statement based on the needs of the organization you are targeting.
4. Stay optimistic; don't let rejection get the best of you.
5. Maintain a sense of humor.

People are always asking me when I'm going to retire. Why should I? I've got it two ways—I'm still making movies, and I'm a senior citizen, so I can see myself at half price.

—George Burns, comedian, (1896–1996)

Write Your Positioning Statement

Keep in mind the most important points you want the hiring person to know about you, review your results from the Seven Stories Exercise (Chapter Ten and Appendix III) and refer to the words in the list above as your guide. For example:

- "I am an *experienced, results driven*, dedicated worker."
- "My skill and ability to develop new business will far *exceed your expectations*."
- "My *long standing knowledge of the industry* will benefit your company."

Confidence is contagious. So is lack of confidence.
—Vince Lombardi, football coach (1913–1970)

If you're having trouble, this may be a good time to seek help from a career coach. You may even be able to deduct on your tax return money spent on career development.

Age and Experience Will Work in Your Favor

"When Shirley, 55 was downsized she followed the Five O'Clock methodology to obtain her new position. When she met with the vice president of the company after she was hired he told her, "I was able to get the organization to meet your salary needs because of your age and experience.'" (D. Madison, *Report from the Front Lines,* Delmar Thompson, Clifton Park, NY, 2006.)

The message? Don't underestimate your value. Many employers will appreciate the experience and maturity that you bring to their company.

Don't Draw Conclusions Until You Have Gathered All the Facts

The following is excerpted from the article, "Is it Age Discrimination? Or Simply Discouragement?" by Kate Wendleton featured in *The Five O'Clock News*, March 2004.

We have a maxim at the Club: If the reason for your difficult search could be anything beyond discrimination (age, gender, race, and so on), what could it be? Identify that, and fix it.

Yes, discrimination exists, but a job hunter may be too quick to blame discrimination. Let's tackle the age issue . . . Generally speaking, those who are older also earn more. Older workers have to determine whether their salaries are keeping them out of work. Salary discrimination is not the same as age discrimination. If salary seems to be getting in the way of finding employment, job hunters can change the salaries they demand. . . .

People over 55 may feel they've paid their dues, have a terrific record of accomplishments, and should not have to put in as much job-search effort as a younger person. But this attitude is unrealistic and can keep an older worker out of the workforce—while he or she is chalking it up to discrimination. The job market has been unusually challenging for everyone recently, not just for those over 55.

Thus for many older people, the problem is perceived discrimination. It's the hopelessness of not seeing a positive response and giving up too quickly. The job market has been unusually challenging for everyone recently, not just for those over 55. Job hunters should also consider whether their field, industry, or geographic area has been hit particularly hard. If so, that's not discrimination either. . . . If age weren't the issue, what Thus for many older people, the problem is perceived discrimination. It's the hopelessness of not seeing a positive response and giving up too quickly. The job market has been unusually challenging for everyone recently, not just for those over 55. Job would it be? If you were 40 instead of over 50, what would you do? Do those things. Forget about your age problem, and try to solve the others, including your own discouragement. You could have 15 more years of work, or maybe not. This is a problem to be solved, and I know you can do it—as long as YOU don't think that your age is the primary issue here."

This article points out the need to be cautious about drawing conclusions based on either too little information or on your preconceived notions about aging. A story I heard a number of years ago about a woman, whom I'll call Peggy, clearly represents what can happen when a person makes inferences based on this type of thinking.

Peggy was returning home to the city after visiting a friend who moved to the country. She was unfamiliar with the roads and was driving fast so she could arrive home before dark. Out of the corner of her eye she saw a farmer standing at the side of the road. Just as she was about to turn around a sharp curve, the farmer yelled out "PIG." Upset, thinking he was being rude because she was unknown to him and was driving really fast, she glared back at him, yelled a rather unkind response, sped around the curve, and—hit a pig.

The Message in This Story?

Peggy was so involved with her own agenda and preconceived notions that she immediately drew a faulty conclusion and missed the more important message. How many times do you or someone you know, who is over 50, approach the job-search process with false assumptions? Keep this story in mind the next time you blame age discrimination for not getting an interview or not being hired for a job for which you felt qualified. Are you drawing conclusions? Are you making assumptions before you gather the facts? Could it be something other than your age that prevented you from getting that call-back or job offer? (See Chapter Seven to review how to dispute a disabling belief and rethink a negative assumption.)

Try Consulting or Working *Pro Bono*

If you are starting out in a new career or want to try a new job function, consider working as a consultant or volunteering your time and working *pro bono* until you get some experience. This strategy works no matter what your previous title or job responsibility may have been. I was honored to hear Howard Putnam speak at the National Speakers Association Convention in Orlando, Florida, in 2006, where he talked about how to grow a new business. Howard, was the former president and CEO of Southwest Airlines, and is credited with making that company a success. After leaving Southwest, he became CEO of Braniff International and was the first CEO to successfully restructure a major airline into, through, and out of bankruptcy. He also is the author *The Winds of Turbulence*, a book about leadership and ethics.

Now in his late 60s, Howard built a successful speaking business after his retirement from the airline industry. He told the audience that he knew he was in trouble when, in the early stages of his speaking career, a prospective client asked whether he believed in The First Amendment, which guarantees free speech. Howard said yes, of course, only to realize he was now committed to speaking for free! But, he stated, he actually did speak for free many times in the beginning of his new career, as a way of building his credentials and establishing his reputation.

His story demonstrates that no matter how successful you have been in the past, when building a new career you have to begin by paying your dues and maybe even working for little or no money. Howard Putnam's other message for success was to let go of old habits and develop a new personal vision. He offered the following advice for beginning a new endeavor, "Feel it, nurture it, and make it happen." What wonderful advice from a man who knows not to let adversity stop him from succeeding.

Don't let your age undermine your enthusiasm toward achieving your goals.

I hope that you will gain a more optimistic outlook about aging as you follow the suggestions in this chapter. Position yourself as a winner and proceed forward.

Energy and persistence conquer all things.
—Benjamin Franklin, founding father of the United States (1706–1790)

15
• • • •

Volunteer Vacations and Leisure Travel

All God's children need traveling shoes.
                    —Maya Angelou, American poet (1928–)

A man practices the art of adventure when he breaks the chain of routine and renews his life through reading new books, traveling to new places, making new friends, taking up new hobbies and adopting new viewpoints.
                    —Wilfred Peterson, author, *Adventures in the Art of Living*

Have you ever dreamed of traveling to exotic locals? Would you like to visit another country and stay longer than a two-week vacation? Do you think it would be fun and stimulating to engage in meaningful work in a foreign country? Now that you have retired, this can all be possible, with a little research and planning.

Retirees I spoke with who didn't intend to work full-time were instead planning to pursue leisure activities beyond sitting by the pool playing shuffleboard or bridge. They were looking forward to hiking trips, scuba diving and snorkeling, wildlife safaris, bicycle tours, living and working in a foreign county, studying language abroad, caring for animals in their natural habitat, teaching children in remote regions, and more. These retirees see themselves as healthy, adventure seekers who don't feel their chronological age.

Many retirees not only want to enjoy leisure and relaxing activities, they also want those activities to be meaningful and have a personal purpose. For this reason, volunteer vacations are becoming extremely popular.

At the end of this chapter I have listed resources for volunteer vacations to give you an idea of the variety and depth of the kinds of programs that are available. I have also listed resources for active leisure travel experiences that do not involve volunteer work.

Alison Gardner, senior travel editor of www.transitionsabroad.com, recommends that before you embark on your travels you should: "Realistically define your travel goals and limitations, ask lots of questions, and carefully review the feedback before making travel decisions." In addition, before you put your money down, commit to anything, or sign a contract, be sure your research is accurate and up-to-date. Use the Internet and search the travel blogs for recommendations and reviews. Speak to travelers who've volunteered or taken the same trip or tour that you are planning.

Experience, travel—these are as education in themselves.
> —Euripides, Greek playwright (480 BC–406 BC)

Senior Travel Discounts Abound

Because of the growing number of travelers over 50, senior travel discounts and the range of travel opportunities for the mature traveler are increasing. Senior discounts can be found on air, rail, train, bus, hotel and tour packages. AARP, for example, offers many discounts through its travel department. Major car rental companies offer 5 to 10% senior discounts. Greyhound Bus Line offers 10% off full-fare tickets to persons over 55. If you're 62 or older and a United States citizen or permanent resident, you can apply for the *Golden Age Passport* booklet that entitles you to free admission to all national parks, monuments, forest, and recreational areas.

Volunteer Vacations

Largely due to travelers between 50 to 80 years old, ecological, educational, cultural, and volunteer vacations are flourishing globally.
> —Alison Gardner

Note: Several of the listings below were adapted from the reviews found on www. transitionsabroad.com.

Amizade, Ltd.

PO Box 110107, Pittsburgh, PA 15232

888-973-4443 or 412-441-6655, fax 757-257-8358

www.amizade.org

Cross-cultural awareness programs, combining work and recreation in 13 communities in 11 countries worldwide. Fifty percent of volunteers are older adults.

Archaeological Institute of America, Boston University

656 Beacon St., Boston, MA 02215-2006

617-353-9361

www.archaeological.org

Online directory of worldwide fieldwork opportunities.

Publishes *Archaeological Fieldwork Opportunities Bulletin*, annual print catalog of volunteer opportunities for amateur archaeologists.

Earthwatch Institute

3 Clocktower Place, Maynard, MA 01754-0075

800-776-0188 or 978-461-0081, fax 978-461-2332

www.earthwatch.org

Assist field researchers engaged in scientific and social science research in 48 countries, with an emphasis on sustainability. Forty percent of participants are older adults.

Global Citizen's Network

130 North Howell Street, St. Paul, MN 55104

800-644-9292 or 651-644-0960

www.globalcitizens.org

Work one to three weeks with local villagers on community projects.

Global Volunteers

375 E. Little Canada Rd., St. Paul, MN 55117-1628

800-487-1074 or 651-407-6100

www.globalvolunteers.org

Teach conversational English and other basic subjects to at risk youth. Assist with healthcare, build schools and community facilities. One to three week programs in 19 countries. Sixty five percent of volunteers are older adults.

Globe Aware

7232 Fisher Rd, Dallas, TX 75214-1917
877-588-4562 or 214-823-0083, fax 214-823-0084
www.globeaware.org
Offers one to two week adventures focusing on cultural awareness and sustainability in Peru, Costa Rica, several Southeast Asia countries, Nepal, and Brazil. Twenty-five percent of volunteers are ages 50 to 80.

Habitat for Humanity (HQ. and International Programs)

121 Habitat St., Americus, GA 31709-3498
800-HABITAT or 912-924-6935, fax 912-924-6541
www.habitat.org
Assist in building homes in areas where a need exists. No building experience necessary. Programs located in over 70 countries.

LANDSCOPE Expeditions

UWA Extension, Univ. of Western Australia
35 Stirling Hwy, Crawley, WA 6009 Australia
08-6488-2433, fax 08-6488 1066
www.naturebase.net/landscope/index.html
Volunteer opportunities to work in natural surroundings. Download a free copy of tour schedule. Seventy-five percent of participants are older adults.

LiFeline Centre

P.O. Box 86, San Ignacio, Cayo, Belize, Central America
www.li-feline.com
Support the rescue, rehabilitation and conservation of Central America's endangered wild cats (jaguars, pumas, ocelots, margays, and jaguarondis) on 60-acre conservation facility in the Belize rainforest.

National Trust Working Holidays

P.O. Box 84, Cirencester, Gloucestershire GL7 1ZP, U.K.
011-0870 429 2429
www.nationaltrust.org.uk/main/w-trust/w-volunteering/w-workingholidays
Assist in caring for vulnerable wildlife species in England, Wales and Northern Ireland. Download catalog online. Older adult projects: Oak, Oak Plus, and Archaeological Holidays.

Oceanic Society Expeditions

Research Expeditions, Fort Mason Center, Building E, San Francisco, CA 94123

800-326-7491 or 415-441-1106

www.Oceanic-society.org

Opportunities to volunteer as research assistants working with academics and field researchers to log, record, and collect data, including bird banding and measuring nesting sea turtles. Sixty percent of clients are older adults.

Orangutan Foundation International (OFI)

4201 Wilshire Blvd., Suite 407, Los Angeles, CA 90010

800-ORANGUTAN or 323-938-6046

www.orangutan.org

Volunteer program assisting in the preservation of orangutans in their rainforest habitat. Fifty to sixty percent of volunteers are older adults.

The Land Conservancy (TLC) of British Columbia

2709 Shoreline Dr., Victoria, BC V9B 1M5 Canada

250-479-8053, fax 250-744-2251

www.conservancy.bc.ca

Offers two-day to one-week conservation trips dedicated to protecting ecologically significant environments and properties with historical, cultural, scenic, or recreational value in Canada's westernmost province.

Online Resources

Avalon Travel Publishing: The Adapter Kit Series

www.adapterkit.com

Information on living or traveling for an extended period in a foreign country.
Guides to Ireland, Mexico, France, and Belize already published. Costa Rica and Italy soon to be added.

Living Abroad In Series

www.travelmatters.com/livingabroadin.html.

Guides to Italy, Japan, Spain, and Costa Rica are already on the shelf, with Ireland, Mexico, France, Belize and more on the way.

Smarter Living's Senior Travel
www.smarterliving.com/senior
Lists discounted transportation, travel tips, and articles focusing on alternative travel. Free Senior Travel E-Newsletter lists late-booking travel discounts.

Travel with a Challenge
www.travelwithachallenge.com
Web magazine updated monthly, geared to the mature/senior traveler. Covers alternative travel themes: ecological, educational, cultural/historical, and volunteer vacations worldwide.

Marco Polo Magazine
695 Central Ave., Ste. 200A, Saint Petersburg, FL 33701
800-523-7274 or 727-894-3343, fax 727-894-3230
www.marcopolomagazine.com
Quarterly dedicated to adventure travelers over 50.

The Mexico File
www.mexicofile.com
5580 La Jolla Blvd., Suite 306, La Jolla, CA 92037
800-563-0345, Tel. /fax 858-456-4419
www.mexicofile.com
Subscription print newsletter published ten times a year and an updated web site geared to the independent traveler. Includes retirement issues and suggested destinations. Over 50 percent of subscribers are senior travelers.

Travel Books

Volunteer Vacations, Short-Term Adventures That Will Benefit You and Others
Bill McMillon, Chicago Review Press, 8th Ed.

The Practical Nomad: Guide to the Online Travel Marketplace
Edward Hasbrouck, How to use the Internet as a travel resource.

Fantastic Discounts & Deals for Anyone Over 50
Janet Groene, Cold Spring Press and distributed by Simon & Schuster.

The Grown-Up's Guide to Retiring Abroad

Rosanne Knorr, Ten Speed Press.
Guide providing tips and info for retiring abroad.

New Golden Door to Retirement and Living in Costa Rica

Christopher Howard, Costa Rica Books.
Guide to living, retiring, and investing in Costa Rica.

No Problem! Worldwise Travel Tips for Mature Adventurers

Janice Kenyon, Orca Book Publishers.
Travel tips for independent senior adventurers.

Unbelievably Good Deals and Great Adventures That You Absolutely Can't Get Unless You're Over 50, 2007-2008

Joan Rattner Heilman, McGraw-Hill.
Tips for persons 50 plus on how to leverage their age for better deals in transportation, accommodations, tours and learning opportunities.

Solo Traveling

Connecting: Solo Travel News

689 Park Road, Unit 6, Gibsons, BC V0N 1V7, Canada
604-886-9099, fax 604-608-2139
www.cstn.org
Annual membership fee includes bimonthly newsletter, *Connecting: Solo Travel News*, three e-publications—*Single-Friendly Travel Directory, Go Solo Tips,* and *Going Solo Tales,* and online travel companion ads, advice, lodging, and hospitality exchanges. Nearly 50 percent of members are 50 plus.

O Solo Mio Singles Tours

160 Main Street, Los Altos, CA 94022
www.osolomio.com
Specializes in group travel for individuals without travel partners. Matches roommates by: age, gender, smoking preference, sleeping habits, snoring issues, and geographic similarities.

Leisure Travel and Other Interesting Ideas

Travel and change of place impart new vigor to the mind.

—Seneca, Roman dramatist (3 BC–65 AD)

The real voyage of discovery consists not in seeking new landscapes but in having new eyes.

—Marcel Proust, French novelist (1871–1922)

Active Travel Programs Designed Specifically for People Over 50

ElderTreks

North America 1-800-741-7956; Outside North America 1-416-588-5000

www.eldertreks.com

Off-the-beaten-path, small-group adventures by both land and sea in over 60 countries.

The Over the Hill Gang International

1820 West Colorado Springs, Co, 80904

719-389-0024

www.othgi.com

Trips to worldwide locations geared to physically active seniors. Group trips include skiing, hiking, horseback riding, biking, golfing and other outdoor activities.

50plus Expeditions

760 Lawrence Ave. W, Unit #18, Toronto, Ontario, Canada M6A 3E7

USA & Canada: 1-866-318-5050; Worldwide: 1-416-749-5150

www.50plusexpeditions.com

Small group adventures, expedition and adventure cruises, and independent adventures. Trips graded on demand level of physical activity, climate, elevation, etc.

Walking the World

P.O. BOX Fort Collins, CO 80522-1186

1-866-393-9255 1-970-498-0500

www.walkingtheworld.com

Offers walking vacations to unique destinations through out the world.

Senior Women's Travel Tours

435 E. 79th Street, #4, New York, NY 10021

212-988-1359

House Exchanges and Home Visits

House-swap agencies abound, some with printed catalogs, most with online listings. Online viewing is usually free. Pay only to list your home. The following provided by AARP Magazine's May/June 2002 issue. (Updated for this book as of June 2006.)

HomeLink

800-638-3841

www.homeline.org

Annual fee to list online; also lists your home in a printed directory.

HomeExchange.com

800-877-8723

www.homeexchange.com

Annual fee to list.

International Home Exchange Network

386-238-3633

www.ihen.com

Annual fee to list. Nonmembers may contact members for free.

Intervac US

800-756-4663

www.intervacus.com

Annual fee to list online. Also can list in printed directory.

US Servas, Inc.

11 John Street, Room 505, New York, NY 10038

252-252-252

www.usservas.org

Worldwide traveler's organization created after World War II to promote peace among people of different countries and nationalities. Provides opportunities for person-to-person contacts, both nationally and internationally including option of 1–2 night visit at home of host. No money is exchanged between host and traveler. Travelers pay annual membership fee, however, participation in the Host and Day Host Programs is free.

16
....

Education, Life-Long Learning and Other Pursuits

It's what you learn after you know it all that counts.
                    —Attributed to Harry S. Truman, US President (1884–1972)

Learning is a treasure that will follow its owner everywhere.
                    —Chinese Proverb

There is divine beauty in learning, just as there is human beauty in tolerance. To learn means to accept the postulate that life did not begin at my birth. Others have been here before me, and I walk in their footsteps. The books I have read were composed by generations of fathers and sons, mothers and daughters, teachers and disciples. I am the sum total of their experiences, their quests. And so are you.
                    —Elie Wiesel, writer, Nobel Peace Prize, 1986 (1928–)

Whether you are interested in life long learning, a second degree, an advanced degree, studying for fun, enriching the skills of a hobby or spiritual growth the choices are vast, the opportunities many. The following stories demonstrate how several individuals returned to school enabling them to change careers after they retired.

Veronica and Phillip (A Husband and Wife Story)

Veronica's Story

When Veronica, a kindergarten teacher for 30 years retired at 55, she joined every organization she could to keep herself busy; she became a trustee in her temple and an officer in the garden club. She enjoyed being involved and connected, but felt she wasn't being fulfilled. She wanted more meaning in her life, and explained to me, "My dream in high school was to become a nurse, but life got in the way and it never came to fruition. My parents wanted me to become a teacher and so I got my Masters in Science and Art Education and began my long teaching career." At 63, Veronica is now pursuing her childhood dream as a second year nursing student. "My life is about studying and books. I'm the oldest student in the class, which began with 84 students and is now down to 38. By the time we finish, we will probably be down to 35 students." Veronica is determined to be one of them, especially since it wasn't easy to be admitted; she had to first obtain her transcripts from the "vault" of a bureaucratic complex and then had to pass rigorous entrance exams.

Now that she's enrolled, she finds nursing school very competitive and difficult. But Veronica is following her passion and is highly motivated. "I find that my brain still works and that's what's keeping me going. I love the challenge—of going back to school and doing what I always wanted to do. I have even been elected vice-president of the nursing club. She adds, "I believe that you have to have a vision. When things get difficult, I see myself walking across the stage to get my pin at graduation. If you see yourself doing something, then you can do it. When I believe in something, it usually happens."

Philip's Story

Veronica's husband, Philip, had owned an automotive repair business for 30 years. When he turned 50, his business started to decline and he knew he had to make a career decision. He decided to retire from welding but not from working. He needed to stay active and involved.

"My choice was to find another business or go back to school. I researched and found the medical field was wide open. Veronica was talking about becoming a nurse. I was always fascinated by medicine and the human body and decided that nursing, considering time and age constraints, was a more realistic option for me. I took the entrance exam and got a very high grade. We applied to nursing school and were both accepted. We waited until we passed a couple of tests to tell anyone. Now we are both in Phi Theta Kappa. Everyone was amazed; a lot of people would like a second career but believe they can't do it. When Veronica and I first started, the other students looked at us as if we were crazy. Now the young "kids" love us. And I love learning. It makes me feel young. I don't feel there is a 'retirement' in my future."

Marsha's Story

Marsha, 63, retired at 52 after 30 years as a Rehabilitation Counselor. While she was still working she began planning for her retirement by assessing her skills and interests and gathering information on possible options. She knew she wanted to continue working, and felt strongly that her next job had to meet all her needs and interests. She wanted a job that had growth potential and where she could make her own hours. She stated, "I wanted work that matures with you, that you only get better at and would always be challenging and new. I also knew I wanted to work in an allied field, one I already had experience in."

After extensive research she decided to become a therapist and enrolled in an analytic training institute while she was still employed. Although she was slated to retire at 55, she left three years ahead of schedule to pursue her plan. She said. "Going back to school was fresh and new. It made me feel very young and excited about learning. I loved being challenged, and getting positive feedback on how well I was doing. I fed on it." At 53, Marsha finished her program and became a licensed psychoanalytic psychotherapist. "I haven't looked back since, she stated, "The work keeps getting deeper and better as I continue to add more skills and grow. I feel that some of the most important work of my life has been accomplished in these last years." Marsha is currently on the executive board of the Training Treatment division of the Institute of Contemporary Psycho-Therapy and a Certified EMDR and Trauma Therapist. She plans to continue in her second career for a very long time, but also knows the importance of keeping a strong life-work balance. She achieves her balance by downhill skiing, hiking, and taking Adventure Travel vacations.

Jeannie's Story

Jeannie, worked as a nurse for 25 years, made the decision to enroll in law school when she was 45. Today at 55 she has combined her nursing background with her law degree and specializes in medical malpractice cases. "I was faced with a lot of negativity when I began. Friends and relatives asked me 'Why are you doing this?' 'Aren't you tired of school?' 'You have a good job and a good career. Why aren't you content to stay where you are?'

I figured I was 45 and in four years no matter what I did I would still be 49, with a law degree or not, so why not go for it?" She went on, "I plan to live into my triple digits. Maybe I'll retire at 100. At first, I was seen as a nurse going to law school; now I'm an attorney with a nursing background. I believe it is a good thing to get a new career every 25 years and to use the old career as a foundation."

Educational Programs

Get over the idea that only children should spend their time in study. Be a student so long as you still have something to learn, and this will mean all your life.
—Henry L. Doherty, American businessman (1870–1939)

The variety and scope of educational opportunities keeps growing. The following list offers a sampling of some available resources. Use these resources as a starting point but always continue to do your own research as well.

Note: These resources are listed for your information. They are in no way endorsed or recommended by the author or publisher.

Elderhostel
Boston, MA
www.elderhostel.org
1-800-454-5768, 1-877-426-8056
Offers programs for persons 55 and over in the U.S., Canada, and internationally in: history, culture, nature, music, outdoor activities, individual skills, crafts, and study.

Oceanic Society
Research Expeditions
Fort Mason Center, Building E, San Francisco, CA
www.Oceanic-society.org
800-326-7491, 415-441-1106
Programs in environmental conservation research protecting marine wildlife and environment. (Also see Volunteer Vacations in Chapter Fifteen.)

Education for Adults

www.educationforadults.com

SeniorNet

www.Seniornet.org

Community based Learning Centers offer low-cost computer classes for adults 50 and older. Curriculum includes introduction to computers, word processing, spreadsheets, e-mail and using the Internet. Offers onsite workshops and technology related conferences, lab time at individual learning center locations, chat room discussion groups and a free book exchange program.

GradSchools

www.gradschools.com

Online directory that lists graduate school programs categorized by curriculum and subdivided by geography.

Senior Audit Programs

Many colleges offer senior audit programs both online or on campus. Below are some examples of what is available. Contact colleges in your local community to find out about programs near you.

My Turn

Kingsborough Community College, City University of New York, Brooklyn, NY

www.kbcc.cuny.edu (click on My Turn)

718-368-5079

Offers NY State residents 60 and over opportunities to take degree or non-degree classes with regular college students on a space available basis. No tuition fee, $80 registration fee per semester.

University of Denver Senior Audit Program

Denver, Colorado

www.du.edu/specpro/specproweb/senioraudit.

303-871-2360

Allows adults 60 or older to audit select undergraduate courses.

Rutgers University Senior Audit

New Brunswick, New Jersey

ur.rutgers.edu/community/senior

732-932-7823 ext 682

Allows retired New Jersey residents 62 or older, at no costs or fees, to audit courses on a space-available, non-credit basis.

University of Central Florida Senior Citizen Registration

Orlando, Florida registrar.ucf.edu/SeniorCitReg

407-823-3531

Offers free courses to adults 60 or older.

George Washington University

Washington, DC

www.gwu.edu/~alumni/educ/courseaudit

202-994-6435

Offers GW alumni and senior citizens residing in the community, for a nominal registration fee, a wide array of the University's courses on a non-credit basis.

Ohio University Lifelong Learning

Athens, Ohio

www.ohio.edu/lifelong

740-593-1776, 877-685-3276

Offers a wide range of affordable online electronic classes in skill enhancing and career development certificate programs.

Columbia University, Lifelong Learners Program

New York, NY

www.ce.columbia.edu/auditing/lifelonglearners.cfm

212-854-9699.

Offers persons 65 or older opportunities to audit courses at a discount rate. No examinations, papers or grades are assigned

Native American Vision Quest Education Programs

Rites of Passage

P.O. Box 2061, Santa Rosa, CA 95404

(707) 537-1927

Education programs offering mind/body/spirit approach to health, healing and personal growth.

Animas Valley Institute

Choosing Conscious Elderhood programs
www.animas.org
970-247-7943
Offers workshops, retreats and vision quests to identify and validate the wisdom and power of being an elder.

Learning Keeps the Mind Active, Alert and Growing

> *Question everything. Learn something. Answer nothing.*
> —Euripides, Greek playwright (480 BC–406 BC)

Education keeps you up-to-date and can increase your earning potential. If your dream involves advancing in your field or beginning a new career then education or additional training is a must. Being a life-long learner can also boost your confidence and make you feel more positive about yourself. Finally, attending classes is a great way to develop intergenerational friendships, stay connected to a community of interesting people, develop a support group, and expand your horizons and your network.

> *The purpose of learning is growth, and our minds, unlike our bodies, can continue growing as we continue to live.*
> —Mortimer Adler, American philosopher (1902–2001)

Mortimer Adler believed that, no matter how old, a person should never stop learning and growing. He was a wonderful example of his philosophy. He wrote more than twenty books *after* his 70th birthday and wrote his 60th book, *The New Technology: Servant or Master* at age 95.

17
· · · ·

Keeping the Balance:
Taking Care of
Yourself

My philosophy is that only you are responsible for your life.
But doing the best at this moment puts you in the best place for the next moment.
— Oprah Winfrey, talk show host (1954–)

Ease into Retirement by Being Proactive

Pat worked as an editor at a major publishing house for 20 years. At 64, a year before she planned to retire, she decided to become involved in meaningful activities she enjoyed and that could be continued into retirement. She joined an ongoing yoga class and enrolled in a three-year certificate program to study food and healing at a well-known cooking school. On weekends, Pat volunteered at an adult learning center, which offered her the opportunity to take reduced tuition classes and workshops.

Pat explained, "I knew I had to keep busy when I retired, so I decided why wait? I wanted to get involved in new things that interested me. I felt if I started before I retired, when I actually left, I would be busy and wouldn't miss my colleagues at work or my job so much." Pat prepared for her retirement by becoming proactive and developing interests and new friendships she could continue to grow in the years ahead.

Are you approaching retirement but are so absorbed at work that you're not able to take time out from your busy schedule to think about retirement? Don't fool yourself by thinking you will plan after you leave. Be proactive; start thinking and planning while still on the job. Along with planning for the future I have observed six additional behaviors successful retirees incorporated into their daily lives. These six behaviors may be familiar to you, but do you actually consider them on a daily basis?

Six Behaviors for Nurturing and Maintaining a Sense of Well-Being

1. Handle stress successfully.
2. Eat wisely.
3. Exercise your body.
4. Put laughter in your life.
5. Challenge your mind with new ideas and activities.
6. Be positive about yourself and your future.

Let's examine each one a little more closely.

1. Handle Stress Successfully

How you adapt to stress is based on your unique personality, needs, attitude and perceptions. However, Deepak Chopra believes that three universal factors common to all people are responsible for creating stress. He explains, "All persons have different levels of stress but what seems to produce the greatest perceived threats in a given situation are: lack of predictability, lack of control, and lack of outlets for frustration." (D. Chopra, *Ageless Body, Timeless Mind*, Harmony Books, *New York, NY, 1993.*)

Are you affected by any of these?

- Do you feel unable to predict what lies ahead for you?
- Do you feel you may have lost control of events within your life?
- Do you feel you don't have a place or a person to go to where you can express your frustrations or upsets?

Some stress is not necessarily a bad thing, it heightens your awareness in dangerous situations and also can motivate you to take action and complete a task. Some people even believe that without it life would be dull and unexciting. Too much stress, however, can be harmful to you both physically and mentally. Prolonged or extreme stress can attack your body, creating situations of distress and illness. The trick is to make stress work for you and not against you.

We all experience stress, but how well do you handle it? Below are suggestions to help you handle unnecessary stress. How many of these strategies are in your life now? Which do you need to add to your life? As you read these suggestions, perhaps you will better understand your major stressors and will be able to use these tips as a guide to developing your own personal strategies to help deal with stress.

Suggestions for Handling Stress

- Plan a regular daily routine. Even if you don't stick to it on occasion, it helps to have planned activities to look forward to.
- Find a close friend who is supportive and listens well.
- Be proactive. Recognize you are in control and have choices.
- Learn the definition of assertiveness and use it as a guide. Ask for what you need. Don't be afraid to ask. Question your doctor, Social Security administrators, your significant other, your children, your friends, and others to get the information you need to make informed decisions about your life.
- Do something you always wanted to do.
- Practice preventive maintenance (for you, your car and your house).
- Keep a pad with you at all times and write down things so you don't have to rely on memory.
- Unclutter your surroundings and simplify your life; give away unnecessary items and replace broken ones.
- Make copies of important papers and keep a written note of where you placed the copies and the originals.
- Ask for help when you need it.
- Reward yourself after you have completed a difficult task.
- Be flexible, but always have a contingency plan so that you don't get caught off guard.
- Use positive affirmations to change a negative habit or thought.
- Create, in your home, a comfortable space of your own, to relax.
- Consistently practice relaxation strategies such as deep breathing and meditation.
- Take action. Stop procrastinating and worrying, just do it.
- Get enough sleep—at least six to seven hours every night.

- Laugh frequently and deeply.
- Allow enough time to do things you enjoy; include leisure time activities and fun hobbies.
- Relax your standards. It's all right not to be the best; perfectionism can be exhausting.
- Be optimistic about your life and the future.

2. Eat Wisely

Let food be thy medicine.

—Hippocrates, Greek physician (460 BC–377 BC)

Take time to examine your health habits. Being overweight and eating the wrong foods is harmful to your body.

How aware are you of how you treat your body? How much and what kind of food do you put into it? Eating too many calories and too much fat could lead to obesity as well as increasing your risk of heart disease. An AARP study, "Beyond 50: A Report to the Nation on Health Security", *AARP Magazine*, May/June 2002, reports that obesity nearly doubled among people 50 + in the last two decades. (The coordinator of this study attributes this new problem not only to overeating, but also to sedentary lifestyles caused by too much time spent watching television and working on the computer.)

AARP is sending to its members a strong message. Could they be talking about you? Take stock of your eating habits. Eat small meals made from simple and nutritious foods. Eat plenty of fruits and vegetables. Start the day with a hardy breakfast. To give your food a chance to digest, chew slowly and relax while eating. The more wisely you eat, the better you will feel; the better you feel, the more you will enjoy your retirement.

For further reading, here are two interesting books on the effects of food on your body: *Food and Healing* by Annemarie Colbin, Ballantine Books, New York, NY, 1986 and *Foods That Heal* by Dr. Bernard Jensen, Avery Publishing Group, New York, NY, 1988.

One-quarter of what you eat keeps you alive. The other three-quarters keep your doctor alive.

—Hieroglyph found in an ancient tomb

3. Exercise Your Body

Physical activity is at the crux of successful aging.
—Dr. John Rowe, president Mount Sinai School of Medicine, Chair,
MacArthur Foundation Research Network on Successful Aging.

With your talents and industry, with science, and that stedfast honesty which eternally pursues right, regardless of consequences, you may promise yourself every thing—but AS, health, without which there is no happiness. An attention to health then should take place of every other object. The time necessary to secure this by active exercises, should be devoted to it in preference to every other pursuit.
—Letter to Thomas Mann Randolph, Jr., July 6, 1787.
—*The Papers of Thomas Jefferson*, ed. Julian P. Boyd, vol. 11, 1955.

In their book, *Successful Aging*, John Rowe and Robert Kahn conclude that exercise is the biggest factor in maintaining health and overall good functioning. They state, "Exercise improves and maintains muscular, skeletal, cardiovascular, and brain functions." (J.W. Rowe. MD and R. L. Kahn, PH.D, *Successful Aging*, Bantam Dell, 1999.)

People often blame age for physical problems that are actually caused by: inadequate exercise, too much smoking, excessive use of alcohol or overeating foods with sugars and fats. I hear people constantly complain about how their body is slowing down and their physical performance is becoming more limited since they reached 50. Some of the comments I have heard are:

- "I was more active when I was younger."
- "I just can't walk up the steps anymore. I feel tired now and prefer the elevator."
- "Ten years ago I would have walked the ten blocks to the library; now I wait for the bus."
- "I feel like I'm falling apart. I have new aches and pains everyday."
- "I wish I could still go dancing, play tennis, go to the gym. My energy is not the same as when I was younger."

Do any of these sound familiar to you?

Are these concerns really caused by aging or are they the result of a *perception* people carry around about aging?

Consistent exercise will dramatically increases your physical fitness; the more you move, the better you will feel. Resistance exercise such as weight lifting increases muscle size and strength, and plays a role in helping to limit osteoporosis and improve balance.

> *They have even taken people in their 90's and put them on a weight-training program and doubled their strength and endurance.*
> —Jack La Lanne, fitness guru still going strong at 92, interviewed at 91 by the editor of the online publication, *Share Guide, 2003.*

Daily exercise won't be exhausting or difficult if you choose activities you enjoy. You can take a brisk walk; ride a bike for half an hour or swim at your local pool. Experiment with a combination of Pilates, jazzercise, spinning, fencing, karate and yoga. You can even exercise from home with exercise videos. Before you decide to purchase one, go to your local library, take several videos home and try them out.

Think about hiring a personal trainer (some even make house calls.) Many personal trainers specialize in bodies over 50. Ask your friends, ask at the gym, do some research and be sure to interview trainers before you commit to working with them. Diane, 70, comments, "I have been working with a personal trainer for five years. I began when I was diagnosed with osteoporosis and didn't want to take medication. Now I'm more aware of my body, and my balance is much improved. I have more respect for what exercise can do. I have become stronger and know if I hadn't done this, I'd be in real trouble."

Don't Take the Mind-Body Connection Lightly

Experts agree about the connection between our bodies and minds. Dr. George Vaillant in his book *Adaptation to Life*, reports that mental health is the most important predictor of physical health (G. Vaillant, Little Brown, Boston, MA, 1977.) Dr. Joan Borysenko, reminds us how the "mind's relaxation response can boost your immune system, overcome chronic pain, and help to rid the body of many symptoms caused by stress." (J. Borysenko, *Minding The Body, Mending The Mind*, Bantam Books, New York, NY, 1987.)

My personal favorite form of exercise is yoga, which works your body as it calms your mind. Even if you have injuries and are unable to sustain vigorous exercise, yoga will strengthen you in a gentle way. Through postures and controlled proper breathing, yoga exercises your internal organs, stimulating the glands, improving digestion, metabolism, balance and focus.

Years ago, I met a yoga devotee, 89, who told an audience how he had been badly injured during WWII and was confined to a wheelchair. He discovered yoga and embarked upon a limited yoga practice. He worked on it conscientiously for many years. "And here I am today," he would tell his amazed audience while bending down and touching his toes without bending his knees.

Since yoga is about relaxing the body to prepare the mind for meditation, I believe it is best to begin your yoga practice at a yoga school and not at a gym. Have patience with yoga and you will gradually begin to see results and experience the effects it has on both body and mind. To locate yoga schools near you, go to www.yoga.com. Two schools to look into are: Sivananda Yoga Institute and Integral Yoga Institute, both have centers in cities nationally and internationally.

Tai Chi, a Chinese exercise that relaxes the muscles rather than tightening them, also provides an excellent opportunity to maintain physical well-being and build endurance and strength. By using slow, low-impact movements, you can increase both concentration and balance. Tai Chi is a wonderful way to assist your body toward recovery after an injury. Before practicing Tai Chi, research to find a teacher with whom you feel comfortable. To be effective, Tai Chi needs to be practiced regularly. Therefore, having a teacher you like is important.

You may also want to consider water aerobics or swimming, stretching exercises, joining a softball team or an organized sport with folks of the same age, a daily walking routine or even just playing with your grandchildren. The most important thing is to stay as active as you can.

Here are some interesting websites you can explore:

- www.50plus.org
- www.over50baseball.com
- www.nsga.com (National Senior Games Association)
- www.seniorgolfersamerica.com

4. Put Laughter in Your Life

Laughter is the sun that drives winter from the human face.

—Victor Hugo, French novelist, statesman,
human rights campaigner (1802–1885)

If people only knew the healing power of laughter and joy, many of our fine doctors would be out of business.
Joy is one of nature's greatest medicines.

—Catherine Ponder, American inspirational writer (1927–)

Most people don't laugh enough. Is that you? Do you feel that you are too busy to laugh? Do you wait to have fun until after you have completed what you are doing? Will you laugh when you have completed that task? Will you *ever* be done?

How often do you laugh during the day, even if you are not feeling especially joyful? Do you smile at yourself and at the world regularly? Don't take yourself too seriously—laughing at yourself is a wonderful release.

Doctor I have a ringing in my ears. "Don't answer!

—Henny Youngman, comedian, king of the one liner (1906–1998)

Take time out to look for the fun things around you. Even when you experience a stressful situation, remember that stress is not an event, but a *perception* of an event. It is your *choice* how you look at that event. Try to change your perception and view the event with humor. Instead of creating feelings of concern, add some laughter to the situation. Keep a laugh journal where you can list funny things that have happened to you or funny things that you have noticed. Do this on a daily basis and you will start to notice how much lighter and happier you'll feel.

Including joy in your life is a wonderful way to help short-circuit negative attitudes and a temporarily stressful situation. I always tell my clients that they should try to substitute laughter for the proverbial "apple a day" that "keeps the doctor away." Not only is laughter good for your health but it has even been proven to aid in healing.

To make mistakes is human; to stumble is commonplace; to be able to laugh at yourself is maturity.

—William Arthur Ward, American writer (1920–)

Robert Holden, founder of the Happiness Project in Oxford, England calls laughter "stationary aerobics." He states that ten minutes of laughter can have the following results:

- cause your pulse and blood pressure to drop
- release endorphins, natural painkillers
- exercise facial muscles to prevent sagging
- give your internal organs a good workout
- raise oxygen levels, benefiting your cardiovascular system, heightening both physical and mental energy while reducing tension
- reduce levels of cortisol, the stress hormone
- contract and relax muscles in the entire body, exercising them and causing them to grow stronger, and
- produce anti-inflammatory agents that can help relieve back pain or arthritis.

(Summarized from an article by Catherine Kalamis, "Laugh Your Way to Health", *Choice Magazine,* March 2001, and from *Relax-You May Only Have A Few Minutes Left*, Loretta LaRoche, Villard Press, New York, NY, 1998.)

My Grandmother is over eighty and still doesn't need glasses. Drinks right out of the bottle.
　　　　—Henny Youngman, comedian, king of the one liner (1906–1998)

The Norman Cousins' Story

Norman Cousins, editor of the *Saturday Review* for 40 years and a staunch optimist, was returning from Russia in 1964 when he was diagnosed with a crippling, irreversible, and life-threatening disease. He decided to "beat the odds" by using his will power and a combination of high doses of Vitamin C, medical advice and laughter. In his book, *Anatomy of an Illness,* he describes how watching funny movies, such as the Marx Brothers, was one of the remedies that helped cure him. After finding ten minutes of deep belly laughs kept him pain-free for two hours, he proclaimed that laughing could be a healing tool. He recovered, wrote several more books, and continued speaking out for world peace until his death in 1990; 26 years later than his doctors predicted he would live. (Norman Cousins, *Anatomy of an Illness as Perceived by the Patient: Reflections on Healing and Regeneration*, New York: WW Norton and Company, 1979.)

Laughter is a form of internal jogging. It moves your internal organs around. It enhances respiration. It is an igniter of great expectation.
 —Norman Cousins, journalist, author, world peace advocate (1915–1990)

The Doctor says, "You'll live to be 60!"
"I AM 60!"
"See, what did I tell you?"
 —Henny Youngman, comedian, king of the one liner (1906–1998)

Try to give yourself daily doses of humor. Look for humor wherever you are. While traveling on a rain-damaged road in a Caribbean country, my husband spotted a sign with an arrow that read, "Danger Depression Ahead." Shopping in a small grocery store in upstate New York, I saw a sign reading, "If you don't see what you want, we don't have it, so don't bother asking." Humor is everywhere if you only look for it.

I like nonsense; it wakes up the brain cells. Fantasy is a necessary ingredient in living. It's a way of looking at life through the wrong end of a telescope and that enables you to laugh at all of life's realities.
 —Theodore Seuss Geisel (Dr. Seuss), author (1904–1991)

Another great way to keep you upbeat and energized is to laugh with others. Victor Borge once said, "A smile is the shortest distance between two people." I believe that laughter is even a shorter distance because laughter is contagious. It can spread from one person to the next in a blink of an eye. Did you ever notice when you are in a group of people and one person starts to laugh that others join in even if they don't know what the laughing is about? In India, in Bombay and other cities, over 100 people gather every morning before work, to laugh together in a large park, for 30 minutes. These "laughing clubs" are so popular that you can now find them in cities in the United States.

The person who can bring the spirit of laughter into a room is indeed blessed.
 —Bennett Alfred Cerf, publisher (1898–1971)

5. Challenge Your Mind with New Activities and Ideas

Physiologist, Dr. Marian C. Diamond, a leader in brain research, explains that development and aging are a continuum and that our brain begins to age when we are born. "A brain forming in the embryo," she explains, "develops 50,000 nerve cells per second and loses at least 50% of these cells before birth. Most are concerned about losing nerve cells at the other end of the life cycle when, in reality, you lost more nerve cells before you entered the world." This sounds rather bleak, but actually Dr. Diamond has good news about our brain as we age. She and her colleagues explain, "The brain when responding to stimulation continues to produce new cells, even in the areas associated with memory. These new connections, called dendrites, grow like the branches of a tree between the nerve cells allowing the cells to communicate with each other." (Dr. M. C. Diamond, *Successful Aging of the Healthy Brain,* article originally presented at the joint Conference of the American Society on Aging and the National Council on the Aging, March 10, 2001, New Orleans, LA.) In other words, by continuing to learn and to challenge yourself, your brain will continue to grow and process information. In order to keep your brain functioning and alert you need to exercise it as regularly as you exercise your body.

Dr. Diamond believes five factors help the brain to function at its fullest:

1. A healthy diet: Include a good percentage of protein.
2. Exercise: Oxygenate all parts of the body, especially the brain.
3. Newness: Search for new things or new ways to do old, familiar things.
4. Challenge: Push yourself one step beyond what you think you can do. Learn complex skills; try word puzzles and other challenges such as sewing, knitting, painting, wood-working, home repair or learning a foreign language. Begin studying a musical instrument; take up piano or learn to play the guitar. (A good resource is *Making Music* magazine, www.makingmusicmag. com, which promotes the concept of recreational music-making as beneficial for all ages.)
5. Nurture yourself and others: Build strong support systems, maintain close ties with family members and friends and take care of yourself with love. Dr. Diamond believes that frequent emotional support from friends and family, along with consistent mental stimulation from relationships, contribute

to good physical well-being. She states, "Social connection is essential for successful aging with a strong link between social support and health. People with close relationships and strong connections to others are happier; they eat healthier, exercise more and manage stress better."

Live life in a way that maximizes contentment, creativity, and love. This is what I call healing.

—Joan Borysenko, contemporary, author

Maureen, 70, who worked for 21 years as the office manager of a well-known restaurant chain seems to be following Dr Diamond's advice. When her job was eliminated, she occupied herself by volunteering at her church's senior center, ran for office and was elected secretary of the church board. She also began knitting scarves for disabled veterans. Maureen also became involved with another church senior group and spent two days a week organizing outings and speakers for their recreation club meetings.

"I enjoy the excitement of working with active seniors. They are always so happy to see me. Not only do I feel energized but I look forward to the attention and love I get from them," she explained. "When I'm alone, I work on crossword puzzles every morning at breakfast. I love the challenge they offer and it keeps my mind alert. I try to be very active each day, walking at least half an hour whenever the weather is good. I do miss my job, but some days I'm so busy I totally forget all about it."

6. Be Positive About Yourself and Your Future

Become a possibilitarian.
No matter how dark things seem to be or actually are, raise your sights and see possibilities.
Always see them, for they are always there.
    —Norman Vincent Peale, Christian preacher, author (1898–1893)

In a study conducted at Yale University's Department of Epidemiology and Public Health, it was found that older people with positive self-perceptions of aging lived 7.5 years longer than those with negative self-perceptions of aging. ("Longevity Increased by Positive Self-Perceptions of Aging", Becca R. Levy, et al., *Journal of Personality and Social Psychology,* August, 2002, Vol. 83, No. 2, published by the American Psychology Association.) (See Chapter Two for more about this study.)

My husband has two aunts, 78 and 81, both with their share of major health problems. You would never know anything bothers them when you are in their company. They are always busy planning activities for the next day, week, month, or year ahead. I asked them how they stay so positive. Their response: "We enjoy life, we have our ups and downs, we stay very physically active, we believe in a higher power. Our family relationships are strong; we stay in touch with all of them even though they live all over the world and we help each other." What follows was drawn from our conversations.

Aunt Barbara and Aunt Margaret's Nine Rules of Positive Thinking

1. Keep a positive attitude, have faith and don't let things get you down.
2. Don't take life too seriously.
3. Don't panic when a situation occurs; take things with a grain of salt and just keep trying until you get it right.
4. Choice is the most important thing you have.
5. You need to find your own way to get out of your depression. Do something active that distracts you and gets you out of that mood—wash dishes, clean floors, etc.
6. Go out and take action; never be passive.
7. Follow your intuition and act without listening to everyone telling you what to do.
8. When facing a problem, keep your objective in mind; get everyone talking and keep moving forward to solve the problem.
9. Don't put on airs. Be yourself. Treat everyone the same way: the garbage man and the queen, until they show you differently.

Aunt Barbara and Aunt Margaret are my role models. They can be yours, too.

Think About Adding Some Form of Spirituality to Your Life

Dr. Harold Koenig, in his book, *Purpose and Power in Retirement,* argues that people who are involved in religious practices are less depressed and lead happier, richer lives. Additionally he states, "Spirituality will help a person to maintain meaning and purpose in life." (H. Koenig, *Purpose and Power in Retirement,* Templeton Foundation Press, Philadelphia, PA, 2002.) Specifically, you might try to:

- Schedule regular time for meditation or spiritual practice.

- Spend a good deal of time in nature. It's good for your soul and your heart to appreciate what nature has to offer—trees, rivers, mountains, waterfalls, flowers, sunsets and much more.
- Cultivate the seeds you started early in life. Cultivate your purpose.
- Give to others.
- Attend religious services.

How does this sound: a balanced life of social, financial, spiritual, emotional and physical well-being, including good health and freedom to make your own decisions? Successful aging encompasses all these factors. It's your choice. Exercise daily, eat healthy, get involved in new situations, meet new friends, laugh frequently, challenge your brain to learn new things and you will be on the road to creating for yourself the best years ahead—the best years of your life.

To laugh often and much; to win the respect of intelligent people and the affection of children; to earn the appreciation of honest critics and endure the betrayal of false friends; to appreciate beauty, to find the best in others; to leave the world a little better; whether by a healthy child, a garden patch or a redeemed social condition; to know even one life has breathed easier because you have lived.
This is the meaning of success.

—Ralph Waldo Emerson, American author,
poet, and philosopher (1803–1882)

18
....

Reflecting on Retirement

I look to the future because that's where I'm going to spend the rest of my life.
—George Burns, American comedian (1886–1996)

What does "retirement" really mean? Let's look at it again.

When talking about retirement, look at it as a change from one circumstance—your job or career, to another circumstance—the uncharted waters of your new life. It's time to reframe your thinking, to see retirement as a process, a series of events or stages that you are moving through. You are leaving full-time, paid employment where you spent many years of your life and you are now discovering who you are and what you want while moving into new stages and life events. The next time someone asks you, "What are you doing now?" Your new response can be: "I am retired from my previous employment as . . . (Fill in your previous job title and then move on.) I am moving into a new phase and I am actively involved in redirecting my life toward exploring new possibilities." If you already have a plan established, you may offer an even more focused answer.

Important Points to Remember:

- There are multiple models of retirement from which to choose.
- Create a plan with long-range and short-range goals.

- You are only as old as you think you are.
- Be flexible.
- Maintain a positive attitude.
- Challenge your mind frequently.
- Think positively and be optimistic about your future.
- Pay attention to your body and your health before you need to.
- Discover your purpose and your passion.
- Support and give to others.
- Realize the journey to achieve a good, self-fulfilled life is ongoing—with many twists and turns.
- Look for the humor in your daily life and laugh frequently.
- Review your notes and reread the chapters in this book as needed

Remember retirement is a process. This is your time to begin anew, to dream, to redirect, to refocus, and to live your life to its fullest, whatever that means for you. Be patient and enjoy the journey.

If you ask what is the single most important key to longevity, I would have to say it is avoiding worry, stress and tension. And if you didn't ask me, I'd still have to say it.

—George Burns, Comedian (1896–1996)

What Will Be Your Next Step?

Every intersection in the road of life is an opportunity to make a decision.
   —Duke Ellington, African/American jazz composer, musician (1899–1974)

The rest of your life is ahead of you. Take your time to experiment and explore: plan and take action. The choice is yours to live well and live fully and wisely.

I would rather be ashes than dust!

I would rather that my spark should burn out in a brilliant blaze than it should be stifled by dry-rot.

I would rather be a superb meteor, every atom of me in magnificent glow, than a sleepy and permanent plane.

The proper function of man is to live, not to exist.

—Jack London, American author (1876–1916)

Carpe Diem!

Rejoice while you are alive; enjoy the day:

live life to the fullest; make the most of what you have.

—Horace, Roman philosopher (65 BC–8 BC)

What Is the Five O'Clock Club?

· ·

America's Premier Career-Coaching Network

How to Join the Club

The Five O'Clock Club:
America's Premier Career-Coaching and Outplacement Service

*"One organization with a long record of success in helping people find jobs is
The Five O'Clock Club."*

—*Fortune*

- Job-Search Strategy Groups
- Private Coaching
- Books and Audio CDs
- Membership Information
- When Your Employer Pays

THERE *IS* A FIVE O'CLOCK CLUB NEAR YOU!
For more information on becoming a member, please fill out the Membership
Application Form in this book, sign up on the web at: www.fiveoclockclub.com,
or call: 1-800-575-3587 (or 212-286-4500 in New York)

The Five O'Clock Club Search Process

The Five O'Clock Club process, as outlined in *The Five O'Clock Club* books, is a
targeted, strategic approach to career development and job search. Five O'Clock Club

members become proficient at skills that prove invaluable during their *entire working lives* as well as their search for paid or non-paid work after they retire.

Getting Jobs . . . Faster

Five O'Clock Club members find *better jobs, faster.* The average retired professional, manager, or executive Five O'Clock Club member who regularly attends weekly sessions finds what he or she is looking for by the 10th session. Even the discouraged, long-term job searcher can find immediate help.

The keystone to The Five O'Clock Club process is teaching our members an understanding of the entire hiring process. A first interview is primarily a time for exchanging critical information. The real work starts *after* the interview. We teach our members *how to turn job interviews into offers* and to negotiate the best possible employment package.

Setting Targets

The Five O'Clock Club is action oriented. *We'll help you decide what you should do this very next week to move your search along.* By their third session, our members have set definite job targets by industry or company size, position, and geographic area, and are out in the field gathering information and making contacts that will lead to interviews with hiring managers.

Our approach evolves with the changing job market. We're able to synthesize information from hundreds of Five O'Clock Club members and come up with new approaches for our members. For example, we now discuss temporary placement for retirees, how to use voice mail and the Internet, and how to network when doors are slamming shut all over town.

The Five O'Clock Club Strategy Program

The Five O'Clock Club meeting is a carefully planned *job-search strategy program.* We provide members with the tools and tricks necessary to get a good job fast—even in a tight market. Networking and emotional support are also included in the meeting. Participate in 10 *consecutive* small-group strategy sessions to enable your group and career coach to get to know you and to develop momentum in your search.

Weekly Presentations via Audio CDs

Prior to each week's teleconference, listen to the assigned audio presentation covering part of The Five O'Clock Club methodology. These are scheduled on a rotating basis so you may join the Club at any time. (In selected cities, presentations are given in person rather than via audio CDs.)

Small-Group Strategy Sessions

During the first few minutes of the teleconference, your small group discusses the topic of the week and hears from people who have landed jobs. Then you have the chance to get feedback and advice on your own search strategy, listen to and learn from others, and build your network. All groups are led by trained career coaches with years of experience. The small group is generally no more than six to eight people, so everyone gets the chance to speak up.

Let us consider how we may spur one another on toward love and good deeds. Let us not give up meeting together, as some are in the habit of doing, but let us encourage one another.

—Hebrews 10:24–25

Private Coaching

You may meet with your small-group coach—or another coach—for private coaching by phone or in person. A coach helps you develop a career path, solve current job problems, prepare your résumé, or guide your search.

Many members develop long-term relation-ships with their coaches to get advice throughout their careers. If you are paying for the coaching yourself (as opposed to having your employer pay), please pay the coach directly (charges vary from $100 to $175 per hour). **Private coaching is *not* included in The Five O'Clock Club seminar or membership fee.** For coach matching, see our website or call **1-800-575-3587** (or **212-286-4500** in New York).

From the Club History, Written in the 1890s

At The Five O'Clock Club, [people] of all shades of political belief—as might be said of all trades and creeds—have met together. . . . The variety continues almost to a monotony. . . . [The Club's] good fellowship and geniality—not to say hospitality—has reached them all.

It has been remarked of clubs that they serve to level rank. If that were possible in this country, it would probably be true, if leveling rank means the appreciation of people of equal abilities as equals; but in The Five O'Clock Club it has been a most gratifying and noteworthy fact that no lines have ever been drawn save those which are essential to the honor and good name of any association. Strangers are invited by the club or by any members, [as gentlepeople], irrespective of aristocracy, plutocracy or occupation, and are so treated always. Nor does the thought of a [person's] social position ever enter into the meetings. People of wealth and people of moderate means sit side by side, finding in each other much to praise and admire and little to justify snarlishness or adverse criticism. People meet as people—not as the representatives of a set—and having so met, dwell not in worlds of envy or distrust, but in union and collegiality, forming kindly thoughts of each other in their heart of hearts.

In its methods, The Five O'Clock Club is plain, easy-going and unconventional. It has its "isms" and some peculiarities of procedure, but simplicity characterizes them all. The sense of propriety, rather than rules of order, governs its meetings, and that informality which carries with it sincerity of motive and spontaneity of effort, prevails within it. Its very name indicates informality, and, indeed, one of the reasons said to have induced its adoption was the fact that members or guests need not don their dress suits to attend the meetings, if they so desired. This informality, however, must be distinguished from the informality of Bohemianism. For The Five O'Clock Club, informality, above convenience, means sobriety, refinement of thought and speech, good breeding and good order. To this sort of informality much of its success is due.

Fortune, The New York Times, Black Enterprise, Business Week, NPR, CNBC and ABC-TV are some of the places you've seen, heard, or read about us.

The Schedule

See our website for the specific dates for each topic. All groups use a similar schedule in each time zone.

Fee: $49 annual membership (includes Beginners Kit, subscription to *The Five O'Clock News,* and access to the Members Only section of our website), **plus** session fees based on member's income (price for the Insider Program includes audio-CD lectures, which retails for $150).

Reservations required for first session. Unused sessions are transferable to anyone you choose or can be donated to members attending more than 16 sessions who are having financial difficulty.

The Five O'Clock Club's programs are geared to recent graduates, professionals, managers, executives, and recent retirees from a wide variety of industries and professions. Most earn from $30,000 to $400,000 per year. Half the members are employed; half are unemployed; some are recent or soon to be retirees. *You will be in a group of your peers.*

To register, please fill out form on the web (at www.fiveoclockclub.com)
or call 1-800-575-3587 (or 212-286-4500 in New York).

Lecture Presentation Schedule

- History of the 5OCC
- The 5OCC Approach to Job Search
- Developing New Targets for Your Search
- Two-Minute Pitch: Keystone of Your Search
- Using Research and Internet for Your Search
- The Keys to Effective Networking
- Getting the Most Out of Your Contacts
- Getting Interviews: Direct/Targeted Mail
- Beat the Odds When Using Search Firms and Ads
- Developing New Momentum in Your Search
- The 5OCC Approach to Interviewing
- Advanced Interviewing Techniques
- How to Handle Difficult Interview Questions

- How to Turn Job Interviews into Offers
- Successful Job Hunter's Report
- Four-Step Salary-Negotiation Method

All groups run continuously. Dates are posted on our website. The textbooks used by all members of The Five O'Clock Club may be ordered on our website or purchased at major bookstores.

**The original Five O'Clock Club was formed in Philadelphia in 1883.
It was made up of the leaders of the day who shared their
experiences "in a spirit of fellowship and good humor."**

Questions You May Have About the Weekly Job-Search Strategy Group

Job hunters are not always the best judges of what they need during a search. For example, most are interested in lectures on answering ads on the Internet or working with search firms. We cover those topics, but strategically they are relatively unimportant in an effective job search.

At The Five O'Clock Club, you get the information you really need in your search—*such as how to target more effectively, how to get more interviews, and how to turn job interviews into offers.* What's more, you will work in a small group with the best coaches in the business. In these strategy sessions, your group will help you decide what to do, this week and every week, to move your search along. You will learn by being coached and by coaching others in your group.

> *We find ourselves not independently of other people and institutions but through them. We never get to the bottom of our selves on our own. We discover who we are face to face and side by side with others in work, love, and learning.*
> —Robert N. Bellah, et al., *Habits of the Heart*

Here Are a Few Other Points:

- For best results, attend on a regular basis. Your group gets to know you and will coach you to eliminate whatever you may be doing wrong—or refine what you are doing right.
- The Five O'Clock Club is a members-only organization. To get started in the small-group teleconference sessions, you must purchase a minimum of 10 sessions.
- The teleconference sessions include the set of 16 audio-CD presentations on Five O'Clock Club methodology. In-person groups do not include CDs.
- After that, you may purchase blocks of 5 or 10 sessions.
- We sell multiple sessions to make administration easier.
- If you miss a session, you may make it up any time. You may even transfer unused time to a friend.
- Although many people find jobs quickly (even people who have been unemployed a long time), others have more difficult searches. Plan to be in it for the long haul and you'll do better.
- Carefully read all of the material in this section. It will help you decide whether or not to attend.
- The first week, pay attention to the strategies used by the others in your group. Soak up all the information you can.
- Read the books before you come in the second week. They will help you move your search along.

To register:

1. Read this section and fill out the application.
2. After you become a member and get your Beginners Kit, call to reserve a space for the first time you attend.

To assign you to a career coach, we need to know:

- your current (or last) field or industry
- the kind of job you would like next (if you know)
- your desired salary range in general terms

For private coaching, we suggest you attend the small group and ask to see your group leader to give you continuity.

The Five O'Clock Club is plain, easy-going and unconventional. . . . Members or guests need not don their dress suits to attend the meetings.
— (From the Club History, written in the 1890s)

What Happens at the Meetings?

Each week, job searchers from various industries and professions meet in small groups. The groups specialize in professionals, managers, executives, or recent college graduates. Usually, half are employed and half are unemployed.

The weekly program is in two parts. First, there is a lecture on some aspect of The Five O'Clock Club methodology. Then, job hunters meet in small groups headed by senior full-time professional career coaches.

The first week, get the textbooks, listen to the lecture, and get assigned to your small group. During your first session, *listen* to the others in your group. You learn a lot by listening to how your peers are strategizing *their* searches.

By the second week, you will have read the materials. Now we can start to work on *your* search strategy and help *you* decide what to do next to move your search along. For example, we'll help you figure out how to get more inter-views in your target area or how to turn inter-views into job offers.

In the third week, you will see major progress made by other members of your group and you may notice major progress in your own search as well.

By the third or fourth week, most members are conducting full and effective searches. Over the remaining weeks, you will tend to keep up a full search rather than go after only one or two leads. You will regularly aim to have 6 to 10 things *in the works* at all times. These will generally be in specific target areas you have identified, will keep your search on target, and will increase your chances of getting multiple job offers from which to choose.

Those who stick with the process find it works.

Some people prefer to just listen for a few weeks before they start their job search and that's okay, too.

How Much Does It Cost?

It is against the policy of The Five O'Clock Club to charge individuals heavy up-front fees. Our competitors charge $4,000 to $6,000 or more, up front. Our average fee is $360 for 10 sessions (which includes audio CDs of 16 presentations for those in the teleconference program). Executives pay an average of $810 for 10 sessions. For administrative reasons, we charge for 5 or 10 additional sessions at a time.

You must have the books so you can begin studying them before the second session. (You can purchase them on our website or at major bookstores.) If you don't do the homework, you will tend to waste the time of others in the group by asking questions covered in the texts.

Is the Small Group Right for Me?

The Five O'Clock Club process is for you if:

- You are truly interested in job hunting.
- You have *some* idea of the kind of job you want.
- You are a professional, manager, or executive—or want to be.
- You want to participate in a group process on a regular basis.
- You realize that finding or changing jobs and careers is hard work, but you are absolutely willing and able to do it.

If you have no idea about the kind of job you want next, you may attend one or two group sessions to start. *Then* see a *coach privately* for one or two sessions, develop tentative job targets, and return to the group. You may work with your small-group coach or contact us through our website or by calling **1-800-575-3587** (or **212-286-4500** in New York) for referral to another coach.

How Long Will It Take Me to Get a Job?

Although our members tend to be from fields or industries where they expect to have difficult searches, *the average person who attends regularly finds a new position within 10 sessions.* Some take less time and others take more.

One thing we know for sure: **Research shows that those who get *regular* coaching during their searches get jobs faster and at higher rates of pay than those who search on their own or simply take a course.** This makes sense. If a person comes only when they think they have a problem, they are usually wrong. They probably had a problem a few weeks ago but didn't realize it. Or the problem may be dif-ferent from the one they thought they had. Those who come regularly benefit from the observations others make about their searches. Problems are solved before they become severe or are prevented altogether.

Those who attend regularly also learn a lot by paying attention and helping others in the group. This *secondhand* learning can shorten your search by weeks. When you hear the problems of others who are ahead of you in the search, you can avoid them completely. People in your group will come to know you and will point out subtleties you may not have noticed that interviewers will never tell you.

Will I Be with Others from My Field/Industry?

Probably, but it's not that important. You will learn a lot and have a much more creative search if you are in a group of people who are in your general salary range but not exactly like you. Our clients are from virtually every field and industry. The *process* is what will help you.

We've been doing this since 1978 and under-stand your needs. That's why the mix we provide is the best you can get.

Career Coaching Firms Charge $4,000–$6,000 Up Front. How Can You Charge Such a Small Fee?

1. We have no advertising costs, because 90 per-cent of those who attend have been referred by other members.

    A hefty up-front fee would bind you to us, but we have been more success-ful by treating people ethically and having them pretty much *pay as they go.*

    We need a certain number of people to cover expenses. When lots of people get jobs quickly and leave us, we could go into the red. But as long as members refer others, we will continue to provide this service at a fair price.

2. We focus strictly on *job-search strategy,* and encourage our clients to attend free support groups if they need emotional support. We focus on getting *jobs,* which reduces the time clients spend with us and the amount they pay.

3. We attract the best coaches, and our clients make more progress per session than they would elsewhere, which also reduces their costs.

4. We have expert administrators and a sophisticated computer system that reduces our over-head and increases our ability to track your progress.

May I Change Coaches?

Yes. Great care is taken in assigning you to your initial coach. However, if you want to change once for any reason, you may do it. We don't encourage group hopping: It is better for you to stick with a group so that everyone gets to know you. On the other hand, we want you to feel comfortable. So if you tell us you prefer a different group, you will be transferred immediately.

What If I Have a Quick Question Outside of the Group Session?

Some people prefer to see their group coach privately. Others prefer to meet with a different coach to get another point of view. Whatever you decide, remember that the group fee does *not* cover coaching time outside the group session. Therefore, if you wanted to speak with a coach between sessions—even for *quick questions*—you would normally meet with the coach first for a private session so he or she can get to know you better. *Easy, quick questions* are usually more complicated than they appear. After your first private session, some coaches will allow you to pay in advance for one hour of coaching time, which you can then use for quick questions by phone (usually a 15-minute minimum is charged). Since each coach has an individual way of operating, find out how the coach arranges these things.

What If I Want to Start My Own Business?

The process of becoming a consultant is essentially the same as job hunting and lots of consultants attend Five O'Clock Club meetings. However, if you want to buy a franchise or existing business or start a growth business, you should see a private coach.

How Can I Be Sure That the Five O'Clock Club Small-Group Sessions Will Be Right for Me?

Before you actually participate in any of the small-group sessions, you can get an idea of the quality of our service by listening to all 16 audio CDs that you purchased. If you are dissatisfied with the CDs for any reason, return the package within 30 days for a full refund.

Whatever you decide, just remember: *It has been proven that those who receive regular help during their searches get jobs faster and at higher rates of pay than those who search on their own or simply attend a course.* If you get a job just one or two weeks faster because of this program, it will have more than paid for itself. And you may *transfer unused sessions to anyone you choose.* However, the person you choose must be or become a member.

When Your Employer Pays

Does your employer care about you and others whom they ask to leave the organization? If so, ask them to consider The Five O'Clock Club for your outplacement help. The Five O'Clock Club puts you and your job search first, offering a career-coaching program of the highest quality at the lowest possible price to your employer.

Over 25 Years of Research

The Five O'Clock Club was started in 1978 as a research-based organization. Job hunters tried various techniques and reported their results back to the group. We developed a variety of guidelines so job hunters could choose the techniques best for them.

The methodology was tested and refined on professionals, managers, and executives (and those aspiring to be) from all occupations. Annual salaries ranged from $30,000 to $400,000; 50 per-cent were employed and 50 percent were unemployed.

Since its beginning, The Five O'Clock Club has tracked trends. Over time, our advice has changed as the job market has changed. What worked in the past is insufficient for today's job market. Today's Five O'Clock Club promotes all our relevant original strategies—and so much more.

As an employee-advocacy organization, The Five O'Clock Club focuses on providing the services and information that the job hunter needs most.

Get the Help You Need Most: 100 Percent Coaching

There's a myth in outplacement circles that a terminated employee just needs a desk, a phone, and minimal career coaching. *Our experience clearly shows that downsized workers need qualified, reliable coaching more than any-thing else.*

Most traditional outplacement packages last only 3 months. The average executive gets office space and only 5 hours of career coaching during this time. Yet the service job hunters need most is the career coaching itself—not a desk and a phone.

Most professionals, managers, and executives are right in the thick of negotiations with prospective employers at the 3-month mark. Yet that is precisely when traditional outplacement ends, leaving job hunters stranded and sometimes ruining deals.

It is astonishing how often job hunters and employers alike are impressed by the databases of *job postings* claimed by outplacement firms. Yet only 10 percent of all jobs are filled through ads and another 10 percent are filled through search firms. Instead, direct contact and networking—done The Five O'Clock Club way—are more effective for most searches.

You Get a Safety Net

Imagine getting a package that protects you for a full year or more. Imagine knowing you can comeback if your new job doesn't work out—even months later. Imagine trying consulting work if you like. If you later decide it's not for you, you can come back to The Five O'Clock Club.

We can offer you a safety net of one full year's career coaching because our method is so effective that few people actually need more than 10 weeks in our proven program. But you're protected for a year.

You'll Job Search with Those Who Are Employed–How Novel!

Let's face it. It can be depressing to spend your days at an outplacement firm where everyone is unemployed. At The Five O'Clock Club, half the attendees are working, and this makes the atmosphere cheerier and helps to move your search along.

What's more, you'll be in a small group of your peers, all of whom are using The Five O'Clock Club method. Our research proves that those who attend the small group regularly and use The Five O'Clock Club methods get jobs faster and at higher rates of pay than those who only work privately with a career coach through-out their searches.

So Many Poor Attempts

Nothing is sadder than meeting someone who has already been getting job-search *help,* but the wrong kind. They've learned the traditional techniques that are no longer effective. Most have poor résumés and inappropriate targets and don't know how to turn job interviews into offers.

You'll Get Quite a Package

You'll get up to 14 hours of private coaching—well in excess of what you would get at a traditional outplacement firm. You may even want to use a few hours after you start your new job.

And you get up to one full year of small-group career coaching. In addition, you get books, audio CDs, and other helpful materials.

To Get Started

The day your human resources manager calls us authorizing Five O'Clock Club outplacement, we will immediately ship you the books, CDs, and other materials and assign you to a private coach and a small group.

Then we'll monitor your search. Frankly, we care about you more than we care about your employer. And since your employer cares about you, they're glad we feel this way—because they know we'll take care of you.

What They Say About Us

The Five O'Clock Club product is much better, far more useful than my outplacement package.

—Senior executive and Five O'Clock Club member

The Club kept the juices flowing. You're told what to do, what not to do. There were fresh ideas. I went through an outplacement service that, frankly, did not help. If they had done as much as the Five O'Clock Club did, I would have landed sooner.

—Another member

When Your *Employer* Pays for The Five O'Clock Club, *You* Get:

- **Up to 40 hours of guaranteed private career coaching** to determine a career direction, develop a résumé, plan salary negotiations, and so on. In fact, if you need a second opinion during your search, we can arrange that too.
- **ONE YEAR (or more) of small-group teleconference coaching** (average about 5 or 6 participants in a group) headed by a senior Five O'Clock Club career consultant. That way, if you lose your next job, you can come back. Or if you want to try consulting work and then decide you **don't like it, you can come back**.
- **Two-year membership** in The Five O'Clock Club: Beginners Kit and two-year subscription to *The Five O'Clock News*.
- **The complete set of our four books** for professionals, managers, and executives who are in job search.
- **A boxed set of 16 audio CDs** of Five O'Clock Club presentations.

Comparison of Employer-Paid Packages

Typical Package	Traditional Outplacement	The Five O'Clock Club
Who is the client?	The organization	Job hunters. We are employee advocates. We always do what is in the best interest of job hunters.
The clientele	All are unemployed	Half of our attendees are unemployed; half are employed. There is an upbeat atmosphere; networking is enhanced.
Length/type of service	3 months, primarily office space	1 year, exclusively career coaching
Service ends	After 3 months—or before if the client lands a job or consulting	After 1 full year, no matter what. You can return if you lose your next job, if your assignment ends, or if you need advice after starting your new job.
Small-group coaching	Sporadic for 3 months; Coach varies	Every week for up to 1 year; same coach
Private coaching	5 Hours on average	up to 14 hours guaranteed (depending on level of service purchased)
Support materials	Generic manual	• 4 textbooks based on over 25 years of job-search research • Sixteen 40-minute lectures on audio CDs • Beginners Kit of search information • 2-year subscription to the Five O'Clock Club magazine, devoted to career-management articles
Facilities	Cubicle, phone, computer access	None; use home phone and computer

The Way We Are

The Five O'Clock Club means sobriety, refinement of thought and speech, good breeding and good order. To this, much of its success is due. The Five O'Clock Club is easy-going and unconventional. A sense of propriety, rather than rules of order, governs its meetings.
   —J. Hampton Moore, *History of The Five O'Clock Club* (written in the 1890s)

Just like the members of the original Five O'Clock Club, today's members want an ongoing relationship. George Vaillant, in his seminal work on successful people, found that "what makes or breaks our luck seems to be . . . our sustained relationships with other people." (George E. Vaillant, *Adaptation to Life,* Harvard University Press, 1995)

Five O'Clock Club members know that much of the program's benefit comes from simply showing up. Showing up will encourage you to do what you need to do when you are not here. And over the course of several weeks, certain things will become evident that are not evident now.

Five O'Clock Club members learn from each other: The group leader is not the only one with answers. The leader brings factual information to the meetings and keeps the discussion in line. But the answers to some problems may lie within you or with others in the group.

Five O'Clock Club members encourage each other. They listen, see similarities with their own situations, and learn from that. And they listen to see how they may help others. You may come across information or a contact that could help someone else in the group. Passing on that information is what we're all about.

If you are a new member here, listen to others to learn the process. And read the books so you will know the basics that others already know. When everyone understands the basics, this keeps the meetings on a high level, interesting, and helpful to everyone.

Five O'Clock Club members are in this together, but they know that ultimately they are each responsible for solving their own problems with God's help. Take the time to learn the process, and you will become better at analyzing your own situation, as well as the situations of others. You will be learning a method that will serve you the rest of your life, and in areas of your life apart from your career.

Five O'Clock Club members are kind to each other. They control their frustrations because venting helps no one. Because many may be stressed, be kind and go the extra length to keep this place calm and happy. It is your respite from the world outside and a place for you to find comfort and FUN. Relax and enjoy yourself, learn what you can, and help where you can. And have a ball doing it.

There arises from the hearts of busy [people] a love of variety, a yearning for relaxation of thought as well as of body, and a craving for a generous and spontaneous fraternity.

—J. Hampton Moore, *History of The Five O'Clock Club*

Lexicon Used at the Five O'Clock Club

Use The Five O'Clock Club lexicon as a shorthand to express where you are in your job search. It will focus you and those in your group.

I. Overview and Assessment

How many hours a week are you spending on your search?

Spend 35 hours on a full-time search, 15 hours on a part-time search.

What are your job targets?

Tell the group. A target includes industry or company size, position, and geographic area. The group can help assess how good your targets are. Take a look at *Measuring Your Targets*.

How does your résumé position you?

The summary and body should make you look appropriate to your target.

What are your backup targets?

Decide at the beginning of the search before the first campaign. Then you won't get stuck.

Have you done the Assessment?

If your targets are wrong, everything is wrong. (Do the Assessment in *Targeting a Great Career.*) Or a counselor can help you privately to deter-mine possible job targets.

II. Getting Interviews

How large is your target (e.g., 30 companies)?
How many of them have you contacted?

Contact them all.

How can you get (more) leads?

You will not get a job through search firms, ads, networking, or direct contact. Those are techniques for getting interviews—job leads. Use the right terminology, especially after a person gets a job. Do not say, "How did you get the job?" if you really want to know "Where did you get the lead for that job?"

Do you have 6 to 10 things in the works?

You may want the group to help you land one job. After they help you with your strategy, they should ask, "How many other things do you have in the works?" If *none,* the group can brainstorm how you can get more things going: through search firms, ads, networking, or direct contact. Then you are more likely to turn the job you want into an offer because you will seem more valuable. What's more, 5 will fall away through no fault of your own. Don't go after only 1 job.

How's your Two-Minute Pitch?

Practice a *tailored* Two-Minute Pitch. Tell the group the job title and industry of the hiring manager they should pretend they are for a role-playing exercise. You will be surprised how good the group is at critiquing pitches. (Practice a few weeks in a row.) Use your pitch to separate you from your competition.

You seem to be in Stage One (or Stage Two or Stage Three) of your search.

Know where you are. This is the key measure of your search.

Are you seen as an insider or an outsider?

See *How to Change Careers* for becoming an insider. If people are saying, "I wish I had an opening for someone like you," you are doing well in meetings. If the industry is strong, then it's only a matter of time before you get a job.

III. Turning Interviews into Offers

Do you want this job?

If you do not want the job, perhaps you want an offer, if only for practice. If you are not willing to go for it, the group's suggestions will not work.

Who are your likely competitors and how can you outshine and outlast them?

You will not get a job simply because "they liked me." The issues are deeper. Ask the interviewer: "Where are you in the hiring process? What kind of person would be your ideal candidate? How do I stack up?"

What are your next steps?

What are *you* planning to do if the hiring manager doesn't call by a certain date or what are you planning to do to assure that the hiring manager *does* call you?

Can you prove you can do the job?

Don't just take the *trust me* approach. Consider your competition.

Which job positions you best for the long run? Which job is the best fit?

Don't decide only on the basis of salary. You will most likely have another job after this. See which job looks best on your résumé and will make you stronger for the next time. In addition, find a fit for your personality. If you don't *fit*, it is unlikely you will do well there. The group can help you turn interviews into offers and give you feedback on which job is best for you.

> "Believe me, with self-examination and a lot of hard work with our coaches, you can find the job . . . you can have the career . . . you can live the life you've always wanted!"
>
> Sincerely,
> Kate Wendleton

Membership

As a member of The Five O'Clock Club, you get:

- A year's subscription to *The Five O'Clock News*—10 issues filled with information on career development and job-search techniques, focusing on the experiences of real people.
- Access to *reasonably priced* weekly seminars featuring individualized attention to your specific needs in small groups supervised by our senior coaches.
- Access to one-on-one coaching to help you answer specific questions, solve current job problems, prepare your résumé, or take an in-depth look at your career path. You choose the coach and pay the coach directly.
- An attractive Beginners Kit containing information based on over 25 years of research on who gets jobs . . . and why . . . that will enable you to improve your job-search techniques—immediately!
- The opportunity to exchange ideas and experiences with other job searchers and career changers.

All that access, all that information, all that expertise for the annual membership fee of only $49, plus seminar fees.

How to Become a Member—by Mail or E-mail:

Send your name, address, phone number, how you heard about us, and your check for $49 (made payable to "The Five O'Clock Club") to The Five O'Clock Club, 300 East 40th Street—Suite 6L, New York, NY 10016, or sign up at www.fiveoclockclub.com.

We will immediately mail you a Five O'Clock Club Membership Card, the Beginners Kit, and information on our seminars followed by our magazine. Then, call **1-800-575-3587** (or **212-286-4500** in New York) or e-mail us (at info@fiveoclockclub.com) to:

- reserve a space for the first time you plan to attend, or
- be matched with a Five O'Clock Club coach.

Membership Application

The Five O'Clock Club

☐ **Yes! I want to become a member!**

I want access to the most effective methods for finding jobs, as well as for developing and managing my career.

I enclose my check for $49 for 1 year; $75 for 2 years—payable to The Five O'Clock Club. I will receive a Beginners Kit, a subscription to *The Five O'Clock News*, access to the Members Only area on our website, and a network of career coaches. Reasonably priced seminars are held across the country.

Name: _____

Address: _____

City: _____ State: _____ Zip: _____

Work phone: (_____) _____

Home phone: (_____) _____

E-mail: _____

Date: _____

How I heard about the Club: _____

For Executives Only (Applying Business Techniques to Your Job Search)
The following optional information is for statistical purposes. Thanks for your help.
Salary range:
☐ $100,000 to $200,000   ☐ $200,000 to $300,000   ☐ $300,000 and above
Age: ☐ 30–39   ☐ 40–49   ☐ 50+
Gender: ☐ Male   ☐ Female

Current or most recent position/title: _____

Please send to:
Membership Director, The Five O'Clock Club,
300 East 40th St., Suite 6L, New York, NY 10016

The original Five O'Clock Club® was formed in Philadelphia in 1893. It was made up of the leaders of the day who shared their experiences "in a setting of fellowship and good humor."

Appendixes

Inspirations:
Ideas, Anecdotes and Advice from Retirees

Are there times when you start feeling down, frustrated with your situation or just plain stuck in your tracks? You may need some inspiration from others who have gone through the same feelings. Use these quotes, taken from the stories and experiences of retirees, to help you move through this period of negative thoughts and low energy.

Return frequently to this section whenever you feel the need for a positive pick-me-up to keep you focused on achieving a good life filled with meaning, purpose and joy.

If any of these statements resonate with you, star them, copy them onto a 3 × 5 index card, and carry the card with you. Read it whenever you need to get out of your rut and begin moving forward again.

Quotes from Retirees

Larry, 67:

- "Stay busy, don't vegetate. Keep following your dream."
- "I look in the mirror and say, 'Do I look like that?' I certainly don't feel like that. The way I feel about myself is great and that's how I'm going to look."
- "My wife managed a busy brokerage firm office of 30 people. Now she designs

flyers and posters for our store. I'm pleased to report that she loves it. I guess it's easy to adapt when you're doing something you really enjoy."

Arthur, 80:

- "When I'm faced with a problem. I always say, 'I can do that."
- "I try to volunteer for work I know nothing about. It seems like a good exercise for staying mentally active."

Charlie, 92:

- "I don't let my mind weaken; I like to learn new things each day."
- "I walk 2 miles every morning. It makes me feel content and fit."

Pete, 58:

- "The Five O'Clock Club's Seven Stories Exercise was the best. It helped me realize what I really wanted to do with my life."

Sarah, 64:

- "I've created my own daily structure to replace the structure I had in my job."
- "It slowly dawned on me: I don't have clothes to wear to an interview. I haven't looked for a job in 20 years. I dreaded looking for the 'right outfit.' Well, I had to do it. So, I went shopping. Not only did I get energized but I realized it was actually fun."

Jack, 59:

- "I had never given myself permission to play. So, I gave myself permission and now I know how to play. I actually learned to have fun. I laugh a lot and don't take myself so seriously any more."

Valerie, 63:

- "I realized how important it was to me to have a sense of achievement. So, I took action. I started learning Spanish. Now I feel pretty good about myself. What a sense of achievement! I never thought I could do it. I guess all I needed was to get started."

Andrea, 58:

- "When I start to feel upset, I remember something funny. I start laughing and instantly feel much better."

Diane, 70:

- "When I was 55 my mother said to me, 'Why are you starting a new business at the end of your work life?' I returned to school, got another Master's degree and had a successful business for 13 years. Am I glad I didn't listen to her!"
- "I first starting learning how to use a computer 5 years ago. I looked at it and I said 'no way!' Now I have become more competent because I see the possibilities."
- "I hate to admit it, but I even like using computers. And it has helped me with my new business. I had to learn and I'm glad I did."

Jean, 64:

- "Once I had crafted and practiced my 'Two-Minute-Pitch,' I felt more confident about myself when I began networking. It gave me added confidence about myself and my ability to speak with strangers."

Marion, 58:

- "I never get bored I always look to learning new things or learning more about old things."

Phil, 62:

- "I'm never sure of the outcome but, whether it works or not, I feel better if I have a contingency plan to fall back on."
- "I feel so much better now that I have developed a weekly schedule of how I will spend my time."

George. 65:

- "Having a plan has kept me focused and enabled me to reach my goal. Sometimes it was tough to keep going, but I persevered and here I am today, happy."

Quotes from the Experts

Suzie Orman, Financial advisor (on Finance):

- "If you want to change your financial ways, just change. Don't stop to analyze, or ask why or how. Just change."

(See Chapter Five)

Jane Northrup, Medical doctor (on Perfectionism):

- "Release your perfectionism. The process of life is always changing. Demanding perfection holds the universe in a strait jacket."

(See Chapter Ten)

Wayne Dyer, Inspirational speaker (on Belief):

- "What you desire is on its way. If you believe something good is coming to you, you will be looking for it."

(See Chapters Six, Seven and Fourteen)

Louise Hay, Inspirational writer (on Finding New Things to Do):

- "Do something new—or at least different—every day. Know that life is never stuck, stagnant or stale, for each moment is ever new and fresh."

Marianne Williamson, Inspirational writer (on Eating):

- "Eating nutritious food supports you in living highly and energetically within the body. In taking care of the body, you take better care of the spirit."

(See Chapter Seventeen)

Cheryl Richardson, Inspirational writer (on Fun):

- "Do something just for fun. Pleasure is one of life's essential nutrients."

(See Chapter Seventeen)

Ruth Graves, Yoga instructor (on Yoga):

- "If you have issues with your body and are limited to exercise, try Yoga. Yoga builds you up in a very gentle way. Yoga means union of the mind, body, and spirit. They are all connected. If the mind is tense, the body gets tense. Relax the body and you relax the mind. Yoga can be especially helpful when you have lost the structure in your life. It will help you develop focus."

(See Chapter Seventeen)

III
·····

The Seven Stories Exercise®

The direction of change to seek is not in our four dimensions: it is getting deeper into what you are, where you are, like turning up the volume on the amplifier.
—Thaddeus Golas, *Lazy Man's Guide to Enlightenment*

In this exercise, you will examine your accomplishments, looking at your strongest and most enjoyable skills. The core of most coaching exercises is some version of the Seven Stories Exercise. A coach may give you lots of tests and exercises, but this one requires *work* on your part and will yield the most important results. An interest or personality test is not enough.

Do not skip the Seven Stories Exercise. It will provide you with information for your career direction, your résumé, and your interviews. After you do the exercise, brainstorm about a number of possible job targets. Then research each target to find out what the job possibilities are for someone like you.

If you're like most people, you have never taken the time to sort out the things you're good at and also are motivated to accomplish. As a result, you probably don't use these talents as completely or as effectively as you could. Too often, we do things to please someone else or to survive in a job. Then we get stuck in a rut—that is, we're *always* trying to please someone else or *always* trying to survive in a job. We lose sight of what could satisfy us, and work be-comes drudgery rather than fun. When we become so enmeshed in survival or in trying to please others, it may be difficult to figure out what we would rather be doing.

When you uncover your enjoyable skills, you'll be better able to identify jobs that allow you to use them, and recognize other jobs that don't quite fit the bill. *Enjoyable skills* are patterns that run through our lives. Since they are skills from which we get satisfaction, we'll find ways to do them even if we don't get to do them at work. We still might not know what these skills are—for us, they're just something we do, and we take them for granted. That's why you should ask other people—your parents and friends—what they see as your enjoyable skills.

Tracking down these patterns takes some thought. The payoff is that our enjoyable skills do not change. They run throughout our lives and indicate what will keep us motivated for the rest of our lives.

Look at Donald Trump. He knows that he enjoys—and is good at—real estate and self-promotion, and that's what he concentrates on. Now remember that you may have 3 to 5 different careers throughout your life—not 3 to 5 jobs, but 3 to 5 *careers*. Still, you can identify commonalities in those careers—aspects that you must have that will make you happier and more successful. In my case, for example, whether I was a computer programmer, a chief financial officer or a career coach, I've always found a way to teach others and often ran small groups—even in my childhood!

You too will find commonalities in your accomplishments, and these may be indicators of the elements you need in a job to be happier and more successful. Let's take one more example. An accountant whose enjoyable accomplishments involve helping the business head and giving advice would probably not be happy sitting in a corner crunching numbers and getting the numbers to balance. If what motivates him is the helping part, then he must be in a job where he is helping—perhaps giving advice to clients. Chances are, this person enjoyed helping people even when he was very young and this is a pattern that runs through many of his accomplishments.

> *One's prime is elusive. . . . You must be on the alert to recognize your prime at whatever time of life it may occur.*
> —Muriel Spark, *The Prime of Miss Jean Brodie*

The Seven Stories Approach: Background

This technique for identifying what people do well and enjoy doing has its roots in the work of Bernard Haldane, Ph.D, who in the 1940s, helped military personnel transition their skills to civilian life. Its overwhelming success in this area won the attention of Harvard Business School where it went on to become a significant part of its *Manual for Alumni Placement*. Haldane's work is being carried on today by practitioners of the Dependable Strengths Articulation Process (DSAP) all over the world through the Center for Dependable Strengths in Seattle, WA. The volunteers of this non-profit public charity have brought Haldane's methods to places as diverse as South Africa and China, to colleges and universities, public education, churches, social service agencies and in their work with people of all ages.

The exercise is this: Make a list of all the enjoyable accomplishments of your life, those things you enjoyed doing *and also* did well. List at least 25 enjoyable accomplishments from all parts of your life: work, from your youth, your school years, your early career up to the present. Don't forget volunteer work, your hobbies and your personal life. Other people may have gotten credit or under-appreciated what you did. Or the result may not have been a roaring success. For example, perhaps you were assigned to develop a new product and take it to market. Let's say you worked on this project for two years, loved every minute of it, but it failed in the market. It doesn't matter. What matters is that you enjoyed doing it and did it well.

Examine those episodes that gave you a sense of accomplishment. You are asked to name 25 accomplishments so you will not be too judgmental—just list anything that occurs to you. Don't expect to sit down and think of everything. Expect to think of enjoyable accomplishments over the course of four or five days. Be sure to ask others to help you think of your accomplishments. Most people carry around a piece of paper so they can jot ideas down as they occur to them. When you have 25, select the seven that are most important to you by however you define important. Then rank them: List the most important first, and so on.

Starting with your first story, write a paragraph about each accomplishment. Then find out what your accomplishments have in common. If you are having trouble doing the exercises, ask a friend to help you talk them through. Friends tend to be more objective and will probably point out strengths you never realized.

You will probably be surprised. For example, you may be especially good interacting with people, but it's something you've always done and therefore take for granted. This may be a pattern that runs through your life and may be one of your enjoyable skills. It *may* be that you'll be unhappy in a job that doesn't allow you to deal with people.

When I did the Seven Stories Exercise, one of the first stories I listed was from when I was 10 years old, when I wrote a play to be put on by the kids in the neighborhood. I rehearsed everyone, sold tickets to the adults for two cents apiece, and served cookies and milk with the proceeds. You might say that my direction as a *general manager*—running the whole show, thinking things up, getting everybody working together—was set in the fourth grade. I saw these traits over and over again in each of my stories.

After I saw those patterns running through my life, it became easy for me to see what elements a job must have to satisfy me. When I interview for a job, I can find out in short order whether it addresses my enjoyable skills. If it doesn't, I won't be as happy as I could be, even though I *may decide to take the job as an interim step toward a long-term goal.* The fact is, people won't do as well *in the long run* in jobs that don't satisfy their enjoyable skills.

Sometimes I don't pay attention to my own enjoyable skills, and I wind up doing things I regret. For example, in high school I scored the highest in the state in math. I was as surprised as everyone else, but I felt I finally had some direction in my life. I felt I had to use it to do some-thing constructive. When I went to college, I majored in math. I almost flunked because I was bored with it. The fact is that I didn't *enjoy* math, I was simply good at it.

There are lots of things we're good at, but they may not be the same things we really enjoy. The trick is to find those things we are good at, enjoy doing, and feel a sense of accomplishment from doing.

To sum up: Discovering your enjoyable skills is the first step in career planning. I was a general manager when I was 10, but I didn't realize it. I'm a general manager now, and I love it. In between, I've done some things that have helped me toward my long-range goals, and other things that have not helped at all.

It is important to realize that the Seven Stories Exercise will *not* tell you exactly which job you should have, but the *elements* to look for in a job that you will find satisfying. You'll have a range of jobs to consider, and you'll know the elements the jobs must have to keep you happy. Once you've selected a few job categories that might satisfy you, talk to people in those fields to find out if a particular job is really what you want, and the job possibilities for someone with your experience. That's one way to test if your aspirations are realistic.

After you have narrowed your choices down to a few fields with some job possibilities that will satisfy your enjoyable skills, the next step is to figure out how to get there. That topic will be covered in our book *Shortcut Your Job Search.*

. . . be patient toward all that is unsolved in your heart and try to love the questions themselves like locked rooms and like books that are written in a foreign tongue.

—Rainer Maria Rilke, *Letters to a Young Poet*

A Demonstration of The Seven Stories Exercise

To get clients started, I sometimes walk them through two or three of their enjoyable accomplishments, and tell them the patterns I see. They can then go off and think of the seven or eight accomplishments they enjoyed the most and also performed well. This final list is ranked and analyzed in depth to get a more accurate picture of the person's enjoyable skills. I spend the most time analyzing those accomplishments a client sees as most important. Some accomplishments are more obvious than others. But all stories can be analyzed.

Here is Suzanne, as an example: "When I was nine years old, I was living with my three sisters. There was a fire in our house and our cat had hidden under the bed. We were all outside, but I decided to run back in and save the cat. And I did it."

No matter what the story is, I probe a little by asking questions: What was the accomplishment for you? and What about that made you proud? These questions give me a quick fix on the person.

The full exercise is a little more involved than this. Suzanne said at first: "I was proud because I did what I thought was right." I probed a little, and she added: "The accomplishment was that I was able to make an instant decision under pressure. I was proud because I overcame my fear."

I asked Suzanne for a second story; I wanted to see what patterns might emerge when we put the two together: "Ten years ago, I was laid off from a large company where I had worked for nine years.

I soon got a job as a secretary in a Wall Street company. I loved the excitement and loved that job. Six weeks later, a position opened up on the trading floor, but I didn't get it at first. I eventually was one of three finalists, and they tried to discourage me from taking the job. I wanted to be given a chance. So I sold myself because I was determined to get that job. I went back for three interviews, said all the right things, and eventually got it."

- "I fought to win."
- "I was able to sell myself. I was able to overcome their objections."

- "I was interviewed by three people at once. I amazed myself by saying, 'I know I can do this job.'"
- "I determined who the real decision maker was, and said things that would make him want to hire me."
- "I loved that job—loved the energy, the upness, the fun."

Here it was, 10 years later, and that job still stood out as a highlight in her life. Since then she'd been miserable and bored, and that's why she came to me.

Normally after a client tells two stories, we can quickly name the patterns we see in both stories. What were Suzanne's patterns?

Suzanne showed that she was good at making decisions in tense situations—both when saving the cat and when interviewing for that job. She showed a good intuitive sense (such as when she determined who the decision maker was and how to win him over). She's decisive and likes fast-paced, energetic situations. She likes it when she overcomes her own fears as well as the objections of others.

What was the accomplishment?

What made her proud?

We needed more than two stories to see if these patterns ran throughout Suzanne's life and to see what other patterns might emerge. After the full exercise, Suzanne felt for sure that she wanted excitement in her jobs, a sense of urgency—that she wanted to be in a position where she had a chance to be decisive and operate intuitively. Those are the conditions she enjoys and under which she operates the best.

Armed with this information, Suzanne can confidently say in an interview that she thrives on excitement, high pressure, and quick decision-making. And, she'll probably make more money than she would in *safe* jobs. She can move her life in a different direction—whenever she is ready.

Pay attention to those stories that were most important to you. The elements in these stories may be worth repeating. If none of your enjoyable accomplishments were work related, it may take great courage to eventually move into a field where you will be happier. Or you may decide to continue to have your enjoyment outside of work.

People have to be ready to change. Fifteen years ago, when I first examined my own enjoyable skills, I saw possibilities I was not ready to handle. Although I suffered from extreme shyness, my stories—especially those that occurred when I was young—gave me hope. As I emerged from my shyness, I was eventually able to act on what my stories said was true about me.

People sometimes take immediate steps after learning what their enjoyable skills are. Or sometimes this new knowledge can work inside them until they are ready to take action—maybe 10 years later. All the while internal changes can be happening, and people can eventually blossom.

> *If one advances confidently in the direction of his dreams, and endeavors to live the life which he has imagined, he will meet with success unexpected in common hours.*
>
> —Henry David Thoreau

Enjoyable Skills—Your Anchor in a Changing World

Your enjoyable skills are your anchor in a world of uncertainty. The world will change, but your enjoyable skills remain constant.

Write them down. Save the list. Over the years, refer to them to make sure you are still on target—doing things that you do well and are motivated to do. As you refer to them, they will influence your life. Five years from now, an opportunity may present itself. In reviewing your list, you will have every confidence that this opportunity is right for you. After all, you have been doing these things since you were a child, you know that you enjoy them, and you do them well!

Knowing our patterns gives us a sense of stability and helps us understand what we have done so far. It also gives us the freedom to try new things regard-less of risk or of what others may say, because we can be absolutely sure that this is the way we are. Knowing your patterns gives you both security and flexibility—and you need both to cope in this changing world. Now think about your own stories. Write down everything that occurs to you.

> *The Ugly Duckling was so happy and in some way he was glad that he had experienced so much hardship and misery; for now he could fully appreciate his tremendous luck and the great beauty that greeted him. . . . And he rustled his feathers, held his long neck high, and with deep emotion he said: "I never dreamt of so much happiness, when I was the Ugly Duckling!"*
>
> —Hans Christian Anderson, *The Ugly Duckling*

The Seven Stories Exercise™ Worksheet

This exercise is an opportunity to examine the most satisfying experiences of your life and to discover those skills you will want to use as you go forward. You will be looking at the times when you feel you did something particularly well that you also enjoyed doing. Complete this sentence: "There was a time when I . . ." List enjoyable accomplishments from all parts of your life: from your youth, your school years, your early career up to the present. Don't forget volunteer work, your hobbies and your personal life. Other people may have gotten credit or under-appreciated what you did. Or the result may not have been a roaring success. None of that matters. What matters is that you enjoyed doing it and did it well.

List anything that occurs to you, however insignificant. When I did my own Seven Stories Exercise, I remembered the time when I was 10 years old and led a group of kids in the neighborhood, enjoyed it, and did it well.

When you have 25, select the seven that are most important to you by however you define important. Then rank them: List the most important first, and so on. Starting with your first story, write a paragraph about each accomplishment. Then find out what your accomplishments have in common. If you are having trouble doing the exercises, ask a friend to help you talk them through. Friends tend to be more objective and will probably point out strengths you never realized.

Section I

Briefly outline below *all* the work/personal/life experiences that meet the above definition. Come up with at least 20. We ask for 20 stories so you won't be too selective. Just write down anything that occurs to you, no matter how insignificant it may seem. Complete this sentence, "There was a time when I . . ." You may start with, for example, "Threw a fiftieth birthday party for my father," "Wrote a press release that resulted in extensive media coverage," and "Came in third in the Nassau bike race."

Don't just write that you enjoy "cooking." That's an *activity,* not an accomplishment. An accomplishment occurs at a specific time. You may wind up with *many* cooking accomplishments, for example. But if you simply write "cooking," "writing" or "managing," you will have a hard time thinking of 20 enjoyable accomplishments.

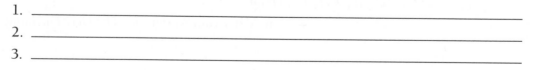

1. _____
2. _____
3. _____

4. _____

5. _____

6. _____

7. _____

8. _____

9. _____

10. _____

11. _____

12. _____

13. _____

14. _____

15. _____

16. _____

17. _____

18. _____

19. _____

20. _____

21. _____

22. _____

23. _____

24. _____

25. _____

Section II

Choose the seven experiences from the above that you enjoyed the most and felt the most sense of accomplishment about. (Be sure to include non-job-related experiences also.) Then **rank them.** Then, for each accomplishment, describe what *you* did. Be specific, listing each step in detail. Use a separate sheet of paper for each.

If your highest-ranking accomplishments also happen to be work related, you may want them to appear prominently on your résumé. After all, those were things that you enjoyed and did well. And those are probably experiences you will want to repeat again in your new job.

Here's how you might begin:

Experience #1: Planned product launch that resulted in 450 letters of intent from 1,500 participants.

    a. Worked with president and product managers to discuss product potential and details.

    b. Developed promotional plan.

    c. Conducted five-week direct-mail campaign prior to conference to create aura of excitement about product.

    d. Trained all product demonstrators to make sure they each presented product in same way.

    e. Had great product booth built; rented best suite to entertain prospects; conducted campaign at conference by having teasers put under everyone's door every day of conference. Most people wanted to come to our booth.

—and so on—

Analyzing Your Seven Stories

Now it is time to analyze your stories. You are trying to look for the patterns that run through them so that you will know the things you do well that also give you satisfaction. Some of the questions below sound similar. That's okay. They are a catalyst to make you think more deeply about the experience. The questions don't have any hidden psychological significance.

If your accomplishments happen to be mostly work related, this exercise will form the basis for your *positioning* or summary statement in your résumé, and also for your Two-Minute Pitch. If these accomplishments are mostly not work related, they will still give you some idea of how you may want to slant your résumé, and they may give you an idea of how you will want your career to go in the long run.

For now, simply go through each story without trying to force it to come out any particular way. Just think hard about yourself. And be as honest as you can. When you have completed this analysis, the words in the next exercise may help you think of additional things. **Do this page first.**

Story #1. _____

What was the *accomplishment?* _____

_____

What about it did you *enjoy most?* _____

_____

What did you *do best?* _____

_____

What *motivated you to do this?* _____

_____

What about it *made you proud?* _____

_____

What *prompted you to do this?* _____

_____

What *enjoyable skills did you demonstrate?* _____

Story #2. _____

What was the *accomplishment?* _____

_____

What about it did you *enjoy most?* _____

_____

What did you *do best?* _____

_____

What *motivated you to do this?* _____

_____

What about it *made you proud?* _____

_____

What *prompted you to do this?* _____

_____

What *enjoyable skills did you demonstrate?* _____

Story #3. _____

What was the *accomplishment?* _____

_____

What about it did you *enjoy most?* _____

_____

What did you *do best?* _____

_____

What *motivated you to do this?* _____

_____

What about it *made you proud?* _____

_____

What *prompted you to do this?* _____

_____

What *enjoyable skills did you demonstrate?* _____

Story #4. _____

What was the *accomplishment?* _____

_____

What about it did you *enjoy most?* _____

_____

What did you *do best?* _____

_____

What *motivated you to do this?* _____

_____

What about it *made you proud?* _____

_____

What *prompted you to do this?* _____

_____

What *enjoyable skills did you demonstrate?* _____

Story #5. _____

What was the *accomplishment?* _____

_____

What about it did you *enjoy most?* _____

_____

What did you *do best?* _____

_____

What *motivated you to do this?* _____

_____

What about it *made you proud?* _____

_____

What *prompted you to do this?* _____

_____

What *enjoyable skills did you demonstrate?* _____

Story #6. _____

What was the *accomplishment?* _____

_____

What about it did you *enjoy most?* _____

_____

What did you *do best?* _____

_____

What *motivated you to do this?* _____

_____

What about it *made you proud?* _____

_____

What *prompted you to do this?* _____

_____

What *enjoyable skills did you demonstrate?* _____

Story #7. _____

What was the *accomplishment?* _____

_____

What about it did you *enjoy most?* _____

_____

What did you *do best?* _____

_____

What *motivated you to do this?* _____

_____

What about it *made you proud?* _____

_____

What *prompted you to do this?* _____

_____

What *enjoyable skills did you demonstrate?* _____

We are here to be excited from youth to old age, to have an insatiable curiosity about the world. . . We are also here to help others by practicing a friendly attitude. And every person is born for a purpose. Everyone has a God-given potential, in essence, built into them. And if we are to live life to its fullest, we must realize that potential.

—Norman Vincent Peale

IV
• • • •

Your Fifteen-Year Vision and Your Forty-Year Vision

In my practice as a psychiatrist, I have found that helping people to develop personal gains has proved to be the most effective way to help them cope with problems.

—Ari Kiev, M.D., *A Strategy for Daily Living*

If you could imagine your ideal life five years from now, what would it be like? How would it be different from the way it is now? If you made new friends during the next five years, what would they be like? Where would you be living? What would your hobbies and interests be? How about 10 years from now? Twenty? Thirty? Forty? Think about it!

Some people feel locked in by their present circumstances. Many say it is too late for them. But a lot can happen in 5, 10, 20, 30, or 40 years. Reverend King had a dream. His dream helped all of us, but his dream helped him too. He was living according to a vision (which he thought was God's plan for him). *It gave him a purpose in life.* Most successful people have a vision.

A lot can happen to you over the next few decades—and most of what happens is up to you. If you see the rest of your life as boring, I'm sure you will be right. Some people pick the "sensible" route or the one that fits in with how others see them, rather than the one that is best for them.

On the other hand, you can come up with a few scenarios of how your life could unfold. In that case, you will have to do a lot of thinking and a lot of research to figure out which path makes most sense for you and will make you happiest.

When a person finds a vision that is right, the most common reaction is fear. It is often safer to *wish* a better life than to actually go after it.

I know what that's like. It took me two years of thinking and research to figure out the right path for myself—one that included my motivated abilities (Seven Stories Exercise) as well as the sketchy vision I had for myself. Then it took *10 more years* to finally take the plunge and commit to that path—running The Five O'Clock Club. I was 40 years old when I finally took a baby step in the right direction, and I was terrified.

You may be lucky and find it easy to write out your vision of your future.

Or you may be more like me: It may take a while and a lot of hard work. You can speed up the process by reviewing your assessment results with a Five O'Clock Club career counselor. He or she will guide you along. Remember, when I was struggling, the country didn't *have* Five O'Clock Club counselors or even these exercises to guide us.

Test your vision and see if that path seems right for you. Plunge in by researching it and meeting with people in the field. If it is what you want, chances are you will find some way to make it happen. If it is not exactly right, you can modify it later—after you have gathered more information and perhaps gotten more experience.

Start with the Present

Write down, in the present tense, the way your life is right now, and the way you see yourself at each of the time frames listed. **This exercise should take no more than one hour.** Allow your unconscious to tell you what you will be doing in the future. Just quickly comment on each of the questions listed on the following page, and then move on to the next. If you kill yourself off too early (say, at age 60), push it 10 more years to see what would have happened if you had lived. Then push it another 10, just for fun.

When you have finished the exercise, ask yourself how you feel about your entire life as you laid it out in your vision. Some people feel depressed when they see on paper how their lives are going, and they cannot think of a way out. But they feel better when a good friend or a Five O'Clock Club counselor helps them think of a better future to work toward. If you don't like your vision, you are allowed to change it—it's your life. Do what you want with it. Pick the kind of life you want.

Start the exercise with the way things are now so you will be realistic about your future. Now, relax and have a good time going through the years. Don't think too hard. Let's see where you wind up. You have plenty of time to get things done.

> **The 15-year mark proves to be the most important for most people. It's far enough away from the present to allow you to dream.**

There are more things in heaven and earth, Horatio, then are dreamt of in your philosophy.

—William Shakespeare, *Hamlet*

Your Fifteen- and Forty-Year-Vision Worksheet

1. The year is _____ (*current year*).
   You are _____ years old right now.

- Tell me what your life is like right now. (*Say anything you want about your life as it is now.*)
  _____
  _____
  _____

- Who are your friends? What do they do for a living?
  _____
  _____

- What is your relationship with your family, however you define "family"?
  _____

- Are you married? Single? Children? (*list ages*)
  _____
  _____

- Where are you living? What does it look like?
  _____
  _____

- What are your hobbies and interests?
  _____
  _____

- What do you do for exercise?
  _____

- How is your health?
  _____

- How do you take care of your spiritual needs?
  _____

- What kind of work are you doing?
  _____

- What else would you like to note about your life right now?
  _____

Don't worry if you don't like everything about your life right now. Most people do this exercise because they want to improve themselves. They want to change something? What do you want to change?

Five Years

2. The year is _____ *(current year 5).*
   You are _____ years old. *(Add 5 to present age.)*

Things are going well for you.

- What is your life like now at this age? *(Say anything you want about your life as it is now.)*

  _____

  _____

- Who are your friends? What do they do for a living?

  _____

  _____

- What is your relationship with your "family"?

  _____

- Married? Single? Children? *(List their ages now.)*

  _____

- Where are you living? What does it look like?

  _____

  _____

- What are your hobbies and interests?

  _____

- What do you do for exercise?

  _____

- How is your health?

  _____

- How do you take care of your spiritual needs?

  _____

- What kind of work are you doing?

  _____

- What else would you like to note about your life right now?

  _____

  _____

Fifteen Year

3. The year is _____ (*current year 15*).
   You are _____ years old. (*Current age plus 15.*)

• What is your life like now at this age? (*Say anything you want about your life as it is now.*)

   _____

   _____

• Who are your friends? What do they do for a living?

   _____

• What is your relationship with your "family"?

   _____

• Married? Single? Children? (*List their ages now.*)

   _____

• Where are you living? What does it look like?

   _____

   _____

• What are your hobbies and interests?

   _____

• What do you do for exercise?

   _____

• How is your health?

   _____

• How do you take care of your spiritual needs?

   _____

• What kind of work are you doing?

   _____

• What else would you like to note about your life right now?

   _____

   _____

   _____

The 15-year mark is an especially important one. This age is far enough away from the present that people often loosen up a bit. It's so far away that it's not threatening. Imagine your ideal life. What is it like? Why were you put here on this earth? What were you meant to do here? What kind of life were you meant to live? Give it a try and see what you come up with. If you can't think of anything now, try it again in a week or so. On the other hand, if you got to the 15-year mark, why not keep going?

Twenty-Fifth Year

4. The year is _____ *(current year 25).*

You are _____ years old! *(Current age plus 25.)*
Using a blank sheet of paper, aanswer all the questions from previous worksheets for this stage of your life.

5. The year is _____ *(current year 35).*

You are _____ years old! *(Current age plus 35.)*
Using a blank sheet of paper, aanswer all the questions from previous worksheets for this stage of your life.

6. The year is _____ *(current year 45).*

You are _____ years old!
Using a blank sheet of paper, aanswer all the questions from previous worksheets for this stage of your life.

(Current age plus 45.)

7. The year is _____ *(current year 55).*

You are _____ years old! *(Current age plus 55.)*
Using a blank sheet of paper, aanswer all the questions from previous worksheets for this stage of your life.

Keep going—don't die until you are past 80!
How do you feel about your life? You are allowed to change the parts you don't like.

You have plenty of time to get done everything you want to do. Imagine wonderful things for yourself. You have plenty of time. Get rid of any "negative programming." For example, if you imagine yourself having poor health because your parents suffered from poor health, see what you can do about that. If you imagine yourself dying early because that runs in your family, see what would have happened had you lived longer. It's your life—your only one. As they say, "This is the real thing. It's not a dress rehearsal."

V
...
Additional Suggested Reading

Throughout this book I have cited articles, books, magazines and studies dealing with the topic of retirement transition. The books named below are additional reading suggestions for your interest that I have used over the years but weren't cited in the text.

Ardell, Donald B. *High Level Wellness: An Alternative to Doctors, Drugs and Disease* (Berkeley, CA: Ten Speed Press, 1986).

Brandon, Nathaniel. *How to Raise Your Self-Esteem: The Proven Action-Oriented Approach to Greater Self-Respect and Self-Confidence* (New York: Bantam, 1988).

Bronte, Lydia. *The Longetivity Factor: The New Reality of Long Careers and How It Can Lead to Richer Lives* (New York: HarperCollins, 1993).

Burns, David. *Feeling Good: The New Mood Therapy* (New York: Avon, 1999).

Canfield, Jack and Mark Victor Hansen. *Chicken Soup for the Soul: 101 Stories to Open The Heart And Rekindle The Spirit* (Deerfield Beach, FL: Health Communications, 1993).

Covey, Stephen. *The 7 Habits of Highly Effective People* (New York: Free Press, 2004).

Foster, Rick and Greg Hicks. *How We Choose To Be Happy* (New York: Berkley, 1999).

Harkness, Helen, *Don't Stop The Career Clock: Rejecting the Myths of Aging for a New Way to Work in the 21st Century* (Palo Alto, CA: Davies-Black Publishing, 1999).

Helmstetter, Shad. *What to Say When You Talk to Yourself* (New York: Simon and Schuster, 1982).

James, William. *The Principles of Psychology* (Chicago, IL: William Benton, 1952).

Johnson, Will. *Aligned Relaxed, Resilient: The Physical Foundations of Mindfulness* (Boston, MA: Shambhala, 2000).

Levoy, Greg. *Callings: Finding and Following and Authentic Life* (Three Rivers Press, 1998).

Rechtschaffen, Stephan. *Time Shifting: Creating More Time to Enjoy Your Life* (New York: Doubleday, 1996).

Riehle, Kathleen A. *What Smart People Do When Losing Their Jobs* (New York: John Wiley & Sons, 1991).

Rogers, Natalie, H. *The New Talk Power: The Mind-Body Way to Speak Like a Pro* (New York: Capital Books, 1999).

Sadler, William A., *The Third Age: 6 Principles For Growth and Renewal After Forty* (New York: Da Capo Press, 2000).

Sheehy, Gail. *New Passages: Mapping Your Life Across Time* (New York: Random House, 1995).

Sher, Barbara. I *Could Do Anything If I Only Knew What It Was* (New York: Dell, 1995).

Sher, Barbara. *Wishcraft: How to Get What You Really Want* (New York: Ballantine, 2003).

Tieger, Paul D. and Barbara Barron-Tieger, *Do What You Are: Discover the Perfect Career for You through the Secrets of Personality Type* (New York: Little Brown, 2001).

Tolle, Eckhart. *The Power Of NOW: A Guide to Spiritual Enlightenment* (Novato, CA: Library, 1999).

Travis, John, MD, Ryan, Regina Sara. Simply Well: Choices For A Healthy Life (Ten Speed Press: Berkeley, CA, 2001).

Index

AARP, 27, 148
    on best employers for workers over 50,
      144
    on employment after retirement, 139
    Job Hub service of, 73
    on obesity, 196
    Resources Senior Community Service
      Employment Program, 149
    travel discounts from, 176
About Schmidt (film), 35
accomplishments, 102–3
    listed in Seven Stories Exercise, 247
accountability, 53–54
Actuarial Foundation, 29
Adler, Alfred, 117
Adler, Mortimer, 191
affirmations, 65–69, 166
age, chronological and functional, 13
aged, history of attitudes toward, 5
age discrimination, xiv, 160, 163–64, 168
    combating, 164–66
    history of, 5
    perceptions of, 172–73
    stereotypes and, 167
ageism, 5, 14–15
aging

    attitudes toward, 10–11
    of brain, 203
    exercise and, 197–99
    myths of, 12–17
    perceptions of, 9–10
    unconscious attitudes toward, 12
Alcott, Louisa May, 64
Allen, James, 100
American Red Cross, 145
America's Job Bank - Job Search, 151
Amizade, Ltd., 177
Anderson, Hans Christian, 251
Angelou, Maya, 175
Animas Valley Institute, 191
Archaeological Institute of America, Boston
    University, 177
assessments
    decision making in, 107–8
    fantasy day, 128–30
    inspiring role models, 130–31
    personal future, 131–32
    procrastination and, 108–10
    for second careers, 154
    of skills and interests, 101–6
    of values, 106–7
    worrying and, 110–12

audit programs, 189–90
autotelic experiences, 104
Avalon Travel Publishing, 179

Babson, Roger, 112
baby boomers, 6–8
    post-retirement plans of, 126
    retirement viewed by, xxii–xxiii
Baldwin, James, 48
Baruch, Bernard, 10, 67, 163
Bellah, Robert N., 219
Benefits Outreach Program, 148
Bergson, Henri, 47
Best Companies for Older Workers, 151
Best Jobs in the USA Today, 151
Big Apple Greeters, 146
Big Brothers Big Sisters, 146
Blanton, Smiley, 59
blogging, 40
Boiste, Pierre-Claude-Victor, 166
Borge, Victor, 202
Borysenko, Joan, 112, 198, 204
brain, 16
    challenging with new ideas, 203–4
Brande, Dorthea, 63
Bridges, William, 33, 34, 38
Bronte, Lydia, 142
Brown, Les, 69
Bucella, Marty, 10
Buddha, 55
Burns, George, 9, 167, 207, 208
Buscaglia, Leo, 56, 110, 134
Bush, Barbara, 134

Calment, Jean, 119
Campbell, Joseph, xxii, 125, 133, 145
CanSupport Visitor Program, 148
Careerbuilder, 150
career coaches, 159
CareerJournal.com, 151

CareerSite, 150
Carnegie, Dale, 54, 108, 110
car rental discounts, 176
Carter, Lillian, 7
Casals, Pablo, 167
Castaneda, Carlos, 8
centenarians, xxi
Central Florida, University of, Senior
Citizen Registration, 190
Cerf, Bennett Alfred, 202
Certified Financial Planner Board of
Standards, 28, 29
Cervantes Saavedra, Miguel de, 16
change, 47
    definition of, 48
    managing, 48–56
    transition distinguished from, 32
Chapman, Elwood N., 108
chat rooms, 40
Child, Julia, 122, 139
Child, Paul, 122
children, relocating closer to, 42
Chopra, Deepak, 194
chores, household
    chart of, 90
    division of labor for, 85–86
Christie, Agatha, 169
chronological age, 13
Churchill, Sir Winston, 21, 55
coaching, by Five O'Clock Club, 215, 220,
222–26
Columbia University, Lifelong Learners
Program, 190
Comfort, Alex, 10, 16–17
communications, with spouses, 83
compassion, 74–75
consulting, 224
Consumer Federation of America, 28
cooking, 89
Cooley, Charles Horton, 53

Cool Works, 149
Corporation for National and Community Service, 147
Corrigan, Chris, 153
Cousins, Norman, 201, 202
cover letters, 158
Covey, Stephen R., 53
Craigs List, 148
Csikszentmihalyi, Mihalyi, 96, 102, 104

death, 115, 116, 119
decision making, in assessments, 107–8
Deets, Horace B., 126
Denver, University of, Senior Audit Program, 189
Dependable Strengths Articulation Process (DSAP), 247
Depression (economic), 18
depression (emotional), xi–xii
    among newly retired women, 41
    temporal orientation and, 116–17
Diamond, Marian, C., 14, 16, 203–4
Dickinson, Emily, 10
disenchantment, 36
disengagement, 34–35
disidentification, 35
disorientation, 36
Doherty, Henry L., 188
Dychtwald, Ken, 127
Dyer, Wayne, 243

Earthwatch Institute, 177
eating, 196
education, 185–88
    for employment after retirement, 144
    Native American vision quest education programs, 190–91
    programs for, 188–89
    senior audit programs, 189–90
Education for Adults, 189

ego fulfillment, as need, 94–96
Elderhostel, 188
ElderTreks, 182
elephants, 6
Ellington, Duke, 208
Ellis, Albert, 59–60
Emerson, Ralph Waldo, xxi, 44, 74, 134, 206
Employee Benefits Security Administration (U.S. Dept. of Labor), 27
employment
    age discrimination in, 163–67
    continuing, after retirement, 138–45
    Five O'Clock Club services for finding, 213–18, 222–24
    full-time, xiv
    job hunting guides, 151
    part-time, xiii–xiv
    planning for continuation of, 122
    pro bono, 173–74
    resources for, 149–51
    volunteering versus, 133, 137–38
endings phase, 33–37
Environmental Alliance for Senior Involvement (EASI), 149
esteem, as need, 94–96
Euripides, 176, 191
exercise, 15, 197–99
Experience Corps, 135, 145

Falk, Gerhard, 5
Falk, Ursula A., 5
families, friends versus, 88–89
fantasy day assessment, 128–30
Ferguson, Marilyn, 17, 38
Fifteen-Year Vision, 120, 122–23, 153, 154, 259–65
50plus Expeditions, 182
finances, 21–25
    adjusting to reduced income, 87–88

as basic need, 93
in paid employment *versus* volunteering
  decision, 133
planning, 25–26
resources for help with, 27–29
Financial Literacy and Education Commission (U.S. Dept. of Labor), 28
financial planning, 26
Fischer, David Hackett, 5
Five O'Clock Club, xv, 213–18, 229–30
  assessment inventories used by, 52–53,
    62
  on career research, 155
  Fifteen-Year and Forty-Year Vision
    exercisies of, 259–65
  history of, 216
  on interviewing, 158
  job-search books from, 144
  lexicon of, 231–34
  membership in, 234
  membership application for, 235
  members of, 164
  Seven Stories Exercise of, 102–6, 154,
    245–58
  weekly job-search strategy groups of,
    219–28
food, 196
Forbes, Bertie Charles, 154
Forrest Gump (film), 47
Forty-Year Vision, 120, 122–23, 153,
259–65
Frankhauser, Jerry, 66
Frankl, Viktor E., 118
Franklin, Benjamin, 16, 174
Freud, Sigmund, 53
Fried, Linda P., 135
Friedan, Betty, 4, 7, 11, 35, 163
friends
  families *versus*, 88–89
  needs for love and belonging met by,
    93–94

full-time employment, xiv
functional age, 13
future
  in assessment exercise, 131–32
  imagining, 118–20
  lack of vision for, 115–17
  positive thinking about, 204–5

Gaberino, Geoffrey, 56
Gandhi, Mohandas K., 50, 92
Gardner, Alison, 176
Geisel, Theodore Seuss (Dr. Seuss), 8, 202
Generations of Hope, 149
Generations United, 149
George Washington University, 190
Gibran, Kahlil, 74
Gide, Andre, 31
Gilbert, Rob, 66, 69
Glasow, Arnold H., 122
Global Citizen's Network, 177
Global Greeter Network, 146
Global Volunteers, 177
Globe Aware, 178
goals, 114–15
Goethe, Johann Wolfgang von, 16, 74
Golas, Thaddeus, 245
Golden Age Passport, 176
government, transitioning out of, 158
GradSchools, 189
Graves, Ruth, 244
Great Depression (economic), 18
Grenfell, Sir Winfred, 125
Greyhound Bus Line discounts, 176

Habitat for Humanity, 178
Haldane, Bernard, 246–47
Hanks, Tom, 47
Harmon, Sidney, 8
Hay, Louise, 243
health
  of brain, 203–4

exercise, 197–99
    laughter and, 201
    nutrition, 196
Helfand, David P., 31
Hendrickson, Marjorie, xx, 81
Heraclitus, 47
Hippocrates, 19
hobbies, 132–33
Holden, Robert, 201
Holmes, Oliver Wendell, 9, 75
home visits, 183
Horace, 209
house exchanges, 183
household tasks
    chart of, 90
    division of, 85–86
Hugo, Victor, 200

Idealist (nonprofit organization), 151
income
    adjusting to reduction in, 87–88
    psychic, 153, 155
    see also employment; finances
informational interviews, 155, 158
intellectual abilities, 16
interests and skills
    assessment of, 101–6
    in Seven Stories Exercise, 251
intergenerational programs, 137
    resources for, 149
Internal Revenue Service (IRS), 28
International Home Exchange Network, 183
Internet, 155
Intervac US, 183
interviews
    employment, 160
    getting, 232–33
    informational, 155, 158
    job offers from, 233

Jagger, Mick, 91
James, William, 3, 17, 66
Jefferson, Thomas, 197
job hunting guides, 151
Johnson, Lynn, 19
Johnson, Samuel, 52

Kahn, Robert L., 138, 197
Kalamis, Catherine, 201
Kaplan, Harvey, xx, 153
Keith, Sir Arthur, 71
Keller, Helen, 96
Kiev, Ari, 259
Killam, Deborah, 19
Kim, Jungmeen, 41
King, Billie Jean, 52
King, Martin Luther, Jr., 123
King, Stephen, 104
Koenig, Harold, 205
Kubler-Ross, Elizabeth, 120

La Lanne, Jack, 7–8, 15, 198
The Land Conservancy (TLC) of British Columbia, 179
LANDSCOPE Expeditions, 178
laughter, 200–202
learned optimism, 60–63
Leider, Richard, 96–97
Levy, Becca R., 17, 204
Lewis, Al, 7
Lewis, Sinclair, 77
life expectancy, xxi, 6, 119
LiFeline Centre, 178
Lincoln, Abraham, xx
Living Abroad In series, 179
Lombardi, Vince, 171
London, Jack, 209
love and belonging, as needs, 93–94, 96

Madison, David, 169, 172

mandatory retirement laws, 5
Marco Polo Magazine, 180
Marcus Aurelius Antoninus, 69, 170
marketing yourself, 158–59
Maslow, Abraham, xii, 92, 99, 103
Matisse, Henri, 16
Matthau, Carol, 11
Maxwell, Florida Scott, 121
Mays, Benjamin, 36
men
    older, in workforce, 167
    recently retired, 41
mental abilities, 16–17
mental health, 198
Metropolitan Museum of Art (New York), 136–37
military, transitioning out of, 158
mind, 203–4
Minkowski, Eugene, 116
Moen, Phyllis, 41
Monet, Angela, 166
Monster.com, 150
Moore, J. Hampton, 229, 230
Moses, "Grandma," 16, 140
motivated skills, 154
My Turn (education program), 189

Napoleon Bonaparte, 59
National Endowment for Financial Education, 28
National Trust Working Holidays, 178
Native American vision quest education programs, 97, 190–91
needs, hierarchy of, 92–96
negative thoughts, 75–77
networking, 155, 158
net worth, 26
neutral zone phase, 38
Nevelson, Louise, 16
new beginnings phase, 38

New York Regional Association of Grantmakers, 151
New York State Department of Labor, 150
New York Times, 151
Nicholson, Jack, 35
Nidetch, Jean, 53, 77
Niebuhr, Reinhold, 54
nonprofit opportunities, 151–52
Nonprofit Times online, 152
North American Securities Association, 28
Northrup, Jane, 243
nutrition, 196

OASIS Institute, 149
obesity, 196
Oceanic Society, 179, 188
Ohio University Lifelong Learning, 190
Ombudsman Volunteer, 148
Opportunity Knocks: Non-Profit Organization Classifieds, 152
optimism, 63
    learned, 62
optimists, 61
Orangutan Foundation International (OFI), 179
orcas, 6
Orman, Suzie, 243
Over the Hill Gang International, 182
Ovid, 47

part-time employment, xiii–xiv
Peace Corps, 147
Peale, Norman Vincent, 38, 65
    on optimists, 166
    on positive thinking, 63, 204
    on purpose of life, 258
    on self-confidence, 169
Pension Benefit Guaranty Corporation, 27–28
Pepper, Claude, 7

personal-awareness, 52–53
pessimists, 61
Peterson, Wilfred, 175
physical strength, 15
physiological needs, 92–93, 95–96
planning, 114
    for post-retirement years, 120–21
    for second careers, 154
Plasker, Barbara, 168–69
Plato, 14
Ponder, Catherine, 200
positioning statements, 171, 254
positive thinking, 57–60, 63–64, 204–5
    compassion in, 74–75
    learned, 60–63
    personal barriers eliminated in, 75–77
    positive affirmations in, 65–69
    responsibility taken in, 72–74
    visualization used in, 69–72
primary research, 155
private coaching, 215
proactive action, 54
pro bono work, 173–74
procrastination, 108–9
Proust, Marcel, 38, 182
psychic income, 153, 155
purpose, defining, 96–99
Putnam, Howard, 173–74

Quinn, Anthony, 139

Rappaport, Herbert, xi, 115–21
relationships, 40–41
    after retirement, 81–89
relaxation exercises, 129
religion, 205–6
relocation, following retirement, 41–42,
    86–87
Repplier, Agnes, 57
research, for retirement careers, 154–55

Restak, Richard, 16
résumés, 158–60, 164
    positioning statements on, 254
retirement
    author's experience with, xxiv
    changes in, xxii–xxiii, 3–4
    continued employment after, 138–45
    current perspectives on, 6–8
    finances for, 21–26
    history of, 4–5
    myth of, 17
    perceptions of, xxiv–xxv
    planning for, 120–21
    relationships after, 81–89
    resistance to, 49–50
    resources for planning, 27–29
    transitioning into, 31–33, 153–61
Richards, Keith, 91
Richardson, Cheryl, 244
Rilke, Rainer Maria, 249
Rites of Passage (Native American vision
    quest education programs), 190–91
role models, 130–31
Roosevelt, Eleanor, 71
Roosevelt, Franklin D., 77
Roosevelt, Theodore, xv
Rowe, John W., 138, 197
RSVP (Retired and Senior Volunteer
Program), 146
Russell, Lord Bertrand, 33
Rutgers University Senior Audit, 190

safety and security needs, 93, 96
Saint-Exupery, Antoine de, 36
salaries, 143
    discrimination by, 172
SARAT technique, 109
Sartre, Jean-Paul, 165
Savings Fitness: A Guide to Your Money and

Your Financial Future (U.S. Dept. of Labor), 21, 25, 26
scheduling time, after retirement, 40
Schlossberg, Nancy, 23
Schorr, Daniel, 140
Schulman, Daralee, 110
SCORE Association (Service Corps of Retired Executives), 146
secondary research, 155
Securities and Exchange Commission (SEC), 28
self-accountability, 53–54
self-marketing, 158–59
Seligman, Martin, 58, 60–62
Seneca, 91, 182
Senesh, Hannah, 97
senior audit programs, 189–90
Senior Community Service Employment Program (SCSEP), 150
Senior Corps, 145–46
seniorNet, 40, 147, 189
Seniors Coalition, 147
senior travel discounts, 176
Senior Women's Travel Tours, 183
Seuss, Dr. (Theodore Seuss Geisel), 8, 202
Seven Stories Exercise, 102–6, 154, 170, 245–46
    analyzing, 254–58
    case study in, 249–51
    history and background of, 246–49
    worksheet for, 252–54
Shakespeare, William, 36, 62, 95, 261
Shaw, George Bernard, 51
skills and interests
    assessment of, 101–6
    in Seven Stories Exercise, 251
Small Business Administration (SBA), 150
Smarter Living's senior travel, 180
Social Security Act (U.S., 1935), 4, 5

Social Security Administration (U.S.), 27, 144
social security benefits
    delay start of, 26
    employment post-retirement and, 144
    history of, 5
Society of Actuaries, 29
space issue, 89
Spark, Muriel, 246
spirituality, 205–6
Spock, Benjamin, 139–40
spouses, 40–41
    friends *versus*, 88–89
stereotypes of aging, 10, 167
Stone, I.F., 16
Stoppard, Tom, xxi, 57
stress
    avoiding, 83
    caused by change, 48
    handling, 194–96
    laughter and, 200
support from others, 53

Tai Chi, 199
Teach for America, 147
temporality, 116–17
Thoreau, Henry David, 97, 251
Thurmond, Strom, 7, 140
timelines, 115
toxic people, 61–62
transition, into retirement, 153–61
    change distinguished from, 32
    phases in, 33–38
    strategies for, 39–43
travel, 40, 175–76
    active travel programs for older people, 182–83
    resources for, 179–80
    solo, 181
    volunteer vacations, 176–79

travel books, 180–81
Travel with a Challenge, 180
Trollope, Anthony, 5
Truman, Harry S., 185
Trump, Donald, 246
Turkel, Studs, 140
Twain, Mark, xii, xxiv, 22, 111, 166
Two-Minute Pitches, 159, 232, 254

US Servas, Inc., 183

vacations
    active travel programs for older people,
      182–83
    planning, 84
    resources for, 179–80
    solo travel, 181
    travel books, 180–81
    volunteer vacations, 176–79
Vaillant, George, 118, 198, 229
values, 106–7
Van Buren, Abigail, 18
Ventrella, Scott W., 63–64
vision quests, 97, 199
visualization, 69–72, 129
volunteering, xii–xiii, 134–37
    intergenerational programs, 137
    paid employment versus, 133
    resources for, 145–52
    volunteer vacations, 176–80
VolunteerMatch, 148

Waitley, Denis, 51, 98, 167
Walking the World, 182
Ward, William Arthur, 200
Washington, Martha, 59

Wendleton, Kate, xx, 52, 233
    on age discrimination, 172–73
    on increased life expectancy, 141–42
    on Seven Stories Exercise, 103
    on taking control of your life, 101
Wetfeet, 150
Whitman, Walt, 12
Whitney, King, Jr., 54
Wiesel, Elie, 185
Willilamson, Marianne, 244
Willing, Jules, xxvi
Winfrey, Oprah, 193
Winton, Arthur, 140
women
    depression among, 41
    older, in workforce, 167
work, see employment
workforce, older Americans in, 167
World Wide Opportunities in Organic
    Farms (WWOOF), 148
worrying, 110–12
Wright, Frank Lloyd, 60

Yalow, Rosalyn S., 14
yoga, 199
Youngman, Henny, 200–202
youth
    in intergenerational volunteer pro-
      grams, 137
    perceptions of, 11

About the Author

Renée Lee Rosenberg, M.A. has over twenty years experience as a career transition coach and a career management consultant and has been a certified Five O'Clock Club coach since 1996.

Renée was an adjunct instructor in Career Development at Baruch College, served as director of a major non-profit employment development program and worked as an outplacement counselor at the New York City United Federation of Teachers Union. She has coached Japanese executives in New York and Tokyo, helping them acclimate to the American business culture.

She is a former Vice President and program chair of the New York chapter of the Association of Career Professionals International, serves on the planning board of The Career Development Specialists Network, is a member of the American Counseling Association and The National Speakers Association.

An accomplished and entertaining speaker, Renée regularly presents to groups on a variety of topics including: retirement issues, résumé preparation, interviewing skills, networking and accessing the hidden job market, mid-life career transition, and keeping up momentum through a difficult job search. Other topics that Renée covers include personality and job search, effective communication, and using positive thinking and optimism as a tool for job search and stress reduction.

Renée holds an MA in Vocational Counseling and is a New York State licensed Mental Health Counselor. She is qualified to administer and interpret various skills and interests inventories, including the MBTI Personality Assessment.

She coached a Five O'Clock Club weekly group at the New York City main branch for over ten years and maintains a private practice, counseling in person and via the phone. A member of the Five O'Clock Club media team she has been interviewed and quoted in print and broadcast media.

Her areas of expertise include: transition coaching for retirees, career coaching lawyers, creative artists, clients over-fifty and any clients who feel stuck in their job search and/or transition process.

On the personal side, Renée had a successful international business in Japan and is an accomplished studio jeweler in New York City. She has personally experienced the retirement journey and now specializes in helping others successfully to do the same.

About the Five O'Clock Club and the "Fruytagie" Canvas

Five O'Clock Club members are special. We attract upbeat, ambitious, dynamic, intelligent people—and that makes it fun for all of us. Most of our members are professionals, managers, executives, consultants, and freelancers. We also include recent college graduates and those aiming to get into the professional ranks, as well as people in their 40s, 50s, and even 60s. Most members' salaries have ranged from $30,000 to $400,000 (one-third of our members have earned in excess of $100,000 a year). For those who cannot attend a Club, *The Five O'Clock Club Book Series* contains all of our methodologies—and our spirit.

The Philosophy of the Five O'Clock Club

The "Fruytagie" Canvas by Patricia Kelly, depicted here, symbolizes our philosophy. The original, which is actually 52.5″ by 69″ inches, hangs in the offices of The Five O'Clock Club in Manhattan. It is reminiscent of popular 16th century Dutch "fruytagie," or fruit tapestries, which depicted abundance and prosperity.

I was attracted to this piece because it seemed to fit the spirit of our people at The Five O'Clock Club. This was confirmed when the artist, who was not aware of what I did for a living, added these words to the canvas: "The garden is abundant, prosperous and magical." Later, it took me only 10 minutes to write the blank verse "The Garden of Life," because it came from my heart. The verse reflects our philosophy and describes the kind of people who are members of the Club.

I'm always inspired by Five O'Clock Clubbers. They show others the way through their quiet behavior . . . their kindness . . . their generosity . . . their hard work . . . under God's care.

We share what we have with others. We are in this lush, exciting place together—with our brothers and sisters—and reach out for harmony. The garden is abundant. The job market is exciting. And Five O'Clock Clubbers believe that there is enough for everyone.

About the Artist's Method

To create her tapestry-like art, Kelly developed a unique style of stenciling. She hand-draws and hand-cuts each stencil, both in the negative and positive for each image. Her elaborate technique also includes a lengthy multilayering process incorporating Dutch metal leaves and gilding, numerous transparent glazes, paints, and wax pencils.

Kelly also paints the back side of the canvas using multiple washes of reds, violets, and golds. She uses this technique to create a heavy vibration of color, which in turn reflects the color onto the surface of the wall against which the canvas hangs.

The canvas is suspended by a heavy braided silk cord threaded into large brass grommets inserted along the top. Like a tapestry, the hemmed canvas is attached to a gold-gilded dowel with finials. The entire work is hung from a sculpted wall ornament.

Our staff is inspired every day by the tapestry and by the members of The Five O'Clock Club. We all work hard—and have FUN! The garden *is* abundant—with enough for everyone. We wish you lots of success in your career. We—and your fellow members of The Five O'Clock Club—will work with you on it.

—Kate Wendleton, President

The original Five O'Clock Club was formed in Philadelphia in 1883. It was made up of the leaders of the day, who shared their experiences "in a spirit of fellowship and good humor."

THE GARDEN OF LIFE IS abundant, prosperous and magical. ❦ In this garden, there is enough for everyone. ❦ Share the fruit and the knowledge ❦ Our brothers and we are in this lush, exciting place together. ❦ Let's show others the way. ❦ Kindness. Generosity. ❦ Hard work. ❦ God's care.